THE DEVELOPING CHILD

Recent decades have witnessed unprecedented advances in research on human development. In those same decades there have been profound changes in public policy toward children. Each book in the Developing Child series reflects the importance of such research in its own right and as it bears on the formulation of policy. It is the purpose of the series to make the findings of this research available to those who are responsible for raising a new generation and for shaping policy in its behalf. We hope that these books will provide rich and useful information for parents, educators, child-care professionals, students of developmental psychology, and all others concerned with the challenge of human growth.

Jerome Bruner
New York University

Michael Cole
University of California, San Diego

Annette Karmiloff-Smith
Medical Research Council, London

SERIES EDITORS

The Developing Child Series

Fatherhood

Ross D. Parke

Harvard University Press
Cambridge, Massachusetts
London, England
1996

Library of Congress Cataloging-in-Publication Data

Parke, Ross D.
   Fatherhood / Ross D. Parke.
      p.   cm. — (The developing child series)
   Includes bibliographical references and index.
   ISBN 0-674-29517-X (cloth : alk. paper).
   ISBN 0-674-29518-8 (paper : alk. paper)
   1. Fatherhood.   2. Fathers.   3. Father and child.   I. Title.   II. Series:
Developing child.
HQ756.P379   1996
306.874'2—dc20
95-49647

To my wife, Barbara, and our children, Gillian, Timothy, Megan, Sarah, Jennifer, and Zachary, all of whom have taught me about fathering

Contents

Acknowledgments

A number of students and colleagues contributed in important ways to my research program at the University of Wisconsin, the Fels Research Institute, the University of Cincinnati College of Medicine, the University of Illinois, and most recently the University of California, Riverside. Their work is acknowledged throughout the book. My own research in this volume has been supported by grants from a variety of agencies: The Grant Foundation, the National Foundation March of Dimes, the National Institute of Child Health and Human Development, the National Science Foundation, the MacArthur Foundation, the Spencer Foundation, the University of California, Riverside, the Graduate School of the University of Illinois, and the Fels Fund of Philadelphia. This book was completed while I was on a sabbatical, which was supported by the University of California, Riverside, and a fellowship from the James McKeen Cattell Fund.

Several scholars provided useful critiques of early versions of the book, including Andrew Cherlin, Scott Coltrane, Carolyn and Philip Cowan, John Gottman, and Barbara Tinsley. Elizabeth Gretz edited the final draft with insight and skill. Karin Horspool and Tracy Bunker did a fine job in preparing the manuscript. A special thanks to my wife, friend, and colleague, Barbara Tinsley, for her continuing support, advice, and insight during all of my endeavors. Finally, I want to express my thanks to other father researchers and to the many families who have consented to be studied to help us learn about fathers and fathering.

Fatherhood

1 / Fatherhood: Myths and Realities

A famous anthropologist once said that fathers are a biological necessity, but a social accident. Throughout much of the present century and all of the last, our culture has conformed comfortably to this view. Traditionally, fathers have been portrayed as uninvolved in child care—pacing the waiting room floor during childbirth, never changing a diaper or warming a bottle, and generally steering clear of the nursery, leaving the responsibility for child rearing almost entirely up to their wives. Specialized to their role as family breadwinner, these mythical fathers provided a strong but distant model for their children and moral and material support for their wives. Otherwise, these fathers truly were something of a social accident, and hardly active participants in the rearing of their children.

Whether this stereotype of the uninvolved father ever actually existed in large numbers is debatable. Several historians have recently argued that the traditional portrait of the uninvolved father is, at best, oversimplified.[1] Over the past century, certainly, there has been a continuing tension between forces that pull for greater participation and opposing influences that push for restraint and uninvolvement. Today and probably in earlier eras as well, there is no single type of father. Some fathers

1

remain uninvolved, others are active participants, and some fathers are even raising children by themselves.

A variety of technological, economic, and ideological changes in our society are redefining what it is to be a father. Whether for reasons of personal fulfillment or economic necessity, more women today work full time outside the home than ever before. Women are also returning to work sooner after the birth of a child. Fathers are taking on more responsibility for early infant and child care. At one time, kin and clan—that supportive network of aunts and grandmothers—could be relied on to help in the care of children as well. Today, the nuclear family is much more isolated because of the high geographic mobility that our economy requires. Legal decisions have also affected fathers; more divorced fathers than in the past are assuming or sharing custody of their children. All of these changes have made it more common for fathers to take an active part in rearing their children.

It is, of course, no accident that just as fathers have moved into a breach created by social circumstances, a new ideology of fatherhood has begun to make inroads into the old stereotype. No longer is the father with a diaper pin in his mouth a comical figure. The ideal father of the newest fashion goes to childbirth class with his wife, coaches her through labor, attends her during delivery, and shares in the care and feeding of the infant, especially when his wife returns to work. A new cultural image of fatherhood has emerged that has pushed aside the earlier portrait of the uninvolved father. No longer a social accident, many fathers are active partners in parenting and a direct influence on their children's development.

Although it is important to correct earlier myths about reluctant and uninvolved fathers, it is equally critical to examine how closely the new cultural ideal matches the reality of fathers' actual involvement. Just how involved the modern father has truly become and the consequences of this involvement for his children, for his wife, for the life of the family, and for himself are issues that will be addressed in this book. In the last twenty years, psychologists and other researchers, undoubtedly stimulated by the new popularity of fathering, have examined a long list of questions concerning how involved fathers are with their children, how fathers actually behave with their children, and what effects this behavior seems to have on the children's development. The picture that emerges may be somewhat surprising and perhaps disappointing. In fact, the amount of change in fathers' involvement has not been as dramatic as current cultural images would lead us to believe. There is less a sense of a father revolution than a slow but steady evolution toward a new conception of fathers and their roles in the family and society. Why is change so slow and so difficult to achieve? What are the determinants or impediments to changing a father's role in the family and with his children? In order to understand fathers' impact on children, we need to better understand the pushes and pulls that govern fathers' involvement. In spite of the modest pace of change, it is now clear that fathers can play an important and unique role in the development of the child.

We will look first at the father's role before the birth of the child. Do fathers change during the mother's pregnancy? Do they make psychological adjustments in anticipation of the addition to the family? How does pregnancy change the relationship between husband and wife? Do childbirth classes make a difference in the way fathers experience the birth, and are there any lasting effects on the way they relate to the child? Do fathers who are present during labor and delivery react differently to their newborns? Even if they miss the delivery, fathers are no longer restricted to the traditional peek through the nursery window. How do fathers respond to newborns when they are given the chance to participate in their delivery? Are fathers similar to mothers in their behavior toward very young babies? How are fathers themselves altered by the transition to fatherhood? Are relationships with their wives, parents, and co-workers modified by becoming a father?

As the child grows older, another set of questions becomes relevant. It is natural to wonder whether boys and girls are affected in different ways by a father's active involvement. Do fathers treat their daughters and sons differently? If so, in what ways and at what ages? How important is a father's influence on a child's developing sense of gender identity and social assurance? How can a father influence his child's intellectual development? Most fathers are also husbands. How does their behavior toward their wives affect their children? Some of a father's influence on his children may be indirectly channeled through the mother; the father may affect the mother's feelings and behavior toward the children.

In modern society families exist in a variety of forms. The traditional family arrangement with mother as primary homemaker and caregiver and father as breadwinner is only one of many possible forms of family organization. Our era's high divorce rate creates many single-parent families, and remarriage brings complicated relationships between stepparents and stepchildren. How does divorce affect the father-child relationship? How do single fathers and stepfathers manage the task of child care? Do children develop in different ways when they live primarily with their fathers or their mothers than when they live with both parents? In many families both parents work, and in a few families mother and father reverse roles so that the mother works outside the home and the father stays home with the children. What are the effects of these arrangements?

Finally, we will explore how society influences fathers and fathering. What forms of support are available for fathers to help them learn their roles and perform them effectively? What are the barriers to fathers' involvement? Individual, relational, societal, and cultural factors all need to be considered. A father's relationship with his own parents and his attitudes toward the importance of being an active father may determine his involvement. How does the timing of entry into fatherhood change men's roles? The quality of a man's marriage and his wife's attitude toward men's roles in child care may be influences. Institutions such as hospitals and the workplace help encourage or discourage father involvement. Finally, societal attitudes concerning both men's and women's roles in work and family have a great impact on fathers and how they play their parenting roles. Fathers are relatively recent objects of study for social scientists, and many of these questions cannot yet be fully answered. Enough is known, however, that we can cast aside many of the myths about fathers.

Theories of Fatherhood

Psychology has a long history of ignoring fathers. One of the main reasons for this neglect of fathers lies in earlier psychological theories of parenthood. Theories are hunches or "best bets" about the way the world probably works. Theories help us to select the problems and issues that are most likely to further our understanding of children's development. But theories also constrain us and lead us away from examining some problems in favor of some others. Fathers were not just forgotten by accident; they were ignored because it was assumed that they were less important than mothers in influencing the developing child. The dominant theories corresponded to the traditional conception of the remote father. Two theorists played particularly important roles in this historical development: Sigmund Freud, the psychoanalyst, and John Bowlby, the British ethologist.

One of Freud's most important and long-lasting contributions was his theory of early social development. According to Freud, different gratifications associated with various body zones (mouth, genitals, and so on) become important at different stages of development. For example, Freud thought that the oral zone and activities associated with eating, sucking, biting, and swallowing are most important to the infant. Because it was the mother who usually fed and cared for the infant—at least in Vienna at the turn of the century—Freud gave the mother a prominent role in infant development. Freud believed that the infant's relationship with its mother significantly shaped its later personality and social relationships. Fathers were virtually ignored. Freud did not consider them an influence in infancy. Fathers did have a place in Freud's theory of development, but not until a later period in childhood. However, many subsequent followers of Freud accepted his emphasis on the importance of infancy for later development and thereby perpetuated his belief that the mother was the primary socializing agent.

The original details of Freud's theory were not accepted by later theorists, but many of his central ideas survived in different form. In the 1940s and 1950s learning theorists like Robert Sears and John Whiting attempted to translate Freud's ideas into the language of modern theories of learning.[2] These scientists assumed that infants gain satisfaction through the reduction of basic biological drives, such as hunger and thirst. The mother became important to the infant because she was the parent who usually fed it (that is, satisfied its hunger drive). Since fathers were typically less involved in feeding, their role in infant development was assumed to be minimal.

John Bowlby's view of early development differed from Freud's, but the end result was the same—mothers were portrayed as the most important figures in infancy. In the 1940s, Bowlby was a prominent critic of institutions and orphanages where infants and children failed to adequately develop, both socially and emotionally. Along with other influential investigators, among them René Spitz and Margaret Ribble, Bowlby saw "maternal deprivation" as the cause of these developmental problems.[3] He built on these early speculations in his classic paper, "The Nature of the Child's Tie to His Mother," an eloquent plea for the special importance of the mother in the child's early development. In later papers and books, Bowlby continued to develop his argument concerning the importance of the attachment bond—the process by which the infant comes to prefer specific adults, especially his mother, over others.[4] Bowlby suggested that attachment is a result of instinctive responses that are important for the protection and survival of the species. Crying, smiling, sucking, clinging, and following all elicit necessary maternal care and protection for the infant and promote contact between mother and infant. Bowlby stressed that the mother is the first and most important object of infant attachment. The mother is biologically prepared to respond to these infant behaviors, just as the infant is predisposed to respond to the sights, sounds, and nurturance provided by his human caretakers. Bowlby believed that it is because of these biologically programmed systems that mother and infant develop attachment to each other. For us, the important message is Bowlby's emphasis on the mother as a central figure in early development. There is room for only one primary attachment figure, according to Bowlby. As a result, fathers were secondary and at most played a supporting role for the mother.

It is true that throughout Western history fathers have generally taken a minor part in the care and feeding of infants and young children. Anthropological evidence shows, furthermore, that this pattern is by no means unique to the West. In the majority of the world's cultures, mothers are the primary caretakers and the fathers play a lesser role in child rearing.[5] It would be a mistake, however, to conclude that there is anything biologically necessary about maternal caretaking. In a significant minority of the world's cultures, males and females divide the care of young children more evenly. Among the Trobrianders of Melanesia, for example, the father participates actively in the care, feeding, and transport of young children. Similarly in a number of other cultures, including the Taira of Okinawa, the Aka Pygmies of Africa, and the Ilocos of the Philippines, father and mother share more equally in infant and child care. These exceptions suggest that the roles played by mothers and fathers are not biologically fixed. Instead the definition of gender roles can vary considerably depending on the social, ideological, and physical conditions in different cultures.

According to another argument, fathers, in contrast to mothers, are biologically ill-equipped to be active contributors to child rearing. The biological uniqueness of maternal caretaking is indicated by the fact that our animal ancestors maintain clear sex-role distinctions, with male monkeys, apes, and baboons generally being uninvolved in infant and child care. For example, Irven De-Vore observed cynocephalus baboons in the wild and found that the adult males took little interest in infants.[6] Instead they played a protective role for the troop as a whole. Studies of rhesus monkeys in captivity tell a similar story. Harry Harlow and his colleagues studied the reactions of male and female monkeys to young infants in a laboratory setting. The males and females played clearly different roles: females were four times as likely as males to express nurturant behavior to infants, and most males were ten times as hostile to infants as females.[7] In short, in animals as well as humans, there is evidence indicating that males are less involved than females in the care and nurturance of infants.

Not all studies of animal behavior, however, support the traditional view of fathers. Animal evidence has demonstrated that males can assume a fatherly role even with infants. The males of some nonhuman primate species occasionally engage in nurturant caretaking of infants in the wild. Marmosets and tamarins—monkeys who live in Central and South America—are among the most involved monkey fathers. They not only carry infants during the day for the first few months of life, but may chew food for very young infants, and sometimes they even assist during birth. Males of other species of monkeys, such as the Barbary macaques of Asia and Africa, participate in caregiving; they hold, groom, carry, and protect infants.[8] Even male rhesus monkeys, who rarely display parental behavior in the wild, "are certainly capable of doing so when given the opportunity in the laboratory."[9] William Redican housed adult male and infant rhesus monkeys together in the laboratory and found that these males played with and protected the infants and groomed them just as much as mothers generally do. There are, however, wide differences from one species of animal to another, and the extent of male participation in caretaking varies, in part, with the amount of involvement the females will allow. If the mother monkey permits it, males may be more involved. The important point is that the animal evidence does not support the view that paternal behavior is biologically impossible. Even in animal species in which the male typically does not demonstrate active fathering, nurturant paternal behavior can be elicited under the right conditions.

Still another version of the biological argument holds that females are primed to engage in "mothering" by hormonal changes that occur in pregnancy and childbirth. Because fathers do not experience these hormonal changes, the argument suggests, they are not biologically prepared for parenting. Animal evidence from Jay Rosenblatt, Alison Fleming, and their colleagues has challenged the argument about the necessity of hormones for caretaking.[10] Their careful studies show that both virgin female and male rats will show parenting behavior with sufficient exposure to newborn infants. Thus it seems that environmental conditions can override the effects of hormones and, in the long run, be more important than short-lived hormonal shifts in determining the reactions of males (and females) to infants.

At the same time, biological differences between the genders may predispose men and women to execute their parenting roles differently.[11] For example, play patterns of fathers and mothers with their infants and children are distinctive, but both men and women seem to be equally competent caregivers and exhibit high degrees of similarity as caregivers.[12] Although biology may produce differences in the style or manner in which roles are carried out, there is little support for the argument that men are biologically unprepared for parenting.

Clearly this perspective cannot be used to justify the limited role that fathers have traditionally played in taking care of infants and children. In short, there is no acceptable theory of fatherhood that necessarily consigns fathers to a secondary role in child care. Nor is there any reason why a parent of either sex should have the greater share of influence on the child's development, although there is every reason to suspect that mothers and fathers will have different kinds of influence on their children. The modern study of fathering has largely turned away from outworn theories of parenthood and toward direct observation of parents and children. We now know a substantial amount about how fathers behave with their children, how this behavior differs from maternal behavior, and just what sorts of influence this behavior can have.

An Orientation to Understanding Fathers

Most of us think of fathers as influencing their children directly through their daily face-to-face contact. In turn this suggests to some that fathers must have less influence than mothers because they spend less time with the children. But this does not necessarily follow.

Estimates of the amount of time fathers spend with their infants vary considerably, but most reports indicate that the amount of time is surprisingly limited. In a classic early study of middle-class Boston parents, Milton Kotelchuck found that mothers had principal child-rearing responsibilities for their six- to twenty-one-month-old infants. Mothers were present with their infants more than fathers (9 hours versus 3.2 hours per day).[13] As we shall see in Chapter 4, the amount of time that fathers spend with their children has shifted upward slightly over the last two decades—especially when mothers are employed outside the home—but mothers still assume the major responsibility for child care in most households. Similar patterns are evident in Great Britain.[14] Other international surveys of the time fathers and mothers spend on child care confirm these findings. In France and Belgium, for example, mothers spend even more time in child care compared with fathers.[15] But the total time spent with a child is not the most important determinant of the impact of a father or a mother. The sheer quantity of time is less important than the quality of interaction. Studies of working mothers have consistently shown that the lessened contact as a result of the mother's work time has limited effect on children's development.[16] A better predictor of development is how effectively the mother uses her time with her children. Just being available is not the most important dimension. Presumably the same is true for fathers: the real question is not how many hours per day a father spends with his child, but what he does with the child when he is present. Quality of involvement is the critical issue.

There is no doubt that fathers can play an important direct role in their children's development. They touch, talk, and tickle, and these are ways of influencing the baby and child. Fathers also manage and organize their children's activities. For example, they may regulate their child's behavior by how they arrange the home environment. Do fathers encourage exploration? Do they permit the infant to crawl around the house and investigate its world? Do they provide interesting toys for the child? Do they make books available as the child begins to read? Do fathers highlight interesting features of the environment by showing and pointing and talking? All of these are ways that a parent manages his child's world and probably influences the child's later social and cognitive development.

Children are not simply passive targets for their father's influence. The father-child relationship is a two-way process, and children influence their fathers just as fathers alter their children's development. Children directly affect the ways that their fathers treat them and thereby contribute to the ways in which they are socialized. The cries of a colicky infant who keeps a father up at night, the plea for understanding from a four-year-old who has broken a favorite vase, and the negotiations of a teenager for the keys to the family car are all examples of how children affect fathers' behavior.

We have begun to recognize that the father is important not only through direct influences on his child but also by means of indirect effects on the infant's early interactions with other people. Within the family context, fathers often indirectly influence their infants and children by affecting the mother's behavior. For example, Frank Pedersen and his colleagues have shown that the quality of the husband-wife relationship is linked to that of the mother-infant relationship.[17] Pedersen observed mothers feeding their four-week-old infants and assessed each mother's competence at feeding her baby. Mothers who were rated highly competent "were able to pace the feeding well, intersperse feeding and burping without disrupting the baby and seemed sensitive to the baby's needs for either stimulation of feeding or brief rest periods during the course of feeding."[18] Through an interview, Pedersen assessed the marital relationship. His findings are worth quoting: "When the father was more supportive of the mother, she was more effective in feeding the baby . . . The reverse holds for marital discord. High tension and conflict in the marriage was associated with more inept feeding on the part of the mother."[19] Fathers as well as mothers are affected by the quality of their relationship. Couples who argue and criticize each other are more likely to act this way with their infants and children, to the detriment, as we shall see, of their children.[20]

These reflections remind us of an important fact: if we are to understand the relationship between parent and child, we have to treat the parents as part of a family system and consider all of the relationships among the family members.[21] In addition, we must remember that families do not exist in isolation from other parts of society. Families are embedded in a wide network of other social systems, including neighborhoods, communities, and cultures. In order to understand how fathers function we need to take account of the links between families and these other social systems.[22] By recognizing that fathers are affected by social influences outside the family, we will gain a clearer understanding of the reasons for the variety of forms that fatherhood can assume.

In recent years, a life course view of fathers has emerged.[23] In contrast to the usual view that all fathers are the same, regardless of their age at the time they become fathers, the life course view emphasizes the importance of the timing of fatherhood. Older and younger fathers may differ in a myriad of ways, including their energy and health as well as their educational attainment and their occupational roles. All of these factors alert us to possible differences among fathers, depending on their age. In addition to "father time," or the point at which an individual becomes a father, family time, or the timing of transitional life events for the family as a unit, is also important for understanding fathers. Family time includes such events as a move or a divorce or separation. A life course view considers historical time as well, which provides the social conditions for individual and family transitions. Examples include the Great Depression of the 1930s, the Vietnam era of the 1960s, or the Farm Belt depression of the 1980s in the United States. These distinctions are important because individual, family, and historical events do not always harmonize. For example, a family occurrence such as the birth of a child and the transition to parenthood may have profound effects on a man who has just begun a career in contrast to one who has advanced to a stable occupational position. Moreover, individual and family time are both embedded within the social conditions and values of the historical time in which they exist.

Finally, we are increasingly recognizing variations in fathers and fathering both in other cultures and across ethnic groups within our own culture. Fathers in Ireland, India, and Indonesia are not necessarily equivalent in the ways they enact their roles, and men's fathering roles are shaped in unique ways in these different cultural niches.[24] It is similarly important to understand how African American, Asian American, Latino, and Native American men approach fatherhood and to appreciate the diversity of fathering activities within different ethnic groups as well as between the groups.[25] Although there are still more similarities than differences, identifying and understanding these variations has become a vital concern in the 1990s.

Fathers affect their children, but men are also affected by fatherhood. Being a father can change the ways that men think about themselves. Fathering often helps men to clarify their values and to set priorities. It may enhance their self-esteem if they manage its demands and responsibilities well, or alternatively it may be unsettling and depressing by revealing their limitations and weaknesses.[26] Under the influence of the theoretical writings of Erik Erikson,[27] researchers have begun to explore the ways in which fathering can enhance men's generativity. By generativity, Erikson means "any caring activity that contributes to the spirit of future generations such as the generation of new or mature persons, products, ideas or works of art."[28] Later we will examine evidence that suggests that fathering does indeed enhance men's generativity. Maureen Green notes, "One of the first things a father learns from his children is that his needs can match theirs. They look to him for instruction; he can enjoy giving instruction. The children look to him as a model and being a model adds an extra dimension to his decisions. His ambitions and achievements look different to him if he can learn to look at them through their eyes as well as his own."[29] Fathering, in short, may be good for men as well as for children.

2 / The Transition to Fatherhood: Pregnancy and Birth

Becoming a father is not a single event but a gradual process of becoming acquainted with the demands and joys of a new family role. The process begins early. Even before pregnancy, decisions about when and whether to have a child, to go ahead and "try" to become pregnant or to adopt a child are all part of the complex transition to fatherhood. The process continues as both parents adjust to the mother's pregnancy. Pregnancy is a family affair. Couples, not just mothers, become pregnant. Since the 1970s we have begun to recognize that fathers can play important roles during pregnancy. But this change is slow and by no means complete. One disappointed observer of the changing father scene observed on a recent trip to his local bookstore: "In the 'Childbirth to Parenting' section, almost 200 books addressed motherhood, pregnancy and birth. There were only 2 books on expectant and early fathering."[1]

Pregnancy as a Family Affair

The changes that occur for fathers as a result of the mother's pregnancy are not independent of the changes that mothers themselves undergo during pregnancy. Indeed, fathers' behavior can best be understood by viewing it in relation to mothers' behavior during this time—unless, of course, the father is a seahorse, a species where the father becomes pregnant, carries the developing offspring in his body, and gives birth to young seahorses. Human fathers still lag behind seahorse fathers and can only indirectly experience the joys and trials of pregnancy.

Each of pregnancy's three stages or trimesters has its own characteristic problems and pleasures for the expectant couple. For the woman the first trimester is often difficult, both psychologically and physically. Nausea, vomiting, fatigue, and headaches are common, and depression, irritability, and anxiety are not unusual. In one study of pregnant couples by Pauline Shereshefsky and Leon Yarrow, "a large proportion of women spoke of tempers more easily aroused, a tendency to be 'edgy,' tense, nervous or 'touchy,' to snap more easily, to become more demanding of their husbands, to dissolve into tears more often—general indications of a greater vulnerability and heightened emotionality."[2] Of course being pregnant is not constantly negative during this period. Many women experience euphoria during these months; some switch back and forth between joy and depression.

In the second trimester of pregnancy, many of the more uncomfortable symptoms disappear. Quickening, the baby's first perceptible movement, usually takes place by the end of the fourth month and is one of the first clear signals that the baby is "on the way." Feeling the baby move can be exciting for both parents. Jerold Shapiro, in his book *When Men Are Pregnant*, described one father's reaction at the moment of fetal movement: "There was a ripple across her belly. I asked, 'What was that?' and we both said together, 'Was that a kick?' It was incredible. I am a father. My father is a grandfather. My life is now changed."[3] As the baby gets bigger and stronger, though, its movements seem to be more pleasing to fathers than to mothers. In one study of pregnant couples, most of the men said they enjoyed feeling the baby move, but half of the women were not enthusiastic. Obviously the appeal of fetal movements may depend on whose abdomen is being kicked.[4]

Recent advances in technology, especially the increasingly routine use of sonograms that allow couples to watch videotapes of their developing fetus, are an encouragement to fathers' interest and involvement. Not only do parents grow increasingly attached to their developing infant while it is still in the womb, but sonogram pictures of the fetus may enhance mothers' feelings of attachment to their developing fetus.[5] Although mothers generally show higher levels of fetal attachment than fathers,[6] perhaps sonogram exposure would enhance father fetal attachment and reduce the differences between maternal and paternal fetal attachment. Sonograms have other benefits as well. The opportunity to observe that the developing fetus is healthy and normal probably reduces parents' anxieties. Tiffany Field and her co-workers found that women who received periodic sonograms had less anxiety as the pregnancy progressed, fewer birth complications, and heavier, more alert, more responsive, and less irritable infants.[7]

The last trimester of pregnancy is, again, often stressful. By this time the mother has gained approximately 25–30 pounds, and carrying the fetus is tiring and frequently uncomfortable. Bothersome physical symptoms such as fatigue, insomnia, swollen limbs, and shortness of breath are common. Perhaps as a result, many pregnant women are anxious and irritable during this period, just as in the first trimester. In addition, worries about the baby's health and about the process of birth itself may become stronger as birth nears.

How do expectant fathers react during pregnancy? The ways men experience pregnancy and birth may vary considerably across cultures. Some primitive cultures mark the transition to fatherhood with special ceremonies. One intriguing phenomenon is called the "couvade"—a term derived from the French word *couver* (which means "to brood" or "to hatch") and coined by the British anthropologist Sir Edward Tylor in 1865:

> In certain primitive societies at the approximate time of their wives' lying-in, men take to bed in a pretense ritual, simulating the agony of labor and birth. This ritual serves at least two vital purposes: it establishes for the community just who the father is and also it decoys all evil spirits to the father's hut where they can spend their wrath on the mock mother, leaving the actual mother unharmed to go through the birthing of her baby at a safe distance.[8]

In some cultures, couvade takes on high drama. Consider this example from the Erickala-Vandu, a tribe in Southern India:

> Directly the woman feels the birth pangs, she informs her husband who immediately takes some of her clothes, puts them on, places on his forehead the mark the women usually place on theirs, retires into a dark room where there is only a dim lamp, and lies down on the bed, covering himself with a long cloth. When the child is born, it is washed and placed on a cot beside the father.[9]

A Western version of the couvade is what a British psychiatrist, W. H. Trethowan, calls the couvade syndrome: a set of physical symptoms that are experienced by an expectant father and that disappear almost immediately after his wife has given birth. How widespread is the couvade syndrome? Estimates vary considerably, but generally range between 10 and 15 percent of fathers. Many more expectant fathers undergo physical and psychological changes, but not of sufficient magnitude to satisfy a strict definition of the couvade syndrome.

In one examination of the syndrome, Trethowan found that the expectant fathers suffered symptoms such as loss of appetite, toothaches, nausea, and vomiting. The symptoms were most frequent in the third month of pregnancy and then lessened until the final month, when there again was an increase. These physical symptoms were often accompanied by psychological problems such as depression, tension, insomnia, irritability, and even stuttering. This pattern is very similar to the course of symptoms for mothers, who suffer more morning sickness, headaches, and fatigue in the first and last trimesters of pregnancy than in the middle period. In another study, Beatrice Leibenberg reported that 65 percent of the first-time fathers studied experienced "pregnancy symptoms," including fatigue, nausea, backache, headache, vomiting, and even peptic ulcers. And J. F. Clinton, in one of the best studies of this issue, found that expectant fathers in comparison with a group of nonexpectant males reported longer-lasting and more frequently occurring colds during the first trimester and more weight gain—though unintentional—during the third trimester of their wives' pregnancy.[10]

Although some psychoanalytic writers believe that pregnancy should be viewed as a crisis for most expectant fathers, it is not necessarily a debilitating experience. Nor are all of the changes in men associated with pregnancy quite so dramatic and unsettling. Some, in fact, are more amusing. For example, according to Carolyn and Philip Cowan's study of the transition to parenthood, many men change their appearance during pregnancy—they grow beards or mustaches, or shave them off; some gain weight or lose weight or nurse obscure injuries.[11] Whether these changes occur because of compassion, empathy, or competition with their wives is not clear.

Physical symptoms are only a small part of the changes that expectant fathers undergo. In anticipation of approaching fatherhood, men show increased interest in babies. Some try to learn about children and parenting by reading books. Many men react to the anticipated financial burden of parenthood by a great increase in work, taking on second jobs, especially during the last few months of pregnancy. Although this increase in work and time away from home is often simply a way of paying for the needed cribs, cradles, and other baby paraphernalia, some writers, particularly those of a psychoanalytic persuasion, interpret this flurry of activity as a sign of worry and anxiety. While fathers worry about work and bills, mothers focus more on the emotional climate of the family.[12]

Husbands do worry a lot during pregnancy. One recent study found that men were more anxious than their wives during this period. They even worried more about their wives' aches and pains than their wives did! Fathers also experience typical anxieties, such as getting to the hospital on time when labor begins and whether the baby will be healthy.[13] Their chief worry is money—to pay the hospital bills, to raise the baby—not an unreasonable concern considering that as of the mid-1990s the average cost of having a baby in the United States is $7,000—or higher, if complications arise such as a cesarean section delivery or a premature birth. Estimates of the cost of raising a child to age eighteen in the United States range from $150,000 to over $250,000. All of these worries may result in more severe psychological symptoms for some expectant fathers. Howard Osofsky and Rex Culp found that 2.9 percent of fathers were clinically depressed and 47 percent suffered from low self-esteem. Fathers with low incomes were more likely to report depressive symptoms than fathers with higher incomes.[14] Other men, especially those with a history of violence, are particularly assaultive to their wives during their pregnancy. And the assaults are mainly directed toward the belly—the site of the developing fetus. Whether jealousy is the reason or some other factor remains unknown.[15]

A word of caution: in spite of the stress and worry associated with pregnancy and the transition to fatherhood, smoking as a way of reducing stress is not a good idea. While it has long been known that smoking by the mother may have adverse effects on the baby, paternal smoking during pregnancy reduces the birthweight of infants as well.[16] Even though mothers did not smoke, if the father smoked during pregnancy, babies were 88 grams smaller at birth than babies of nonsmoking fathers.[17] Paternal second-hand smoke clearly has a negative effect on the developing fetus during pregnancy. As fathers (and mothers) become more aware of the adverse effects of smoking on babies, "the choice between a desiccated weed and a well-developed seed" should become less difficult.[18] One simple way that fathers can contribute during pregnancy is to stop smoking.

Sexual patterns change during pregnancy, too. According to Samuel Bittman and Sue Zalk, some men report an increase in sexual attraction to their pregnant wives; others show less interest.[19] Meanwhile the woman's sexual desires may change over the course of the pregnancy. In the first three months, when nausea and irritability are often high, she may not be interested in sex. During the middle trimester, however, her sexual appetite is usually restored. Sexual interest sometimes decreases again in the last stage because of discomfort and fatigue. Although sexual activity is generally not harmful during the later stages of pregnancy, many obstetricians still discourage it. According to William Masters and Virginia Johnson, 77 percent of the women they interviewed were told by their doctors not to have sex during the last trimester.[20] Men's desire may decline as well owing to fatigue, anxiety, or fear. Some men may even view sex as incompatible with their new identity as fathers. Occasionally these conditions trigger an increase in extramarital affairs, but Cowan and Cowan estimate that the frequency is a relatively low 5 percent.[21] Overall, there is a decrease in sexual relations during pregnancy.

Men vary in terms of their readiness for fatherhood, and this sense of readiness may also affect how they react during pregnancy. On the basis of interviews with "expectant" fathers, Kathryn May identified several factors that are important in men's emotional preparedness for fathering.[22] The most basic factor is whether a man has ever wanted to become a father. Some men who become fathers never wanted to have children; others see being a father as part of their life plan. Another component is stability in the couple's relationship. The belief that their marital relationship is a stable one contributes to men's sense of readiness. Not surprisingly, given the expense involved, financial security is also viewed as an important part of being ready for fatherhood. In addition, men who felt a sense of closure to the childless period of their life felt more prepared for fatherhood than those who wanted to complete other goals before the onset of parenthood. Men who are clearly unready for fatherhood may be less involved in the pregnancy, and possibly less committed as fathers. But readiness varies widely from individual to individual, and most men experience some ambivalence during pregnancy.

Providing Emotional Support

Fathers do not simply show their concern for their wives during pregnancy by having backaches. Men tend to react positively to their pregnant wives' increased need for emotional support. Harold Raush and his colleagues found that husbands were highly conciliatory during pregnancy.[23] They asked couples to settle a conflict such as what television program to watch. The strategies that the couples used to settle their dispute were observed and analyzed. The husbands in pregnant couples were more supportive than husbands in nonpregnant couples, and more supportive than they themselves had been before the pregnancy. Pregnancy is no panacea, however, for unhappy marriages: the emotional support that the husband provided slipped back to its prepregnancy level by the fourth month after the birth. The extra support that the husband provides during pregnancy is important, however. In an investigation of twenty-six couples in California, Johanna Gladieux found that emotional support from the husband during pregnancy made it easier for the wife to adjust to pregnancy and enjoy it.[24] Husbands are particularly important as support figures in the early stage of pregnancy—before the public announcement that comes with "showing."

During the second trimester, when pregnancy becomes a public event, friends and relatives become even more important determinants of the expectant mother's satisfaction than the marital relationship. "During this time the acceptance, interest and support of her social community, the opportunity to exchange and share stories or folklore about childbearing and the chance to compare her experiences with others, all become invaluable for the pregnant woman."[25] Friendship patterns change during pregnancy as couples spend more time with other expectant couples or parents with babies and young children. Less time is spent with childless couples. Parents as well as friends become more important now than in the first trimester: Bittman and Zalk found that 40 percent of the women in their study had more overall contact with their own parents during this period. Support from co-workers may decrease for some women, however, as they reduce their work hours and sometimes their commitment.[26] Together this means that support from grandparents and from their spouses becomes especially important for mothers during the latter stages of pregnancy.

Just as the mother looks beyond her spouse for support, information, and reassurance, fathers tend to look for support from friends who are already parents. In addition, expectant fathers turn to their own parents during pregnancy—especially their mothers. "A man may feel he needs more mothering for himself during this stressful period—a little extra stroking at a time when he may feel pressured to be constantly strong and responsible and 'adult' . . . expectant fathers telephoned and wrote letters to their families more during the pregnancy than before."[27] Gladieux found that the availability of these kinds of people, who can serve as experienced guides concerning labor, delivery, and subsequent parenthood, was linked with higher satisfaction for expectant fathers.

Additional evidence concerning the father's importance as a support figure during pregnancy comes from studies that show clear links between the mother's emotional state and early infant development. In one study in Boston, infants were found to be less irritable in the first three days after birth if the mother had been calm and relaxed during pregnancy. Moreover, the more positively parents rated their marriage (and presumably how supportive the husband was during pregnancy), the better the infant appeared physiologically at two months, as assessed by such measures as irritability and ability to recover from being upset.[28]

High interest in pregnancy has consequences for later fathering as well. A father's interest in his wife's pregnancy has been found to be positively related to how much he holds the baby in the first six weeks of life and also to whether he attends to the baby when it cries. The husband's attitude also affects his wife's enjoyment of motherhood—the happier he is about the pregnancy, the more she enjoys the first few weeks of the baby's life.[29]

Helping the Older Child

In families with older children, the wife is not the only one who needs support during pregnancy. The father may play a special role in helping the older child adjust to the birth of a new family member. Bittman and Zalk found that over 34 percent of the expectant fathers they studied spent more time with their children during pregnancy than they had before; only 2 percent reported a decrease. Cecily Legg, Ivan Sherick, and William Wadland found a number of negative reactions in older siblings following the birth of a new baby—including lapses in toilet training, sleep disturbances, and a renewed interest in pacifiers, bottles, and thumbs. They also found that increased involvement of the father during the pregnancy and after the birth helped the older sibling to adjust more easily.[30] By "taking up the slack," devoting time and attention to the older child while the mother is preoccupied with the new baby, the father helps the older sibling to accept the changed situation.

It is just as well that fathers contribute in this way. Pregnancy makes mothers not only less available but also less patient, and older children are often the target of their mother's increased irritability. Alfred Baldwin documented these shifts years ago.[31] He found that mothers changed their child-rearing style after they became pregnant, spending less time with the older child, behaving less warmly and affectionately, and generally becoming less effective in their child-rearing practices. At the same time, they became more restrictive, more severe in their penalties, more coercive, and less democratic. That older children sometimes resent their younger brother or sister is not surprising.

The Father's Presence during Labor and Delivery

Fathers' involvement in pregnancy doesn't stop at the hospital door. Until the 1980s, fathers were routinely excluded from participating in childbirth. This exclusion was in part an effort to reduce infection in the delivery unit; fathers were viewed as a possible source of contamination. The waiting room became the celebrated place where the father could fret, pace, and sleep, but he could not be with his wife during labor and delivery. Although fathers can still occasionally be seen pacing in hospital corridors, hospital practices have changed and fathers are no longer strangers in the labor and delivery room. Even as late as 1972, fathers were permitted in the delivery room in only 27 percent of the American hospitals in one survey. Not until 1974 did the American College of Obstetricians and Gynecologists endorse the father's presence during labor. And yet by the 1990s fathers were admitted to delivery rooms in nearly all U.S. hospitals, and 85 percent of all American males in two-parent families expected to witness the birth of their infants.[32] Why did the rules change?

For one thing, early fears that the father's presence would cause infection proved incorrect.[33] In one survey of 45,000 husband-attended births, there was not a single instance of infection caused by the presence of the father in the delivery room. Second, parents demanded more control over the birth process and put pressure on their obstetricians to change the rules and allow fathers to be present. The way that many parents think about birth has changed. Rather than being treated as a crisis, giving birth is now more often viewed as a normal phase in family development. As part of this shift, many people have sought to make the process of birth more relaxed. Many hospitals have created birthing rooms, which look very much like comfortable bedrooms and give the impression that the home atmosphere has moved into the hospital.

Here is a description of a birth in one of the New Alternative Birth Centers in San Francisco, which are attempting to introduce a homelike atmosphere in the traditional hospital:

> Sarah Katherine Bell was born at 8:56 P.M. Tuesday, May 11, at Mount Zion Hospital. Unlike the experience of her 4-year-old brother, Sarah's first glimpse of the world was not a sterile delivery room bathed in harsh lights and filled with the latest medical equipment, but a room that could have been anyone's bedroom. Her mother, Judy, delivered in a standard double bed with a wicker headboard. Around the bed were plants suspended from macrame hangers, an orange carpet and sofabed where father could relax when he wasn't coaching his wife's breathing. The lights were low and there was a stereo system for music.
>
> Soon after Sarah's birth, the father picked up the couple's son from a babysitter and brought him to the hospital to meet and touch his new sister. By the next morning the Bells were ready to take their baby home.[34]

This shift to birthing rooms helps to make birth a more normal part of family life while maintaining proper safeguards for the newborn baby and the mother. Fathers feel more welcome in such settings than in the cold, antiseptic, and sterile atmosphere of the traditional delivery room. Because of childbirth education classes, fathers are better prepared not only for what to expect but also for what to do to help the mother during labor and delivery. This training helps explain why fears that fathers would "faint" or otherwise be a nuisance if present during the birth process were also shown to be ill founded. Few fathers cause the havoc that obstetricians once suspected would occur if the delivery room doors were opened to them.

Childbirth preparation classes are a standard part of the services of most hospitals, and fathers as well as mothers can be observed doing preparatory exercises and timing breathing patterns. One estimate indicates that between 50 and 80 percent of all pregnant women and often their male partners attend childbirth preparation classes.[35] One popular type of preparation is the Lamaze method. Future parents attend prenatal classes to learn about the physiological processes of pregnancy and birth. Under the guidance of an instructor, the expectant parents learn and practice breathing exercises appropriate for the different stages of labor. These exercises help the mother to relax and therefore reduce the pain that accompanies the contractions. The father plays a supporting role in this process. Robert Fein interviewed fathers after childbirth and found that they reported several ways in which they had helped their wives during labor and delivery:

> Men timed contractions, breathed along with their wives to help them stay "on top" of contractions, massaged backs, brought ice chips and juice, translated and transmitted requests from their wives to doctors and nurses, gave constant caring attention and encouragement and were consistent reminders to their wives when the labor

was most difficult that the women were not alone and that labor would end.[36]

Another benefit of training for birth is that mothers who have learned these relaxing skills require less medication for pain during labor and delivery. This is especially true if fathers are also present during the delivery. Using medication during birth affects the baby, causing drowsiness, lethargy, and possibly poor attention; therefore, reducing the need for medication benefits the child. Not all investigators, however, have agreed that childbirth classes themselves reduce the need for drugs. A self-selection factor may operate: only certain types of people take the classes, particularly the better educated. Perhaps such people would do well in childbirth and need less medication whether they attended these classes or not. Yet recent evidence makes this explanation seem unlikely. A group of investigators in Germany assigned certain women to a childbirth preparation group and others to a control group who received no preparation. The results were striking: the "prepared" women had shorter labors, needed less medication, and reported enjoying the birth experience more then the women who had not received preparation for childbirth.

It is not clear that classes *alone* always yield benefits such as making labor and delivery easier. Other research has shown that childbirth preparation has an effect by making it more likely that fathers will be present during labor and delivery. The father's presence may be a necessary ingredient to the effectiveness of the classes. William Henneborn and Rosemary Cogan studied two groups of couples who had all attended childbirth education classes. In one group the fathers were present throughout labor and delivery; in the other group the fathers attended only the first stage of labor. The women whose husbands participated in both labor and delivery reported less pain, received less medication, and felt more positive about the birth experience than the women in the other group.[37]

Other investigators confirm that the father's presence is significant in the birth process. Doris Entwisle and Susan Doering compared deliveries in which the husband was present during the second stage of labor with deliveries in which he was not. The father's presence increased the mother's emotional experiences at the birth; mothers reported the birth as a "peak" experience more often if the father was present.[38] Fathers are not merely an extra nurse in the labor and delivery suite. They act differently than other support figures and in one study were five times more likely to touch their wives during labor and delivery than nurses were. Remember that nurses are often in and out of the room during labor, while fathers are a more continuous source of support. According to mothers' postpartum reports, the husband's presence was rated as most helpful.[39] Moreover, fathers' participation was rated by mothers as increasing the meaning of the labor experience and by the couple as strengthening their relationship.[40] As might be expected, being present and being actively involved in the delivery affected the quality of the father's experience too. Sharing the delivery was more important to men than being in the labor room. Of the husbands in the Entwisle and Doering study who were not in the delivery room, 88 percent felt negative about missing the delivery. One said, "I felt anxious. Very anxious. Boy it's taking a long time. And disappointed, like I'd let her down. Because I heard her—a nurse came out, and I heard my wife saying, 'I want my husband!' and I thought: Oh, God what's happening? I felt like—possibly—I hadn't done my job. I don't know why he [the doctor] made me leave." Those who were present were enthusiastic about the experience—95 percent of them were positive. One man recalled, "I felt tremendous. It was just an experience I'd never—had before and it's a good experience. I felt like I was part of it too. I was feeling great, tremendous."[41]

Overall, the fathers' reaction at the moment of birth was more positive than their wives'. This may not be surprising—fathers had experienced no physical pain and had been given no dulling drugs. In comparison, fathers who spent time in the waiting room were generally neutral in their emotional reaction to the news of the birth. Only the fathers who were present were positive, and about a quarter of them reported an "ecstatic peak experience"; none of the fathers in the waiting room reached this emotional peak. One elated father remembered, "[I was] as joyful as I've ever been in my life. That is—the greatest experience of anything I've ever done. It was just—a very happy time—a feeling I've never had before."

Being present at the child's birth has other advantages for fathers: in this same study, more fathers (51 percent) than mothers (25 percent) held their babies while still in the delivery room. As the investigators noted, "The father, of course, is not lying down with an intravenous tube inserted in one arm and perhaps a blood pressure cuff on the other."[42] In view of the real possibility that early contact with babies may strengthen feelings of fatherhood, being present at the delivery may facilitate later involvement with the infant. The husband's experience is closely tied to his wife's experience. Women who have a positive birth experience contribute to their husbands' enjoyment of the birth. Preparation for childbirth leads to more active participation by fathers in labor and delivery, which, in turn, makes the whole birth event better for both mother and father—and perhaps gets the father's relationship with his infant off to a better start.

Fathers are not always eager participants in the labor and delivery process, and many feel unprepared—in spite of classes—for the childbirth experience. One observer noted that "men are now invited in, cajoled in, threatened in" to the delivery room.[43] Some men are queasy, anxious, and fearful; others feel that they are letting down their wives if medication is needed for pain. In some cases, fathers may be better off outside the delivery room, and the couple needs to decide what makes sense for them. The father's presence is a choice, and it may not be the best way to provide the full benefits that a supportive partner can offer. In other cultures such as Guatemala, for example, a supportive female partner is commonly provided for women during the labor and delivery process. These support partners are called *doulas*. John Kennell and Marshall Klaus have shown that the provision of continuous emotional support from a trained and experienced figure during labor has clear beneficial effects. Supported mothers were less likely to require cesarean deliveries (8 percent) in comparison with a nonsupported control group (18 percent). Supported mothers who delivered vaginally were less likely to require epidural anesthesia (7.8 percent) than nonsupported mothers (55.3 percent).[44] Recently it has been found that the presence of the father alone was less effective in reducing the need for cesarean deliveries than a combination of a trained support figure and the father (27 percent versus 14 percent).[45] In sum, the father's presence may be helpful, but dads may need more training and support themselves if their full potential as labor partners is to be realized.

More radical innovations aimed at increasing the father's involvement in the birth process are being tried on an experimental basis. A team of New Jersey obstetricians, Myron Levine and Robert Block, encourage fathers to "play doctor" for the day and deliver their babies themselves (in normal, noncomplicated births) under the supervision of the obstetrician.[46] Their intent is "to bring the home aspect into the safety of the hospital setting and to make giving birth more family-centered." Fathers who deliver their babies are enthusiastic; their typical comments include: "On a real high!" "Pretty fantastic!" "As if I'd just caught the winning pass in the Super Bowl!" These fathers also become more involved in the daily care of their infants at home. Three months after the delivery, more than twice as many of the fathers who had delivered their infants were spending an hour or more with their babies daily, compared with fathers who had not delivered their babies. Although these results are intriguing, we cannot leap to conclusions. Most of the fathers were volunteers, and it is possible that only the fathers who were already likely to be highly involved with their babies agreed to help out in the delivery.

Fathers and Cesarean Childbirth

In spite of the increased number of couples choosing natural childbirth, more than 20 percent of deliveries in the United States are carried out by cesarean section.[47] The father's presence has positive effects during cesarean deliveries, as well, and fathers are increasingly allowed to be present. When regional anesthesia is used, the mother can remain conscious and alert, able to benefit from her husband's presence in the same way that vaginally delivered mothers do. According to a study of women whose babies were delivered by cesarean section, women whose husbands were present during delivery were more positive about the birth experience than women whose husbands were not present.[48] Fathers are more likely to be included in cesarean deliveries as time goes on, and in view of the benefits, this is a promising trend.

Surprisingly, perhaps, cesarean delivery—regardless of whether or not the father is present in the delivery room—affects the relationship between father and infant. Pedersen and his colleagues observed the impact of cesarean delivery of the father-infant relationship five months after birth.[49] In contrast to the fathers of infants who were delivered vaginally, the "cesarean" fathers spent more time in routine care and feeding of their infants in the home. Why? Cesarean delivery implies a variety of changes for the family. The father may be pressed into service earlier because mothers who deliver by cesarean take longer to recover than those who deliver vaginally. The mother is unable to carry as much of the burden of newborn care, and so the father takes over some of these duties. Other evidence, from a Swedish study by John Lind, indicates that fathers who are permitted to care for the baby (to feed and diaper it) in the hospital do more caretaking in the home three months later.[50] Together these studies suggest that roles that are organized early after birth may persist, at least for a time. Mode of delivery—vaginal versus cesarean—may have major consequences for the level of involvement between father and infant. Whether greater involvement by the father affects the child's development will be explored in later chapters.

Father-Infant Bonding: Fact or Myth?

The concept of parent-infant bonding emerged in the 1970s. Two pediatricians, Marshall Klaus and John Kennell, argued that opportunities for extended mother-infant contact during the early postpartum period would enhance the mother-infant attachment bond.[51] In the 1980s several researchers tested the bonding notion with fathers as well. Some evidence suggests that fathers who have more extended contact with their newborn infants in the hospital (for example, four hours of extra contact), as opposed to a traditional schedule of only briefly visiting their wife and baby together, are more involved with the baby later on at home. In comparison with the traditional fathers, the extended contact fathers vocalized more during feeding, had a more positive attitude toward the baby's care, and reported playing with their infant longer each day.[52] However, the number of studies that did not find that extended contact had such an effect far exceeds those that support the extended-contact argument. Most scholars now view the early bonding notion with considerable skepticism—not just for fathers, but for mothers as well.[53] The process of developing a close relationship between parent and infant is a gradual one that emerges slowly over the course of the first year of life. Fathers who are not present at the birth of their baby, mothers who deliver by cesarean section, and, of course, adoptive parents all have been found to develop healthy relationships with their infants and children. Katherine May, a researcher and nurse, recently noted: "This bonding business is nonsense. We've sold parents a bill of goods. They believe that if they don't have skin-to-skin contact within the first fifteen minutes, they won't bond. Science just doesn't show that."[54] This "epoxy theory" of early parent-infant relationships has simply not held up under close scrutiny.

The Transition to Fatherhood

The changes in fathers' sense of self and their social relationships that begin during pregnancy continue after men make the transition to fatherhood. These further changes are not surprising if we remember that development does not stop at adolescence, but continues during the adulthood years. One of the major life transitions for men during adulthood is becoming a father. Life course theorists such as Erik Erikson and Robert Havinghurst argue that the transition to fatherhood is "both a crisis and a developmental opportunity for maturation and new growth."[55] Or as Philip Cowan has said, in trying to reconcile these two views of the transition to fatherhood: "It feels as if I am watching an out-of-synch 3-D movie with the picture on the left representing the transition to parenthood as a time of disequilibrium, stress and crisis, while the picture on the right portrays becoming a father as a time of joy with a potential for significant individual and marital growth."[56] Both of these views are correct, of course; as in the case of most life course transitions there is simultaneously stress and difficulty and potential for positive developmental change.

What happens to men during the transition to parenthood? As life course theorists suggest, the impact on fathers is mixed. As individuals, men's self-esteem may suffer in their struggle with the competing demands of work, marriage, and parenting.[57] Many fathers, in comparison with men who are still childless, report more anxiety, stress, and fatigue, a reminder that diaper changing, 3 A.M. feedings, and the increased financial load takes its toll on new fathers.

Men's sense of themselves shifts as a function of the transition to fatherhood. Roles change for both men and women after they become parents. Carolyn and Philip Cowan, in their longitudinal study of the transition to parenthood, assessed shifts in roles between pregnancy and fatherhood. They found that men who became fathers showed a decrease in the "partner/lover" aspect of their self and increased the "parent" portion of their self-definition.[58] In contrast, men who remained childless significantly increased the "partner/lover" aspect of their relationship over the twenty-one-month assessment period. Frances Grossman, who studied men's transition to parenthood, found that first-time fathers who were both more affiliative (that is, importantly connected to others, enjoying empathetic relationships) and more autonomous (that is, viewing themselves as separate and distinct from others) had scores that indicated that they were better adjusted. Fathers who were more affiliative were also reported to be higher in emotional well-being when their firstborns were one year old. These findings suggest that "separateness and individuation are not sufficient for men's well being; they need connections as well."[59] Does fatherhood have a longer-term impact on men's psychological development? D. H. Heath, in a longitudinal study of college men, found that fatherhood related to men's ability to understand themselves, to understand others sympathetically, and to integrate their own feelings.[60]

Does fatherhood affect marital relationships? In contrast to common wisdom that children bring couples closer together and "save marriages," the evidence suggests that there is a decline in marital satisfaction, especially on the part of men, as a consequence of the birth of a child.[61] The marital adjustments associated with the transition to fatherhood are evident in the Cowans' longitudinal study.[62] These investigators found that fathers' marital satisfaction showed a modest decrease from pregnancy to six months, but a sharp decline between six and eighteen months. In contrast, mothers show a much more linear decline, beginning in the postpartum period and continuing across the first two years. In this same period of eighteen months, 12.5 percent of the couples separated or divorced; by five years of age, this figure was up to 20 percent.

In spite of the dip in marital satisfaction, two caveats

should be noted. First, even though marital satisfaction decreases for men (and women) after the onset of parenthood, marital stability (that is, the likelihood of staying in the marriage) increases relative to childless couples, for whom the national average is 50 percent. The Cowans note, "The marital stability of couples who have preschool children is protected. Although new parents may be experiencing increased tension or dissatisfaction as couples, their joint involvement with managing the baby's and the family's needs may lead them to put off, or possibly work harder on, the problems in their marriage—at least while the children are young."[63]

Not all of the couples showed a decline in marital satisfaction; 18 percent of couples showed increased satisfaction with their marital relationship. This figure rose to 38 percent for couples that participated in a supportive intervention program during the transition to parenthood.[64] Similar diversity in the pattern of change in fathers' marital satisfaction is evident in Jay Belsky's longitudinal study.[65] During the transition to parenthood, marital quality declined in about 30 percent of the families, improved in another 30 percent, and in nearly 40 percent showed no change.

A variety of reasons has been suggested for this decline in men's marital satisfaction, including the physical strain of child care, increased financial responsibilities, the emotional demands of new familial responsibilities, the restrictions of parenthood, and the redefinition of roles and role arrangements.[66]

One father in the Cowans' study lamented: "Well I wouldn't give her back, but we don't have any spontaneity any more . . . And we still haven't slept all the way through the night. Partly I'm lying awake worrying about how I'm gonna get everything done at work the next day and still have some time left to play with her when I get home."[67] As the Cowans discovered, however, there is little support for the hypothesis that as the number of negative changes increase, marital satisfaction declines. In their study, they found little relation between declining marital satisfaction and any single negative change.[68] Perhaps it is the cumulative increase—regardless of quality—of negative shifts that is associated with declines in marital satisfaction.[69] At the same time, evidence suggests that discrepancies in expectations on the part of mothers and fathers concerning the relative roles that each will play may be an important determinant of postpartum marital satisfaction. The Cowans found that when a larger discrepancy existed between the wives' expectations of their husbands' involvement in infant care and the actual level of participation, there was a greater decline in wives' marital satisfaction between late pregnancy and eighteen months.[70] Other researchers reported a similar decrease in marital satisfaction when there was a discrepancy between spouses' gender-role attitudes and the division of household and childcare labor. Even traditional fathers who held conservative attitudes about gender roles but were nonetheless involved in child care reported lower levels of dissatisfaction.[71]

On the positive side, when expectations and behaviors match, some evidence suggests that marital satisfaction is correspondingly high. Osofsky and Culp reported that in a three-year longitudinal study of the transition to fatherhood, when fathers were satisfied with the division of family tasks and decisions, marital and sexual adjustment was satisfactory.[72] Research thus suggests that discrepancies in expectations about roles, rather than the level of change per se, may be a key factor in men's marital satisfaction after the onset of fatherhood.

Becoming a father changes not only one's self and

one's marriage but the links with one's parents. The process of increasing contact with parents that begins during pregnancy continues after men become fathers.[73] One father remarked: "Since I've become a father, I just feel more grown up. My parents are finally letting me in on family secrets they thought I was too young to know before."[74] And, as we saw earlier, the social support for expectant fathers from friends and co-workers that begins in pregnancy increases over the first six months of new fatherhood.

Men's involvement in their work may change after the transition to fatherhood as well. Here too there are conflicting pushes and pulls. On the one hand, fathers are more serious about their job obligations—a reflection of the economic reality of parenthood. On the other hand, there is increased pressure to participate in the care and rearing of a new child. Listen to these two fathers:

> "On the job, I've become more serious. I've really had to get my act together. It's not just me and Mary now. I've got a family to provide for."[75]

> "I'm used to working in the evenings, but now, either I don't get to do it at all or I finish and I'm exhausted. I'm in a bind. I miss watching every detail of Sarah's development. But if I really want to build my career and get off on a solid footing, now's the time to do it."[76]

The issue of how to balance work and family is a recurring one for fathers and mothers and extends well beyond the period of pregnancy and the transition to fatherhood. In later chapters we will return to this central issue of modern family life.

As our discussion suggests, the transition to fatherhood is a two-sided coin, with both costs and benefits. This balance continues to fluctuate across the life cycle, as children and fathers develop together. The benefits of involvement in fatherhood for men's own personal development, however, seem to clearly outweigh the costs of becoming a father.

Looking at pregnancy from the perspective of the couple rather than considering it an experience that happens to the mother alone has made us aware of the myriad ways that fathers participate in pregnancy. Not only do they offer comfort and support to their wives, but they go through a process of defining for themselves what it means to become a father. Shifts in hospital practices are allowing fathers to participate more actively in childbirth, and couples vary widely in how much they take advantage of this option. To date the evidence suggests that fathers who choose to become more involved in pregnancy and childbirth seem to benefit themselves and their wives, as well as their infants.

3 / Fathers' Involvement: Infancy and Beyond

Research on fathers and the effects of fathers' behavior on children is a relatively new field, in comparison with research on other aspects of child development. As I suggested in Chapter 1, only recently have we moved beyond the consideration of the mother-child relationship as the sole critical familial influence on children.

As is often the case when scientists begin to study new questions, researchers first started to study fathering and its effects on children by observing and describing fathers' behavior with children. These earliest efforts focused on several issues that flowed from our cultural assumptions about fathers and their potential and actual roles. The image of fathers as incompetent in caregiving and limited in their nurturing capacity—especially with young babies—is highly ingrained in Western culture. This view led researchers to ask, "Are fathers capable of providing nurturance and care for infants and young children? Do they provide such care? Do fathers have distinctive styles of relating to children?" These early descriptive studies of fathers' behavior, carried out in the late 1960s and 1970s, laid important groundwork for subsequent studies. Later research, which I will discuss in detail in Chapters 4 and 5, sought to reveal the predictors, processes, and products of fathering. But without the early studies describing fathers' behavior, the later studies could not have been accomplished. The early studies also helped us set aside some of the cultural myths about fathers' incompetence and disinterest in caring for infants and children. This work gave credibility to the calls for greater participation by fathers in children's lives and provided a firmer scientific basis for the emerging cultural ideal of the new "involved" father.

Fathers and Newborns

The days when fathers were permitted no more than a glance at their new offspring through the nursery window are well past. For the last twenty to thirty years, most fathers have been permitted to have direct contact with their babies in the hospital rather than waiting until they go home. Because fathers and newborns have been getting together more frequently, researchers have been watching more often. The aim has been to determine how fathers interact with very young babies and whether fathers and mothers differ in their early interaction with their infants. Traditionally it was assumed that fathers were disinterested in and uninvolved with newborn babies, but these studies suggested a very different picture. Martin Greenberg and Norman Morris were among the first researchers to notice how delighted and pleased fathers are with their newborns. They interviewed new fathers and discovered that "fathers begin developing a bond to their newborn by the first three days after birth and often earlier. Furthermore, there are certain characteristics of this bond which we call 'engrossment' . . . a feeling of preoccupation, absorption and interest in their newborn."[1]

Although these interviews were suggestive, this verbal evidence was supplemented by other researchers' direct observations of fathers with their babies to determine whether these self-reports of feelings and interest were reflected in actual behavior. A series of my own studies helped put the issue on a firmer basis.[2] Instead of asking fathers how they felt about their newborns, Sandra O'Leary and I observed the fathers when they joined mother and baby in the mother's hospital room. The results were clear: as shown by a wide variety of parenting behaviors such as touching, holding, kissing, exploring, and imitating the infant, fathers were just as interested as mothers in their babies. Fathers even tended to hold the infant more and to rock the infant in their arms more than the mothers.

This study by itself, however, did not provide conclusive evidence that fathers are involved with their infants. For one thing, since both mother and father were in the room, the high degree of father-infant interaction might have been due to the supporting presence of the mother, who might have encouraged the father and provided physical assistance and verbal instructions. Second, most of the fathers in this study had attended childbirth classes and had been present during the delivery. They therefore might have been more interested in their parental role and more likely to involve themselves with their infants than other fathers. Third, the men we observed were middle class and well educated; do working-class fathers show a similar pattern?

To investigate these questions, we studied working-class fathers who had not participated in childbirth classes and had not been present during delivery.[3] We observed the father alone with the infant, the mother alone with the infant, and the father, mother, and infant together. Again the fathers were interested and active participants in the first few days after delivery. Whether alone with their newborn or together with their wife and baby, the fathers were just as nurturant and stimulating as the mothers. The only nurturant behavior in which mothers surpassed fathers was smiling. It has been well established, however, that women smile more than men, not just at babies but at all kinds of people.

Being nurturant, affectionate, and loving may be good for fathers as well as for babies. The opportunities to express these emotions to their children may allow men to become more expressive and gentle in their relationships with other people too. Whether a man truly changes in this way after becoming a father, however, is not yet known.

The father can also indirectly affect his infant by influencing the way in which the mother treats the baby. We observed an example of this kind of indirect influence when we compared mothers alone with their babies and mothers with their babies when their husbands were also present. In the fathers' presence mothers stimulated the babies less—talking, touching, and holding them less often. However, they also smiled at the babies and "explored" them (by counting toes, checking ears, feeling the baby's head, and so on) more. This suggested to us that the father's presence may increase the mother's interest in the new baby.

David Phillips and I took a closer look at the types of speech that fathers and mothers use in talking to their newborns.[4] Talking to babies is different from talking to adults, and earlier researchers have found that mothers use a special form of speech when talking to infants. Often called "motherese," it is characterized by slow and exaggerated speech, repetition, and short phrases.[5] Catchwords such as *hey, hi,* and *hello* are often part of motherese. To discover whether fathers make these same kinds of speech adjustments, we recorded fathers' speech while they were either feeding or playing with their newborns. We found that just as mothers adjust their speech, so do fathers. In contrast to the way they talk to other adults, fathers slow their rate of speech, shorten their phrases, and repeat words and phrases much more when they talk to their newborn infants. Such "baby talk" helps to attract and maintain the baby's attention better than talking in a normal adult voice. This kind of simplified speech also elicits more positive reactions, such as smiles, and may increase the chance that the child will understand the message.[6] This is true whether fathers or mothers use this kind of modified or baby talk. Such speech, moreover, may help babies learn to recognize their parents' and other caregivers' faces and voices. These findings provide another piece of evidence that fathers are sensitive to infants. Like mothers, they talk to babies at the babies' level.

Reading the Baby's Messages

Other evidence indicates that fathers are not just actively involved with their infants but competent social partners as well. One part of being a competent social partner is recognizing and correctly labeling the baby's signals. Infants cry, move, smile, and fuss, and parents need to be able to interpret the different behaviors. Are fathers as sensitive as mothers to these signals?

A series of studies by Ann Frodi, Michael Lamb, and their colleagues has helped to provide an answer. They measured sensitivity to infant behavior by using psychophysiological measures such as heart rate and blood pressure as well as the parents' own reports of how they felt about their baby's behavior. Both mothers and fathers perceived an infant cry as unpleasant, while the sight of a smiling, gurgling infant elicited positive feelings. The psychophysiological measures told a similar story: the parents' blood pressure rose in response to the crying infant but not in reaction to the smiling baby. Most important, the physiological reactions of mothers and fathers were not different. These data contradict the claim that women but not men are innately predisposed to respond to infant signals. The researchers commented, "Our data do not prove that there are no biological sex differences, but they do speak against the notion that 'maternal' responsiveness reflects predominantly biological influences."[7]

Fathers, like mothers, are capable of discriminating among different types of crying patterns. The cry of a premature infant, for instance, differs from the cry of a full-term baby; it is shrill and high pitched. When listening to tapes of premature and full-term babies crying, both mothers and fathers found the cry of the premature infant more unpleasant than the cry of a full-term baby.[8] Even more impressive are data that indicate that men and women are equally able to discriminate among different crying patterns. Babies of course, cry for various reasons: because they are hungry, or because a pin is pricking them, and so on. Mothers can tell the difference between different types of cries such as pain and anger cries, particularly when listening to their own infant.[9] Can men do the same? Although fathers can accurately identify the cries of their own infants, fathers are not as capable as mothers in distinguishing among different kinds of cries. While fathers are better than males who are not fathers in diagnosing why an infant is crying, mothers are better crying detectives than their spouses.[10] Mothers' greater experience with infants as well as their increased caregiving responsibility probably accounts for their superiority in reading babies' cries. It is important to remember, however, that there are wide individual differences across fathers, and some men may be very good at reading these kinds of signals.

There is more to a successful interchange than merely recognizing the baby's signals. The competent caretaker must learn to react appropriately to a baby's messages by behaving responsively. As in any other form of social interaction, the timing or pacing of a person's behavior is just as important as the amount and kind of stimulation he provides.

Fathers not only are able to recognize infant signals, but also are able to use these signals appropriately to guide their own behavior. In my studies of fathers and newborns I have consistently found that fathers are just as responsive as mothers to infant signals such as sounds and mouth movements.[11] Both mothers and fathers talk to the infant more, touch the infant more, and look more closely at the infant after an infant vocalization. Fathers, however, are more likely than mothers to respond to infant vocalization by talking to the baby; mothers are more likely to react with touching. The baby's mouth movements, like vocalizations, elicit responses from both parents: both fathers and mothers increase their talking, touching, and stimulation in response to mouth movements. These data indicate that both fathers and mothers react to the newborn infant's cues in a sensitive and functional manner even though they differ in their specific responses. As the infant develops, parents do differ in their reaction to some signals, such as smiling. Just as mothers smile at their newborn infants more than fathers do, when infants begin to smile, mothers react to their smiles more than fathers do.[12]

Together these findings remind us that the relationship between father and infant is bidirectional. Fathers and infants, just like mothers and infants, continually influence each other. Fathers react to babies' signals, and babies, in turn, learn to use their developing communication skills to affect the ways their fathers treat them. These exchanges teach infants an early and important lesson in social control: that they can influence other people through their own behavior.

Role Differentiation Begins Early

Although I have emphasized the similarities between mothers and fathers, one important difference should be mentioned. Although mothers and fathers are equally involved with their babies from the beginning, fathers are less likely to be involved in direct caregiving activities than mothers. However, direct contact, such as caregiving and diaper changing, is not the only way in which fathers are involved with their children. Several types of paternal involvement can be distinguished. Michael Lamb, a longtime father researcher, suggests three components: interaction, availability, and responsibility. Interaction refers to the father's direct contact with his child through caregiving and shared activities. Availability is a related concept concerning the father's potential availability for interaction, by being present or accessible to the child whether or not direct interaction is occurring. Responsibility refers to the role the father plays in ascertaining that the child is taken care of and arranging for resources to be available for the child.[13] At least two further distinctions can be made. Specifically, it is important to distinguish involvement in child-care activities and involvement in play or leisure activities with the child, since children may learn different lessons from their interactions with their fathers in different situations such as caregiving and play. In addition, absolute and relative involvement need to be distinguished. These two indices are independent and may affect both children's and adults' views of role distributions in different ways.[14] Fathers may spend a great deal of time with their children in an absolute sense, but the impact on the children will depend on how much time the mother is spending as well. For example, families in which the relative involvement of mothers and fathers is equal are very different environments for children than families in which the relative level of parental involvement is very uneven.

Owing to circumstances such as divorce or out-of-wedlock birth, not all fathers reside with their children. By focusing only on fathers in two-parent families, we may overestimate the degree of fathers' involvement. At the same time that fathers in two-parent families seem to be increasing their involvement and moving slowly toward more equal participation with their wives in the care and rearing of children, there has been another trend as well. Increases in fathers' absence, nonpayment of child support, and denial of paternity reflect the less desirable side of fatherhood. These two trends reflect what Frank Furstenberg has labeled "Good dads, bad dads."[15] In Chapter 7, I will address the patterns of involvement of noncustodial fathers. In this section I focus on how fathers and mothers in two-parent families divide the responsibilities of parenting.

Mothers, according to our observational studies of parents and newborns—even mothers of bottle-fed babies—spend more time in feeding and related caretaking activities, such as wiping the baby's face, than do fathers.[16] From the earliest days of the baby's life, a clear division in parental roles is evident. A traditional division of roles is found even in families where the couples hold egalitarian views. This finding seems to reflect a more general tendency: pregnancy and the birth of a first child often shift a couple toward a more traditional division of roles. This is confirmed by a study by Carolyn Cowan and Philip Cowan of couples during pregnancy and up to eighteen months after the birth of a first child.[17] They found that couples shifted toward a traditional arrangement in a variety of areas such as household tasks, decision making, and baby care—regardless of whether their prior role division had been traditional or egalitarian.

Most evidence suggests that this pattern persists well beyond the hospital stay and the newborn period. In a study in Boston, Milton Kotelchuck found that mothers spent an average of an hour and a half per day feeding their year-old infants, compared with fifteen minutes for fathers. Most of the fathers were not present at home during the day, of course, and most of the mothers were. But that is not the only reason for the difference. Seventy-five percent of the fathers had no regular responsibilities for taking care of their infants, and 43 percent reported that they had never changed their babies' diapers.[18] More recent studies confirm this profile. In a longitudinal study of middle- and working-class families in which mothers, fathers, and their infants were observed at one, three, and nine months of age, Jay Belsky and his colleagues found that mothers responded to, stimulated, expressed positive affection toward, and provided more basic care for their infants at all three time points. Fathers exceeded mothers in the extent to which they engaged in reading and television viewing.[19] In Euro-American families, fathers spend 20 to 25 percent as much time as mothers in direct care of children, and this increases to about 33 percent as much as mothers when both parents are employed outside the home.[20]

What about fathers in other ethnic groups in the United States? Recent studies of African American and

Hispanic American families confirm the general picture just described. Just as in Euro-American households, middle-class African American fathers were less likely to be involved in feeding, bathing, and diapering their infants.[21] For example, mothers spent 2.55 hours per day in feeding and cleaning their infants and toddlers; fathers spent 1.47 hours per day in these activities. A similar profile was evident for lower-class two-parent African American families with young infants—fathers were involved in caregiving but to a lesser degree than their wives.[22] Lower-income Hispanic American fathers of four-month-old infants estimated that they spent about half as much time each day (1.8 hours) as mothers (3.6 hours) in basic caregiving activities (bedtime routines, physical care, feeding, and soothing the infant).[23] Comparisons between African American and Hispanic American lower-income families suggest that these two groups of fathers show similar patterns of involvement. Moreover, the fathers in this study by Ziarat Hossain, Tiffany Field, and their colleagues proved to be just as involved with their infants as Euro-American fathers and perhaps even more so. Mothers, however, for both African American and Hispanic American families, remained even more involved in caregiving than fathers—a pattern that is found in Euro-American families as well.[24] Other studies confirm that African American and Hispanic American fathers are involved, accessible, and sensitive parents.[25] These findings are important in light of the past negative characterizations of low-income African American and Hispanic American fathers as uninvolved. Clearly the stereotypes surrounding American fathers of different ethnic backgrounds need to be discarded as outdated and inaccurate. Much of the earlier work was based on single-parent families and failed to recognize the large differences within cultural groups.

Nor is this a uniquely American picture. Martin Richards and his colleagues have reported similar findings for Great Britain. Only 35 percent of the fathers in their study regularly fed their thirty-week-old infants. By the time the infants passed their first birthday, 40 percent of the fathers were regularly helping with feeding.[26] Even more impressive evidence of mother-father differences in involvement comes from the longitudinal study of traditional and nontraditional families in Sweden executed by Lamb and his colleagues. Families in which the father elected to stay home as primary caregiver for one month or more (nontraditional) were compared with families in which the father elected to be a secondary caregiver (traditional). In an analysis of home observations at eight and sixteen months, mothers surpassed fathers in holding and affectionate behavior regardless of family type.[27] Further support for this pattern of sex-of-parent differences comes from a study of Israeli families. In Israel, Charles Greenbaum and Rivka Landau observed middle- and lower-class families when their babies were two, four, seven, and eleven months. At every infant age, mothers greatly exceeded fathers in verbal interactions—regardless of social class.[28] In another Israeli study, kibbutz-reared infants and their parents were observed in the parents' living quarters when the infants were eight and sixteen months of age.[29] Kibbutzim are collective agricultural settlements in which infants are reared in group houses rather than in traditional families. Although child care is the primary responsibility of nonparental caregivers (metapelot) rather than either parent, sex differences in parental behavior similar to those observed in the United States and Sweden were found. Kibbutz mothers were more likely to vocalize, laugh, display affection, hold, and engage in caregiving than were fathers. Because mothers and fathers on Israeli kibbutzim both work full time and have their children cared for by other caregivers, the findings suggest that "more sex-role expectations and/or biological predispositions—rather than immediate competing role demands—appear to account for the widely observed differences between maternal and paternal behavior."[30]

These findings are consistent with the more general proposition that pregnancy and birth of a first child, in particular, are occasions for a shift toward a more traditional division of roles. Of special interest is the fact that this pattern holds regardless of whether the initial role division between husbands and wives is traditional or egalitarian.[31] The Cowans suggest, "Despite the current rhetoric and ideology concerning equality of roles for men and women, it seems that couples tend to adopt traditionally defined roles during times of stressful transition such as around the birth of a first child."[32]

The overall pattern of contact that is evident in infancy continues into middle childhood and adolescence. In a study of middle childhood (six- to seven-year-olds), Graeme Russell and Alan Russell found that Australian mothers were available to children 54.7 hours a week compared with 34.6 hours a week for fathers. Mothers also spent much more time alone with children (22.6 hours/week) than did fathers (2.4 hours/week). When both parents and child were together, however, mothers and fathers initiated interactions with children with equal frequency and children's initiations toward each parent were similar.[33] Adolescents and parents show a similar pattern: in another study, fifteen- to sixteen-year-olds were found to spend twice as much time with their mothers alone than with their fathers alone each day.[34]

From infancy through adolescence, fathers are generally less available on a routine basis than mothers. We will return to this issue later as we explore the reasons for this discrepancy and search for the determinants of fathers' involvement.

The Father as Manager

The focus of research on fathers has been primarily on face-to-face parent-child interaction. To a large degree this emphasis reflects the common assumption that parental influence takes place directly through face-to-face contact or indirectly through the impact of the interaction on another family member. Only recently have researchers and theorists begun to recognize the managerial function of parents and to appreciate the impact of variations in this function on child development.[35] By "managerial," I mean the ways in which parents organize and arrange the child's home environment such as setting limits in the home. The father's managerial role may be just as important as the father's role as stimulator, because the amount of time that children spend interacting with the inanimate environment in the home far exceeds their social interaction time.[36]

Mothers and fathers differ in their degree of responsibility for the management of family tasks. From the time children are babies through middle childhood, mothers are more likely to assume the managerial role than fathers. In infancy, this means setting boundaries for play, taking the child to the doctor, or arranging daycare. Mothers take more responsibility in all of these domains than fathers.[37] In middle childhood, Russell and Russell found that mothers continue to assume more managerial responsibility (for example, directing the child to have a bath, to eat a meal, or to put away toys).[38]

The managerial role also includes initiating and arranging children's access to peers and playmates. In addition, parents function as supervisors or overseers of children's interactions with age-mates, especially with younger children. Although laboratory studies indicate that both mothers and fathers are equally capable of this type of supervisory behavior, in home contexts, fathers are less likely than mothers to perform this supervisory role.[39]

Even in the 1990s and even in the case of families where husbands and wives share roles, fathers are less likely to engage in management of the household and child care. The sociologist Scott Coltrane recently noted: "In most families, husbands notice less about what needs to be done, wait to be asked to do various chores and require explicit directions if they are to complete the tasks successfully . . . most couples continue to characterize husbands' contributions to housework or child care as 'helping' their wives. And when they stay with their children alone, dads often view themselves as 'babysitters.' "[40]

Competence versus Performance

Are fathers the secondary caregivers because they are less talented at child care than mothers? When Douglas Sawin and I tested this hypothesis, it turned out to be wrong. We observed mothers and fathers feeding their babies and measured the amount of milk consumed. The babies took almost the same amount from fathers as from mothers.[41] But of course there is more to being a competent caregiver than merely getting food into a baby. Parental competence, as explained earlier, is best measured by how sensitively parents interpret and respond to infant cues and signals. Consider the feeding situation. The aim of the caregiver is to ensure that the infant continues to receive enough milk. By behaviors such as sucking, pausing, coughing, or spitting up, babies indicate whether the feeding is going smoothly or whether some adjustment is in order. One way to measure how capable parents are as feeders is to examine how quickly they modify their behavior in response to the infant's distress signals. Sawin and I observed fathers and mothers feeding their babies and found that fathers were just as sensitive to these signals as mothers. Fathers, like mothers, responded to these infant cues by momentarily stopping the feeding, looking more closely to check on the baby, and speaking to the baby. Although they tend to spend less time feeding their babies, fathers are as sensitive and responsive as mothers to infant cues in the context of feeding. The only difference between mothers and fathers was that fathers were less likely than mothers to stimulate their babies by touching them when the baby signaled that there was a momentary difficulty.

Even when fathers do not participate directly in feeding their babies, they can still influence the success of feeding in indirect ways, through their relationship with the mother. In Chapter 1, I discussed Frank Pedersen's finding that mothers who had tense and conflicted relationships with their husbands were not as skilled in feeding their babies. Fathers' indirect influences can be observed in other ways as well. Consider the father's role when the mother is breastfeeding. Doris Entwisle and Susan Doering found that mothers who were supported in their breastfeeding efforts by their husbands continued to breastfeed longer than mothers with less supportive husbands.[42] Fathers, of course, can be helpful when mothers are breastfeeding by sharing in other caregiving activities such as bathing and diapering and occasionally relieving the mother of her feeding responsibilities by giving the infant supplemental bottles. In sum, fathers can influence their babies, as well as their wives' behavior with their babies, by both direct and indirect contributions to early feeding.

Cesarean Section and Prematurity as Elicitors of Fathers' Involvement

Fathers do participate in infant care more actively under some circumstances. As we saw in Chapter 2, fathers spend more time in caregiving when mothers have had a cesarean delivery. Another situation that may increase fathers' role in early caregiving is the premature birth of a baby. Having a baby earlier than expected can be stressful for the family, thereby increasing the importance of the father's support for the mother. Investigators in both England and the United States have found that fathers of premature infants are more active in feeding, diapering, and bathing their infants than fathers of full-term babies, both in the hospital and later at home.[43] These fathers' more active participation in caregiving is particularly helpful because premature infants usually need to be fed more often than full-term infants and experience more feeding disturbances. Premature infants can also be less satisfying to feed and to interact with, because they are often less responsive to parental stimulation.[44] Thus by sharing more than usual in caregiving, the father of a premature infant relieves the mother of some of this responsibility, giving the mother some much-needed rest, and thereby may indirectly influence the baby by positively affecting the relationship between mother and baby.

The father's support is important in other ways as well. Often a premature infant is kept in the hospital for a period of time, and the father can play an important role by visiting and becoming acquainted with the baby during this period. Research in Canada by Klaus Minde has shown that mothers who have supportive husbands tend to visit their premature babies in the hospital more often, and that mothers who visit more have fewer parenting problems later than mothers who visit less frequently.[45] Again we find that fathers can influence their infants by affecting the mother-infant relationship. Understanding the paternal role in infant development clearly requires that the father's behavior be viewed in the context of his role within the family.

Play

Play is one of the chief occupations of infants and children. Play begins very early in infancy, and babies are well prepared for playful interaction with other humans. Recent research on perception indicates that babies are particularly responsive to human faces and voices. Rudolph Schaffer notes:

> From the beginning of life, [the infant] is able to regulate what he takes in by selective attention. Given the choice, he will seek out those features of his surroundings to which, by virtue of his physical make-up he is most sensitive . . . If we were to design an object that would contain all these features and thus be maximally attention-worthy, we would end up with a human being . . . It is as though the infant is biologically "set" to be triggered by certain quite specific yet primitive stimuli— stimuli found in other human beings, and one can, of course, readily understand that it would be biologically useful for a baby to be prepared from the very beginning for interaction with other human beings.[46]

Just as babies respond to the sight of a human face, they are more likely to respond to human voices than to other types of sounds.

Both fathers and mothers are active playmates for the infant. In fact, though mothers contribute to their infant's development in a wide variety of ways, fathers probably make their contribution primarily through play. If the mother is not working outside the home, she typically spends more total time in playing with her baby than the father does. Fathers, however, devote a higher proportion of their time with the baby to play than mothers. For example, in his study of middle-class Boston families, Kotelchuck found that fathers devote nearly 40 percent of their time with their infants to play, while mothers spend about 25 percent of their time in play.[47] Fathers are usually secondary caregivers, but they have an important role as play partners. Lamb and his associates watched mothers and fathers interacting with their infants at seven to eight months of age and again at twelve to thirteen months. There were marked differences in the reasons that led fathers and mothers to pick up their infants: fathers were more likely to hold their babies to play with them; mothers were more likely to hold them for caretaking purposes such as feeding and bathing. In spite of fathers' limited availability, their commitment to playful activities probably contributes to their attractiveness to the child.[48]

In a recent study of African American fathers, Ziarat Hossain and Jaipaul Roopnarine found that mothers devoted 38 percent of their involvement time to play in contrast to 54 percent for fathers.[49] Studies of Hispanic American families reveal a similar pattern: fathers spend more of their time with their children in play.[50] In a study of English parents, Martin Richards and his colleagues found that play was the most common form of interaction for fathers of thirty- and sixty-week-old infants. Ninety percent of the fathers played regularly with their infants, while less than half participated in caretaking.[51] The situation is similar in the United States.

Is Fathers' Play Style Unique?

Do fathers and mothers have different styles of play? Consider these two examples: a father picks up his son, seven-month-old Zachary, tosses him in the air, and throws his head back so that he and Zachary are face to face. As Zachary giggles and chortles, his father lowers him, shakes him, and tosses him up in the air again. A mother sits her daughter, ten-month-old Lisa, on her lap and pulls out her favorite toy, a green donkey that brays when you squeeze it. Lisa smiles, and for the next few minutes her mother moves the donkey in front of Lisa's eyes, makes it bray, and talks and sings to her daughter. Lisa watches intently, smiles, and occasionally reaches for her donkey. Are these examples merely cultural stereotypes, or do mothers and fathers really play with their babies in different ways?

A series of studies confirm that differences in parental play styles do exist. Michael Yogman, T. Berry Brazelton, and their colleagues explored differences in mothers' and fathers' play by studying five infants from the ages of two weeks to twenty-four weeks.[52] In a laboratory setting, they observed each infant with three different play partners: father, mother, and a stranger. The infant was placed in a reclining chair (or baby seat) and the face-to-face interactions that developed between the infant and the adult as they played together were filmed. There were clear differences in the ways the adults played with the infants, as revealed by talking and touching patterns. Mothers spoke softly, repeating words and phrases frequently and imitating the infant's sounds more than either fathers or strangers. A burst-pause pattern was common for these mothers: a rapidly spoken series of words and sounds, followed by a short period of silence. Fathers were less verbal and more tactile than mothers. They touched their infants with rhythmic tapping patterns more often than mothers or strangers. Father-infant play shifted rapidly from peaks of high infant attention and excitement to valleys of minimal attention; mother-infant play demonstrated more gradual shifts. Brazelton commented:

> Most fathers seem to present a more playful, jazzing up approach. As one watches this interaction, it seems that a father is expecting a more heightened, playful response from the baby. And he gets it! Amazingly enough, an infant by two or three weeks displays an entirely different attitude (more wide-eyed, playful and bright faced) toward his father than to his mother. The cycles might be characterized as higher, deeper, and even a bit more jagged.[53]

Even though fathers and mothers differ in style in their early face-to-face play, they both show a high degree of sensitivity to their babies. Both the mother's and the father's play is characterized by reciprocity: the parent and infant engage in a dialogue with a clear cycle of approach and withdrawal on the part of both players. With young infants, the parents probably contribute most to this reciprocity; they elicit the baby's attention, gauge their behavior to keep the baby interested, and reduce their level of stimulation when the baby is tired or bored. As infants get older they develop more skill in adjusting their behavior to keep the interaction going. Jerome Bruner has demonstrated that one-year-old infants can play turn-taking games, which rely on each partner doing his part to keep the interchange alive.[54]

Mothers and fathers also have different styles of play with older infants and in situations other than face-to-face play. Thomas Power and I examined the types of games that fathers and mothers played with their eight-month-old infants in a laboratory playroom.[55] Unlike the earlier studies of face-to-face play, this situation was relatively unstructured and toys were available for the parents and infants to use. We were able to identify a number of distinctive games that were played. These ranged from "distal" games, which involve stimulating the baby at a distance by shaking or showing a toy, to "physical" games, which involve directly touching, lifting, or bouncing the baby. Other games, such as grasping and retrieving games, require the infant to hold or retrieve a nearby toy.

Mothers and fathers played many of the same games, but their styles differed. Fathers engaged in significantly more physical games, such as bouncing and lifting, than mothers. Mothers, in contrast, used a more distal, attention-getting approach and played more watching games. A favorite game of the mothers was to show the baby a toy and then shake and move it to stimulate the baby. Fathers were particularly likely to play "lifting" games with their boy infants and were less physical with their girls.

These differences between mothers' and fathers' styles of play are found in the home as well as in the laboratory. Observing infants from eight to twenty-four months of age, Lamb found that fathers engaged in more physical games such as rough-and-tumble play and more unusual or idiosyncratic games than mothers. Mothers, in contrast, engaged in more conventional play activities (such as peek-a-boo and pat-a-cake), stimulus-toy play (jiggling a toy to stimulate the child), and reading than fathers.[56]

Nor are these effects evident only in infancy. Kevin MacDonald and I observed the play interaction patterns between mothers and fathers and their three- and four-year-old children in their homes.[57] We found that fathers engaged in more physical play than mothers. Mothers, in contrast, engaged in more object-mediated play with their offspring than fathers. In a variety of studies, a clear pattern emerges: fathers are tactile, physical, and arousing, while mothers tend to be more verbal, didactic, and object-oriented in their play. Infants and young children get not just more stimulation from their fathers but a qualitatively different pattern of stimulation.

These patterns shift across development. Seeking to profile the developmental changes that occur across childhood, MacDonald and I telephoned nearly four hundred families with over seven hundred children ranging in age from under one year of age to ten years of age and asked them about the frequency of physical play interactions with their children.[58] A curvilinear developmental effect was found, with comparatively low levels of physical play prior to age one, a peak in the preschool years (ages one to four) and a decline after, to very low levels of parent-child physical play after ten years of age. Overall dads still played more physically than moms. Others confirm that play activities are most common in the infancy and preschool periods. As children mature, play declines in frequency as fathers interact with their children in leisure activities, private talks, or helping with schoolwork or reading.

In adolescence, maternal and paternal roles continue to differ. In a study of parent-adolescent relationships, Reed Larson and Maryse Richards asked mothers, fathers, and their adolescents to wear beepers and to record whom they were with and what they were doing whenever their beepers went off. They found that most of the time fathers spend alone with their adolescents is leisure time: watching television, resting, or active recreation.[59] In contrast, mothers spend more time with their adolescents in a wider range of activities, including housework, personal care, and socializing. Moreover, just as in infancy, joking, clowning, and teasing are much more common when adolescents interact with their fathers. Larson notes: "Yet while humor is ice-breaking and fun, it can also have costs. If fathers make everything into a joke, their adolescents may start to suspect them of not taking their feelings seriously."[60] Indeed, when fathers and adolescents are together, teenagers rate their interactions with fathers as less enjoyable than their fathers do. While dad thinks everything is fun, the adolescent may think otherwise. Larson comments:

> One explanation for this gap lies in the relative place of family time in fathers' and adolescents' lives . . . Men's happiest times were in the home sphere, because this is their time of respite from work . . . Adolescents, in contrast, report that their happiest times are with friends . . . Another explanation lies in the asymmetry within the father-adolescent interactions. Fathers have more status and power in the relationship than do adolescents . . . Given the comparative power, it may not be surprising that fathers find these times more gratifying.[61]

Although the style of fathers' involvement as a play or recreational partner appears to be consistent from infancy through adolescence, the meaning of this interaction shifts across development. The fun of fathers' play that we see in infancy is not so evident in adolescence. Perhaps the adolescents' goals of individuation and separation from the family are facilitated by the nature of the father-adolescent relationship. Larson, however, reflects on changes that may lie ahead: "With the rate of women's employment continuing to increase many families need and expect fathers to share more household responsibilities, including those of parenting. Strangers in the home only a generation ago, fathers now need to develop means of relating to their children that are more sensitive and empathic."[62]

These differences in parental play styles are not lost on infants. Infants appear to respond more positively to play with their fathers than to play with their mothers. In one study, K. Alison Clarke-Stewart gave two-and-a-half-year-olds a choice of play partners, and more than two-thirds of the children chose to play with their fathers rather than their mothers.[63] Hildy Ross and Heather Taylor found that boys prefer the paternal play style—whether mothers or fathers are the play partners.[64] Boys were observed as they played with each parent in each of two playrooms—one containing books and puzzles conducive to maternal play and one containing large soft balls and pillows conducive to paternal play. Boys reacted more positively to both mothers and fathers when their play style was more physical and active, resembling the typical paternal style. This study suggests that boys may not necessarily prefer their fathers, but rather prefer their physical style of play. Other evidence suggests that a child's preference for play with one parent or the other may depend on whether the child is a boy or girl. According to David Lynn, while boys always prefer their fathers as playmate, girls between two and four years of age show a shift away from father to mother as a preferred play partner.[65] This shift may occur because as girls develop they increasingly identify with their mother and become more attentive to their mother as a model for learning female gender-role behavior.

Games that fathers and mothers play may have an important impact on the child's later social and cognitive development. Both mothers and fathers are important play partners, but they may have different types of effects on their children's development. The father's physical stimulation complements the mother's verbal inter-action. Some games have short-term effects; their main purpose is to engage the infant's attention and maintain the social interaction between parent and infant. Watch-ing, toy touching, and bouncing and lifting games are play of this type. Other games may affect the infant's long-term development. Grasping and retrieving games, for example, may help the infant learn to explore objects or the larger environment. Face-to-face games may teach the infant turn-taking skills and provide early lessons in control of the social environment. As we will see in later chapters, fathers, more than mothers, seem to affect their child's later development mainly through their play.

Is There a Universal Father Play Style?

Is fathers' physical play an American style? Do fathers in other cultures use this same style of play? The evi-dence is mixed. In some cultures that are very similar to that of the United States, such as England and Australia, there are similar parental gender differences in play style. But studies from several other cultures do not find physical play to be a central part of the father-infant relationship.[66] Neither in Sweden nor among Israeli kib-butz families were fathers more likely to play with their children or to engage in different types of play. Similarly, Chinese Malaysian mothers and fathers reported that they rarely engaged in physical play with their children. Studies in India tell a similar story. Among middle-class Indian families in New Delhi, fathers and mothers were more likely to display affection than to play with infants while holding them. Although mothers engaged in more object-mediated play than fathers, there were no other differences in the play styles of mothers and fathers. Most interesting was the finding that the frequency of rough physical play was very low—less than one instance per hour. Observations of Aka Pygmies of Central Africa by the anthropologist Barry Hewlett are consistent with this pattern. In this culture mothers and fathers rarely, if ever, engage in vigorous or physical play with their children. Instead, both display affection and engage in plenty of close physical contact. In other cultures, such as Italy, neither mothers nor fathers play physically with infants, but other women in the extended family or within the community are more likely to do so.

Even in the United States, fathers do not show this predominantly physical style of play with all types of infants. My colleagues and I observed fathers' and mothers' behavior with full-term infants in contrast to infants born prematurely.[67] (In the United States approximately 14 percent of all infants are born prematurely.) Both in the hospital and soon after the infants were brought home, fathers exhibited their characteristic higher rate of physical play only with full-term infants. Fathers did not play with preterm infants in this physical manner. Tiffany Field, however, found that fathers do play games, laugh, and smile just as much with full-term and preterm infants at four months of age.[68] Perhaps they begin to play more physically when their premature baby is older and perceived as more robust.

Why do mothers and fathers play differently? Do the differences have a biological basis, or are they due to environmental influences? Experience with infants, the amount of time routinely spent with infants, the usual kind of responsibilities (caretaking versus play) that a parent assumes—all of these factors may significantly affect the parent's style of play, regardless of gender. Field compared fathers who serve as primary caretakers—a trend in family organization that is on the increase in the United States—with fathers who are secondary caretakers, the traditional father's role.[69] Using the same face-to-face interaction setting that I described earlier, she found that the two groups of fathers played with their infants differently. Primary-caretaker fathers smiled more and imitated their babies' facial expressions and high-pitched vocalizations more than secondary-caretaker fathers. In these ways the first group of fathers acted very much like mothers who are primary caretakers. Being a primary caretaker and, therefore, spending more time with the baby seems to affect the fathers' style of play significantly—a reminder that fathers' behavior can be modified and is not entirely biologically determined. But not all aspects of the fathers' play style changed. The primary-caretaker fathers were just as physical as the secondary-caretaker fathers, which means that there may be limits on how much fathers' typical style can be altered. Mothers' distinctive verbal play style shows the same kind of persistence across different forms of family organization. In Pedersen's study of mothers who worked outside the home, mothers played more but did not show a different style of play.[70] The working mothers stimulated their babies verbally more than before; they did not become more like fathers and play more physically with their babies.

Whether these distinctively female and male play styles are attributable to cultural influences or biological factors remains a question for future researchers to answer. The fact that male monkeys show the same rough-and-tumble physical style of play as human fathers, however, suggests that we cannot ignore a possible biological component in play styles of mothers and fathers.[71] Male monkeys, moreover, tend to respond more positively to bids for rough-and-tumble play than females.[72] Perhaps "[both monkey and human] males may be more susceptible to being aroused into states of positive excitement and unpredictability than females"[73]—a speculation that is consistent with gender differences in risk taking and sensation seeking.[74] In addition, human males, whether boys or young men, tend to behave more boisterously and show more positive emotional expressions and reactions than females.[75] Together these threads of the puzzle suggest that predisposing biological differences between males and females may play a role in the play patterns of fathers and mothers. At the same time, the cross-cultural data clearly underscore the ways in which cultural and environmental contexts shape play patterns of mothers and fathers and remind us of the high degree of plasticity of human social behaviors.

Fathers are interacting much more with their infants and children than in the past, but many of the traditional role divisions between mothers and fathers remain. Generally, mothers care for children more than fathers, who in turn spend more of their time with their children in play or recreation. However, both parents contribute to both caregiving and play, although they contribute in different ways. No single profile of the relationship between father and child does justice to all fathers. Fathers can and do play a significant role in infancy and childhood, but how and how much individual fathers influence their children varies considerably from one family to another.

4 / What Determines Fathers' Involvement?

In the 1960s and early 1970s many were optimistic that men would soon be equal contributors with their partners to the care of infants and children. The women's movement was in full swing and the men's movement was beginning. How has this expected revolution fared? How much change has actually occurred in men's fathering roles? The short answer is that while change has taken place, its degree and pace have led observers of the fathering scene to characterize the shifts as gradual rather than as revolutionary.

In taking a closer look at the changes that have occurred, we need to remember that these shifts are part of more general societal changes across the last half century. In a unique comparison of U.S. families in the 1920s and in the late 1970s, the researchers Caplow and Chadwick found that both mothers and fathers spent more time with their children in 1977 than they did in 1924.[1] About 10 percent of the fathers spent no time with their children in the 1920s, while only 2 percent were not involved with their children in the late 1970s—a change from one father in ten to one in fifty. The percentage of fathers spending more than an hour per day with their children grew significantly from 66 to 77 percent over this same period. Fathers' involvement is thus increasing over the long term, and since the 1960s the pace of change has increased. Many factors have contributed to this acceleration, including increases in women's employment as well as changes in cultural views about the appropriateness of fathers' involvement in child care.

Joseph Pleck, in his book *Working Wives, Working Husbands*, reports that the time men spend in housework and child care—unfortunately these two aspects of men's family participation are often treated together—increased between the mid-1960s and the early 1980s.[2] Men's share of the total family workload in 1965 was 20 percent and rose to 30 percent by 1981, a gradual increase. Later studies have confirmed this trend. The demographer John Robinson, using a 1985 national survey, found that men's family participation has continued to rise.[3] At the same time, women's average time spent on family work has decreased. In 1985, married men were doing 34 percent of housework—a 14 percent increase from twenty years earlier. Although these studies often fail to distinguish between general household tasks such as cleaning and cooking and child-care tasks, they suggest that men are taking increasing responsibility for family and household workloads.

Others have separately examined these different aspects of family work. Not only are similar trends evident for child care alone, but the research suggests that fathers' involvement with their children shows an even more dramatic increase than their contribution to more general household responsibilities. Tracing changes in fathers' time spent with young children over three decades, Pamela Daniels and Kathryn Weingarten found that men were twice as likely to provide regular daily care for their children during the 1970s than men whose children were born in the 1950s and 1960s.[4] Between 1975 and 1981 husbands increased their time in child care from 2.20 to 2.88 hours, or about half an hour per week.

More recently, Robinson compared levels of child care by fathers in a small American city in 1966 and 1988 and again found an increase.[5] Employed fathers' time with children increased from 1.21 to 1.53 hours per week. This trend appears to be continuing. A national survey of men's child-care responsibility found that the percentage of children whose fathers cared for them during their mothers' work hours rose to 20 percent in 1991 in contrast to a relatively steady level of 15 percent since 1977. Pleck notes: "Fathers are the primary care arrangement almost as often as are family day care homes (22%) and far more often than group care centers (14%) or grandparents (9%)." The fact that fathers are the primary caregivers during mothers' working hours in almost one out of five dual-career families with preschool children suggests that a much higher proportion of fathers have significant child-care responsibility than is usually thought. Some estimate that fathers' involvement in all aspects of child care—not just during their wives' working hours—is nearly a third of the total child care by U.S. dual-career couples in the 1990s.[6]

Similar shifts toward greater involvement by fathers is evident in cross-cultural studies. Fathers in a variety of countries, including Australia, Great Britain, Ireland, Sweden, and Israel, all report that fathers are becoming more involved with their infants and children than in earlier eras.[7] Even in countries such as Japan, where fathers are less involved with their children than American fathers,[8] there are indications that fathers' involvement is on the rise.

Determinants of Fathers' Involvement

Although comparisons across time and cultures are useful,we need to look beyond mere description and search for the causes of fathers' involvement with their children.

Surprisingly, we know much more about what fathers do than why they do it. Examining the factors that alter their actions aids us in understanding the paternal role, which is less culturally scripted and determined than the maternal role, and for which fewer clear role models exist.[9]

The role of the father is multiply determined, and many factors need to be considered in order to make sense of variations in fathers' involvement. Fathers do not simply decide to be involved or uninvolved; rather, their participation in family routines evolves out of a system of influences.[10] In my view, this system involves several levels of determinants—individual, familial, extrafamilial, and cultural—each of which has multiple components (see Table 1). As in any system, these levels of influence do not operate independently but act upon each other in determining fathers' level of involvement. Some factors, such as our culture's attitude concerning roles for males and females, may be most helpful in accounting for overall differences in levels of involvement in caregiving between mothers and fathers as a group or as a member of a particular gender category. Other factors are most useful in understanding differences among individual fathers. For example, the amount of support a father receives from his spouse may be an important determinant of the degree to which he is involved as a caregiver.

Individual characteristics of the father include his gender-role attitudes and his relationship with his own family. The timing of entry into the fathering role is also important. Early-onset fatherhood in adolescence is a very different experience than late-onset fatherhood when a man is in his thirties or forties. At the family level, several dyadic relationships are important. Fathers develop different relationships with different kinds of children. Infants vary in temperament, gender, and birth

Table 1 Determinants of Fathers' Involvement: A Systems View

Individual Influences
  1. Attitudes, beliefs, and motivation of father
  2. Relationship with family of origin
  3. Timing of entry into parental role
  4. Child gender

Family (Dyadic and Triadic) Influences
  1. Mother-child relationships; father-child relationships
  2. Husband-wife relationship
  3. Father-mother-child relationship

Extrafamilial Influences
  Informal Support Systems
    1. Relationships with relatives
    2. Relationships with neighbors
    3. Relationships with friends

  Institutional or Formal Influences
    1. Work-family relationships
    2. Hospital and health-care delivery systems

Cultural Influences
  1. Childhood cultures of boys and girls
  2. Attitudes concerning father/mother gender roles
  3. Ethnicity-related family values and beliefs

order, and these factors shape the father's involvement. Fathers may develop different relationships with temperamentally difficult babies versus easy babies or with sons versus daughters. Even the timing of the child's birth may alter the degree of the father's involvement, as we have seen; babies that are born prematurely may require a different level of father involvement than on-time babies. Mode of delivery matters too; fathers may be more involved with babies delivered by cesarean section.

The husband-wife relationship has a profound impact

on fathers' involvement with their children as well. The quality of the marital relationship is a major determinant of fathers' involvement and the quality of the father's relationship with his children. Do mothers encourage and support fathers' involvement or do they function as gatekeepers and limit fathers' access to their children? Recognizing the interplay among relationships among family members is consistent with a family systems view of fathering.

Fathers and families do not exist in isolation, but are embedded in a variety of informal support systems, such as extended family members, friends, and neighbors, and institutional or formal support networks, such as workplaces, hospitals, and health-care delivery systems. Both types of support systems shape fathers' level of involvement. Institutions such as hospitals help shape fathers' relationships with their infants from the earliest moments of the baby's arrival.

The type and schedule of work that fathers engage in will have an impact on both the quality and the quantity of their involvement with their children. Is a father's work stressful or not? How much control does he have over his work decisions? Does his employer have family-friendly workplace policies and benefits, such as on-site daycare or paternity leave opportunities? Does he work shifts? Are work schedules flexible? Whether both the mother and the father are employed outside the home is a major institutional determinant of fathers' involvement.

In addition, cultural beliefs and attitudes about appropriate roles for men and women in the care and rearing of children also play an enormous role. James Levine has noted: "There is still the widespread belief that a man does not belong at home taking care of children."[11] Only by recognizing that this system of influences, from individual to cultural, needs to be considered will we begin to understand why women take more responsibility for child care than men and why some men are more involved than others with their children.

Individual Factors

Men's own psychological and family background, attitudes toward the fathering role, motivation to become involved, and child-care and child-rearing knowledge and skills all play a role in determining their level of involvement with their children.

Men's Relationship with Their Family of Origin

The quality of the relationships that fathers have with their own mothers and fathers has been viewed as a possible determinant of their involvement with their own children. Evidence in support of this proposition is complex, however, and by no means clear-cut. Two views have guided this inquiry.[12] First, from social learning theory comes a modeling hypothesis suggesting that men model themselves after their fathers, and that this process will be enhanced if their fathers were nurturant and accessible.[13] Men are thought to learn their fathering skills and attitudes from their own fathers. In support of this modeling hypothesis, a number of studies suggest that positive relationships with fathers in childhood are related to higher levels of involvement as fathers later on.[14] Second, a compensatory or reworking hypothesis argues that fathers tend to compensate or make up for deficiencies in their childhood relationships with their own fathers by becoming better and more involved when they themselves assume this role. Support for the second hypothesis is also evident in both classic studies and more recent reports.[15] Grace Baruch and Rosalind

Barnett found that men who viewed their own relationships with their fathers as negative tended to be more involved with their five- and nine-year-old children.[16] As several researchers have noted, the predictive power of earlier familial relationships is especially evident in single-earner families in which wives are not employed.[17] In this setting, fathers have more discretion in determining their level of involvement with their children.

These two positions are unlikely to be mutually exclusive, but probably represent different pathways followed more or less by different fathers. Kerry Daly has interviewed fathers of young children about the sources of their role models for their own fatherhood identity.[18] His work supports the view that some fathers emulate their own fathers, while others compensate; still others report that their fathers had little influence as mentors or models. In support of the father as a positive role model, consider the reflection of this young father: "I would say that with my father, we don't discuss parenting . . . I don't go to him so much for advice on parenting, although I think that much of what I base my parenting practices on are his model. The type of father that he was, I am trying to emulate. He was very solid, always around, and was never not there."[19] This view, however, was a minority perspective. Most of the fathers interviewed by Daly either did not view their fathers as a model or wanted to do better than their own fathers.

Listen to this father's memories: "I don't want to be like him as far as fathering goes . . . He feels the children are to be seen and not heard. We don't have the same feeling."[20] Another father distinguished between his attitude toward work and family and his own father's views: "If I could fault my dad in any way, he didn't spend time with us; he was always working . . . I told him that I regretted that we didn't get to spend enough time together when I was little. He feels bad about that, but I think we have a lot more freedom to spend time with our kids today than maybe our parents did."[21] This father's appreciation of changing societal expectations is seen in his continued reflections about his own father's circumstances: "And maybe it was the values of society at the time but dad was supposed to work and mom to look after the kids. And that has sort of changed; nowadays, dads are also supposed to participate in raising a kid."[22]

Many fathers in Daly's study opted for a piecemeal approach to defining fathering. Instead of emulating one person, these men tried to piece together an image of fathering from different sources. "From this perspective, learning to be a father is somewhat akin to the thoughtful consumer who stands before the shelves making a careful selection of products that are to be added to the cart."[23] Here is how one dad expressed this "multiple models" approach to defining the fathering role: "No I don't think I try to emulate anybody saying, 'this is a good father, I want to be more like him.' You know I look at people I know and I say, 'Well he does that well with his kids,' or 'he handles these sorts of situations well with his kids'—maybe draw on that and someone else."[24]

Men thus draw on models from their own generation as well as fathers from earlier eras and past generations. As men become fathers, they appear to be struggling to reconcile past and present images and models of fathering behavior with the changed circumstances that face modern fathers. Even if they chose to emulate their own fathers, the rapid changes in our society make it difficult for current fathers to apply these lessons from the past in any simple way. A central aspect of learning to be a father is the construction of a set of images that make sense in the contemporary era. It is clear that the inter-generational transmission of parenting is an active process in which the father himself plays a central role in sorting, retaining, and discarding images and guidelines from a variety of sources. There is no simple or single route to developing an identity as a father; just as there are many different fathers, there are many different paths.

Attitudes, Motivation, and Skills

Some men pay much more attention to babies than others do. What distinguishes men who coo and fuss over new babies—other people's babies as well as their own—from men who show little interest? Paternal attitudes, motivation, and skills provide clues about this variation in interest and involvement. Sandra Bem suggests that our definitions of how masculine or feminine we are may affect how nurturant we are willing to be. She argues that normal adults are not either completely masculine *or* feminine, but have some combination of traits traditionally considered masculine and feminine. Therefore some men are tough and assertive (traditional masculine traits) as well as sensitive and empathic (traditional feminine traits). Bem calls individuals who rate themselves high on both masculinity and femininity "androgynous." To find out if the way we perceive our gender role affects our treatment of infants, she watched men who differed in their gender-role perceptions interact with five-month-old babies. She found that androgynous men showed more interest, approached closer to the baby, and smiled, touched, and vocalized at the baby more than men who viewed themselves as traditionally masculine.[25]

This early work may have oversimplified the situation, because later studies of the relationship between gender-role attitudes and fathers' involvement with their own children failed to find clear links. But this does not mean that fathers' attitudes are unimportant. When the focus is more specifically oriented toward beliefs about parental roles, clearer connections between attitudes and behavior are evident. Men who valued the father's role more, rejected the biological basis of sex differences, and perceived their caregiving skills to be adequate were found to be more involved with their three-month-old babies.[26] A variety of types of involvement are related to paternal attitudes, including play, caregiving, and indirect care (for example, packs diaper bag, changes crib linen). Other studies have found that paternal attitudes are important beyond infancy. Graeme Russell found that Australian men who do not accept the notion of maternal instinct participate in child care more with their three- to six-year-old children. In Russell's study, however, 51 percent of mothers and 71 percent of fathers believed in a "maternal instinct" with regard to child care.[27] And although 60 percent of the mothers felt that their husbands had the ability to care for children, only 34 percent of the fathers considered themselves capable of doing so. Moreover, most fathers perceived their involvement as beginning after the baby stage and believed that their role was more important later in the child's life, especially during adolescence.

In spite of the fact that men are competent caregivers, they differ widely in their perceived or actual level of skill in caregiving.[28] In turn, these variations in skill may be related to the degree of their involvement. Some of the most convincing evidence comes from intervention studies, which show that skill-oriented training has a positive effect. These studies indicate that fathers who receive training in caregiving and/or play that presumably increases their skill engage in higher levels of involvement with their infants.[29] I will review this work in Chapter 8.

Timing of Parenthood

The timing of parenting has undergone profound changes over the last several decades. An increasing number of women have had babies both earlier and later than in previous decades. Although the actual teen birth rate between 1960 and 1992 has declined, the number of births to young mothers (under seventeen years old) has risen slightly.[30] African American teens are most at risk for early parenthood, with one out of five black children born to an unmarried teenager.[31] The other trend—delayed childbearing—is even more dramatic. Between 1972 and 1982 the percentage of women who waited until their thirties to have their first child doubled.[32] In 1988 women over thirty accounted for 35 percent of births to women.[33] This trend toward later parenthood has been especially marked among white women; black women, on average, have had their children at earlier ages than white women.[34] What are the consequences of this divergent pattern of childbearing for fathers?

A number of factors need to be considered in order to understand the impact on parenting of childbearing at different ages. First, the life course context, which is broadly defined as the point at which the individual has arrived in his or her social, educational, and occupational timetable, is an important determinant. Second, the historical context, or the societal and economic conditions that prevail at the time of the onset of parenting, interacts with the first factor in determining the effects of variations in timing.

Early Fatherhood

The most significant aspect of early entry into parenthood is that it is a nonnormative event. Achieving parenthood during adolescence can be viewed as an accelerated role transition. Kathleen McCluskey comments: "School age parenting may produce heightened stress when it is out of synchrony with a normative life course. Adolescents may be entering parenting at an age when they are not financially, educationally, and emotionally ready to deal with it effectively."[35] Early childbearing has consequences for mothers, fathers, and offspring. For young women, these include higher medical risk, lower educational attainment, and diminished income. When the fathers are adolescents too, they are often unprepared financially and emotionally to undertake the responsibilities of parenthood—just as in the case of their young female partners.[36] Robert Lerman notes: "Young unwed fathers were generally less well educated, had lower academic abilities, started sex at earlier ages and engaged in more crime than did other young men."[37] Low family income and having lived in a welfare household increase the likelihood of entry into young unwed fatherhood. This profile is especially evident for Euro-American unwed fathers. In spite of the fact that African American males are four times as likely to be unwed fathers as Euro-American males, African American unwed fatherhood is less likely to be linked with adverse circumstances and is a more mainstream event. Several factors reduce the likelihood that an African American adolescent male will become a teenage father, including church attendance, military service, and higher reading scores.

Often a pregnant teen and her partner do not marry, and even if marriage occurs, teenage marriages tend to be highly unstable. Separation and divorce are two to three times as likely among adolescents as among couples who are twenty years old or older.[38] With low rates of marriage and high rates of separation and divorce for adolescents, adolescent fathers have less contact with their offspring than "on-schedule" fathers. Contact is not absent, however; studies of unmarried adolescent fathers indicate a surprising amount of paternal involvement for extended periods following the birth. Recent data based on a national representative sample of over six hundred young unwed fathers indicated that three-fourths of young fathers who lived away from their children at birth never lived in the same household with them.[39] Yet many unwed fathers remain in close contact with their children, with nearly half visiting their youngest child at least once a week and nearly a quarter almost daily. Only 13 percent never visited and 7 percent visited only yearly. These estimates were based on the father's own reports. Other work that relies on maternal reports yields lower contact estimates: Frank Mott found that about 40 percent visited once a week and a third never visited or only yearly.[40]

The pattern of involvement of adolescent fathers is mixed, but some young men do try to stay involved and provide a measure of child care and support. As one young man put it: "I would try the best I could to make their life best for them."[41] Others, in contrast, don't seem to care. Consider this exchange:

Interviewer: Do you know guys who make babies and don't care?

Harold: Yeah, I know quite a few who say, "I got a daughter who lives over here and a son who lives over there" and the way they say it, it seems like they don't care.[42]

On balance, the stereotype of the uncaring and irresponsible teenage father is probably overstated and more myth than reality—at least for some young fathers. One of the major barriers to continued involvement is the difficulty of finding employment and the instability of available jobs.[43] Even though there is more time for child care if you don't have a job, many young men who are unemployed feel that they cannot contribute to the support of their child and often avoid contact with their new family—as if they haven't earned the right to be part of their child's life. One young father commented: "Sometimes a guy got a nice job, you know, he don't mind trying, but if he ain't got no job, maybe he's afraid to try."[44]

Several studies report declines in contact as the child develops.[45] According to Lerman's analysis of the national survey data, 57 percent of fathers visited once a week when the child was 2 or under, 40 percent for ages 2 to 4.5 years, 27 percent for ages 4.5 to 7.5, and 22 percent for 7.5 and older.[46] Nearly one-third of the fathers of the oldest group never visited their offspring.

These declines in fathers' participation appear to continue across childhood and adolescence. In a recent follow-up, Frank Furstenberg and Kathleen Harris traced the pattern of contact between adolescent fathers and their offspring from birth through late adolescence.[47] Under half of the children lived with their biological father at some time during their first eighteen years, but only 9 percent lived with their father during the entire period. Instead, children spent about one-third of their childhood with their fathers, and this was more likely to occur in early childhood. During the preschool period, nearly half of the children were either living with their father or saw him on a weekly basis. By late adolescence, 14 percent were living with him, and only 15 percent were seeing him as often as once a week; 46 percent had no contact, but 25 percent had seen him occasionally in the preceding year.

Fathers who rarely or never visit are less likely to pay child support, which in turn adds to the mother's financial burden and may indirectly have negative effects on the children.[48] Euro-American (30 percent) and Hispanic (37 percent) fathers are more likely to have no contact with their offspring than African American fathers (12 percent).[49]

How have increases in the rate of adolescent childbirth altered the father's role? Or, to pose the question differently, how was being an adolescent father different in a period when adolescent childbearing was relatively rare as compared with a period when the rate is significantly higher? As rates of adolescent childbearing rise and the event becomes less unusual or deviant, the social stigma associated with it may decrease. In combination with increased recognition that adolescent fathers have a legitimate and potentially beneficial role to play, adolescent fathers' opportunities for participation have probably expanded. In addition, the increased availability of social support systems such as daycare may make it easier for adolescent fathers (and mothers) to balance educational and occupational demands with parenting demands. More longitudinal studies of the long-term impact of achieving parenthood during adolescence are necessary, as well as more investigation of the impact of adolescent parenthood during different periods of history.[50]

Finally, early childbearing has a variety of deleterious effects on the offspring. One significant concern is the greater risk of a lower IQ.[51] Being born to adolescent parents also affects children's academic achievement and retention in grade.[52] Nor are the effects short-lived; they tend to persist throughout the school years.[53] Social behavior is affected as well, with several studies showing that children of teenage parents are at greater risk of social impairment (for example, undercontrol of anger, feelings of inferiority, fearfulness) and mild behavior disorders (for example, aggressiveness, rebelliousness, impulsivity).[54] In assessing the effects of early childbearing, it is important to remember that the negative impact on children derives from both teenage mothers and teenage fathers. Both contribute to these outcomes, and it is an oversimplification to attribute the effects to fathers or mothers alone.

Early fatherhood clearly has profound consequences for men, their partners, and their offspring. At the same time, we must keep in mind that there is variation among early fathers as well as among late fathers. The image of all young fathers as uninvolved and uncaring is an outdated stereotype. In Chapter 8, we will revisit early fatherhood and explore recent programs that are aimed at increasing the involvement of teen fathers with their children.

Late Fatherhood

In spite of the increases in teenage fatherhood, most men reach parenthood in their twenties. An increasing number, however, are delaying fatherhood until their thirties or forties. Childbearing when parents are in their twenties may have advantages for fathers. Men who have their children relatively early have more energy for certain types of activities that are central to the father role, such as physical play.[55] The economic strain that occurs when offspring are young is offset by the financial problems that are avoided in retirement because children are grown up and independent earlier. Early fathering also generally means beginning grandfathering at a younger age, which in turn permits a man to be a more active grandparent.[56] But in spite of these advantages, when men become fathers early, they face two main problems: financial strain and time strain. Trying to establish both a career and a family at the same time leaves them open to competing demands that may be difficult to meet.

In contrast, the late-timed father who begins parenting in his thirties or forties avoids these problems. When childbearing is delayed, considerable progress in the educational and occupational spheres has potentially already taken place. Education is completed and career development is well under way for both males and females. If the father's career is more settled, he has more flexibility and freedom in balancing the demands of work and family. Further, patterns of preparental collaboration between the parents may already be established and persist into the parenthood period.

What are the effects of late parenthood for the father-child relationship? Are fathers who delay parenthood more or less involved with their offspring? Are their styles of interaction different from early or on-time fathers?

Retrospective accounts by adults who were the firstborn children of older parents report that having older parents was an important influence in their lives. Many felt especially appreciated by their parents; they described fathers who were between the ages of thirty and thirty-nine when the respondent was born as more accepting than fathers who were younger or older.[57] Parents' retrospective accounts of parenting also vary with timing. C. N. Nydegger found that late fathers expressed greater self-confidence in the parental role as well as greater ease and composure in discussing the role than early fathers.[58] Both mothers and fathers have reported that delayed fathers are more interested than younger first-time fathers in parenting, and they are more likely to engage in caregiving.[59] Pamela Daniels and Kathy Weingarten found that early fathers are less involved in the daily care of a preschool child: three times as many late fathers, in contrast to their early-timed counterparts, had regular responsibility for some part of the daily care of a preschool child.[60] Cooney and colleagues found in a nationally representative sample that late fathers were more likely to be classified as being highly involved and experiencing the paternal role positively than on-time fathers.[61] In another study, men whose first child was not born until their late twenties contributed more to indirect aspects of child care, such as cooking, feeding, cleaning, and laundry.[62]

Qualitatively different styles of interaction are associated with on-time versus late fathers. In a self-report study, Kevin MacDonald and I found that the age of the parent is negatively related to the frequency of physical play.[63] After controlling for the age of the child, the size of the relation is reduced but generally reveals the same pattern. This relation appears stronger for some categories of play than for others, however. Some physical activities, such as bounce, tickle, chase, and piggyback, that tend to require more physical energy on the part of the play partner, decrease as parents become older. The negative relation between age of parent and physical play may be due to either the unwillingness or inability of older parents to engage in high-energy activities, such as physical play, or to the fact that children may elicit less physical activity from older parents. Moreover, Brian Neville and I found older parents likely to engage in more cognitively advanced activities with children and to report holding their children more than younger fathers. These and other studies suggest that older fathers may be less tied to stereotypic paternal behavior, adopting styles more similar to those that have been considered traditionally maternal.[64]

Observational studies of father-child interaction confirm these self-report investigations. Brenda Volling and Jay Belsky, who studied fathers interacting with their infants at three and nine months, found that older fathers were more responsive, stimulating, and affectionate toward their babies at both ages.[65] In another observational study, Brian Neville and I examined the play patterns of early and late fathers interacting with their preschool-aged children. Early and delayed fathers' play styles differed; the early fathers (average age twenty-five years) relied on physical arousal to engage their children, whereas the delayed fathers (average age thirty-six years) relied on more cognitive mechanisms to remain engaged.[66]

Timing effects are important not just for fathers but for grandfathers as well. Not only is age per se important, but the timing of entry into familial roles may be a determinant of interactional style as well. In our study of grandfathers interacting with their seven-month-old grandchildren, Barbara Tinsley and I found that grandfather age related to the level of stimulating play. Grandfathers were divided into three categories: younger (ages thirty-six to forty-nine), middle (fifty to fifty-six), and older (fifty-seven to sixty-eight).[67] Grandfathers in the middle age group were rated significantly higher on competence (for example, confident, smooth, accepting), affect (warm, interested, affectionate, attentive), and play style (playful, responsive, stimulatory). From a life-span developmental perspective, the middle group of grandfathers could be viewed as being optimally ready for grandparenthood, both physically and psychologically. Unlike the oldest group of grandfathers, they were less likely to be chronically tired or to be ill with age-linked diseases. And unlike the youngest grandfathers, they had completed the career-building portion of their lives and were prepared to devote more of their time to family-related endeavors. Indeed, the age of the middle group of grandfathers fits the normative age at which grandparenthood is most often achieved; for these men, the role of grandfather was more age-appropriate than it was for the youngest and oldest groups of grandfathers. Timing is thus a major determinant of fathers' involvement. The choice to enter into fatherhood early, on time, or at a later point in the life span has important consequences for the father's role.

The Infant's Sex

Before their baby is born, many parents have a clear preference for a boy or a girl—especially if the infant is to be their first child. Both mothers and fathers prefer boys, not just in the United States and Britain, but in India, Brazil, and a variety of other countries as well. This preference is particularly strong in men; between three and four times as many men prefer boys as prefer girls. This preference is probably culturally determined and derives from the higher status ascribed to males in many cultures. Reproduction patterns are influenced by these preferences. According to Lois Hoffman, who conducted an extensive survey of 1,500 women and 400 men, couples are more likely to continue to have children if they have only girls. They will have more children than they had originally planned in order to try for a boy.[68]

If parents and particularly fathers prefer sons, do they treat them any differently from daughters once they are born? Fathers do treat male and female infants differently—even in the newborn period. In our study of fathers and babies in the hospital, I discovered that fathers touched and vocalized more with their boys. Not only do fathers talk more to their boys, they are also more likely to respond to their sons' vocalizations. These patterns are particularly marked for first-born boys. Girls are not ignored by their parents: according to Evelyn Thoman and her colleagues, mothers are more active simulators of girls. In their studies of mothers and newborns during feeding they found that mothers talked to and touched their daughters more than their sons.[69]

This pattern is not restricted to the first few days after the baby is born. In our observations of fathers at home with their infants at three weeks and three months of age, Sawin and I found that fathers continue to treat boys and girls differently.[70] In a play situation, fathers consistently stimulated their sons more than their daughters. Fathers touched their sons and visually stimulated them by showing them a toy more often than their daughters. Fathers even looked at their boys more often than their girls. Of course fathers did play with their daughters, but it was the mothers who were the main source of stimulation for the baby girls in this study. Mothers more frequently stimulated their daughters with the toy and touched and moved daughters more than sons. This same kind of effect was present during feeding: fathers made more frequent attempts to stimulate feeding by moving the bottle for their sons than for their daughters. Mothers appeared to compensate by stimulating their daughters' feeding more than their sons'. The picture is more complicated than this, however. For example, fathers do not hold their sons close and snugly—they reserve this type of holding for their daughters. Mothers, in contrast, tend to hold their sons closer than their daughters. In part, these holding patterns can account for the other observations: if you hold your baby more closely, active moving, touching, and other stimulation are difficult to manage.

This pattern of fathers expressing affection for their daughters and stimulating their sons may be the earliest form of gender-role typing. Fathers, as we know from other research, want to encourage the physical and intellectual development of their sons. For daughters, the fathers' aim may be to encourage femininity. As I will discuss in Chapter 6, others contribute significantly to their girls' intellectual development: the mother's early stimulation of her infant daughter may be an antecedent of later intellectual encouragement.

These patterns appear to persist throughout infancy. Kotelchuck found that fathers play about half an hour a day longer with one-year-old firstborn sons than with firstborn daughters. In addition, fathers play different kinds of games with boys and girls. Fathers play physical games such as lifting and tossing more with their boy infants than with their girl infants and vocalize more to their girls than to their boys.[71] In part, this differential treatment may relate to fathers' and mothers' early expectations concerning what baby boys and girls are like. Jeffrey Rubin and his colleagues found that even before fathers had ever picked up their newborn infants—when they had only looked at them—they rated their sons as firmer, larger featured, better coordinated, more alert, stronger, and hardier, while daughters were rated as softer, finer featured, inattentive, weaker, and more delicate. As Rubin and his colleagues suggest, it appears that gender typing has already begun at birth, when the parents have only minimal information about their infant. Furthermore, "the labels they ascribe to their newborn infant may well affect subsequent . . . parental behavior itself."[72] Subsequent research confirms that adults treat infants who are labeled boys or girls differently. Adults play in more masculine ways with a baby that they think is a boy and in a gentler and more nurturant fashion with an infant that they believe is a girl—regardless of the infant's actual sex.[73]

The differential treatment of boys and girls by their fathers continues as children grow. According to Philip and Carolyn Cowan, fathers are more involved with their sons at three and a half years of age, especially if the mother works outside the home.[74] Others report that fathers of nine- to eleven-year-old children spend more time in dyadic interaction with their sons than with their daughters—but only in single-earner families; dual-earner families spent equal amounts of time with sons and daughters.[75] Possibly "these patterns reflect gender role attitudes; single-earner fathers were significantly more traditional in their views of gender roles than were dual-earner fathers. In addition, mothers in more traditional single-earner families may provide a 'gatekeeper' function, engaging daughters in domestic activities in which fathers are seldom involved."[76] As the sociologists Kathleen Harris and Philip Morgan have found, fathers continue to be more involved with sons than daughters in adolescence as well. However, there is an important qualifier. If the sibling pair consists of a boy and a girl, the daughter receives more attention than she would if she had only sisters. "The presence of sons draws the father into more active parenting and this greater involvement benefits daughters, who, in turn, receive more (but unequal) attention from their father."[77]

These patterns are not restricted to the United States and Great Britain. An examination of the Israeli kibbutz provides further information. Jacob Gewirtz and Hava Gewirtz recorded the visiting patterns of parents and noted how long they stayed when they came to the infant group house for a visit with their sons or daughters. Fathers of infant sons visited longer than fathers of infant daughters. Other evidence provided by the anthropologists Mary West and Melvin Konner suggests that these effects may be present in nonmodern cultures as well. In the Kung San of Botswana, a hunting and gathering culture, fathers also spend more time with boys than girls, especially as the infants get older.[78]

Nonhuman primates show this pattern too. Laboratory studies reveal differences in the reactions of adult males to male and female infants. Among rhesus monkeys, studied by William Redican, "mothers tended to play with female infants whereas adult males did so with male infants. In general mothers interacted more positively with female infants and adult males with male infants."[79] The greater attention that fathers direct to boys may not always be positive. Murray Straus, an expert on physical punishment and child abuse, has found that fathers tend to spank and hit their boys more than girls.[80] Parents also argue and fight more in the presence of boys than girls.[81] Father involvement clearly has a negative side for boys as well.

There are exceptions to this apparent universal pattern. Studies of African American fathers reveal that fathers do not interact more with boys than girls—a finding consistent with the observation that in African American families, there is less gender-role distinction than in Euro-American families.[82] Fathers in the Caribbean also tend to treat infant boys and girls similarly, although as children become older, there is an increased preference for sons over daughters.[83] The sociologist Masako Ishii-Kuntz compared fathers' roles in the United States and Japan. Although she confirmed the results of earlier studies by finding that American fathers interact more with their children than do Japanese fathers, she found that Japanese fathers interact slightly more with their daughters than their sons. She observes:

> Japanese parents tend to be much more protective of their daughters than their sons from birth to adult years . . . To many Japanese fathers, their daughter's wedding day is the saddest time of life because their daughters have been "taken away" from them. On the other hand, adult sons are much more likely to form extended family households. Because of these differences . . . Japanese fathers

feel that they need to spend more time with their daughters than their sons.[84]

Across cultures, species, and infants of various ages, the sex of the infant or young child significantly affects interaction between parent and child. Parents treat boys and girls differently from birth, and this suggests that the gender-typing process (that is, the process of learning the behavior usually considered appropriate for one's sex) may begin much earlier than had previously been thought.[85]

Family Factors

Maternal Attitudes: The Mother as Gatekeeper

Consistent with a family systems view, maternal attitudes need to be considered in determining how involved fathers are likely to be with their infants. The majority of women, one study indicates, do not want their husbands to be more involved with their children than they currently are.[86] At the same time, this survey suggests that 40 percent of fathers would like to spend more time with their children than they currently are able to do. As Lamb noted, mothers may play a gatekeeping role, either supporting or inhibiting fathers' involvement with their infants.[87] Although the attitudinal dimensions that define such a gatekeeping role are poorly understood, there is general support for the notion that maternal attitudes toward their own caregiver role and the father's caregiver role make a difference in fathers' level of involvement. Fathers' involvement is positively related to wives' views of their husbands' competence as caregivers.[88] Mothers who view their male partners as competent may facilitate their involvement; alternatively, competent men may be more involved with children which, in turn, shapes their wives' attitudes about their competence.

Ashley Beitel and I examined the relation between maternal attitudes and father involvement with three-to five-month-old infants.[89] A variety of maternal attitudes concerning fathers' involvement with infants were related to the actual level of their involvement in a sample of over three hundred first-time parents. Mothers' assessments of their husbands' child-care skills, of their husbands' interest in participating in child-care activities, and of the value of fathers' involvement all made a difference in fathers' participation in infant care. Mothers' belief in innate sex differences in the ability to nurture infants and the extent to which mothers viewed themselves as critical or judgmental of the quality of their husbands' caregiving were negatively related to fathers' involvement. As these results suggest, maternal attitudes play a significant role in understanding fathers' involvement. Moreover, maternal attitudes predicted levels of fathers' involvement even after controlling for a variety of factors, including amount of maternal outside employment, type of feeding (bottle versus breast), father involvement in birth preparation classes, and family history (parents' recollection of their relationship with their own parents).

These studies emphasize the ambivalence that mothers have about giving up their own sense of control over the domain of caregiving. Although many mothers say they want fathers to be more involved, they are struggling to retain aspects of a role that historically and culturally is a central part of their maternal and female identities at the same time that they are trying to make gains toward equal cultural status in other domains such as work and education. Maternal gatekeeping reflects women's effort to balance the new pieces of their world with the important and cherished old pieces.[90] Many women may recognize that the movement to equity in the workplace has not been as swift or as easy as many had hoped; they are then even less likely to give up their control over the caregiving sector of their lives.

The Mother-Father Relationship

Fathers are involved in many relationships, and one of the most important for understanding fathering is the marital relationship. Several studies have found that the quality of the marital relationship is an important determinant of fathers' involvement with their children. Here is one example. In one short-term longitudinal study of the antecedents of fathers' involvement, Shirley Feldman and her colleagues found that fathers in more satisfying marriages, during the third trimester of their wives' pregnancy, were subsequently more involved in caregiving and play with their six-month-old infants.[91]

Is marital support equally important for mothers and fathers? Apparently not. Researchers have found that the quality of the marriage is much more likely to affect the father-infant relationship than the mother-infant relationship. Belsky and his colleagues, in their series of home observations of mothers and fathers with their infants at one, three, and nine months, found stronger links between fathering and marital interaction than between mothering and marriage.[92] Other studies support this general pattern, finding that spousal support is a stronger correlate of competence in fathers than in mothers. The level of emotional and cognitive support provided by spouses was linked to more and less competent fathers but failed to show such a link in the case of mothers.[93] A similar picture holds for adolescent parents as well. Adolescent fathers interacted more positively with their infants if there was a high level of mother-father engagement. In contrast, the quality of the mother-infant relationship was unrelated to the adolescent female's engagement with her male partner.[94] Moreover, fathers react more to changes in marital relationships than mothers. As marriages deteriorated, men became more negative and intrusive fathers, whereas mothers were less affected by shifts in marital quality.[95] One researcher noted: "The quality of the marital dyad, whether reported by the husband or wife, is the most consistently powerful predictor of paternal involvement and satisfaction."[96]

Together these findings suggest that successful paternal parenting is more dependent on a supportive marital relationship than on maternal parenting. How do we explain this relation? First, as we saw earlier, the father's level of participation is, in part, determined by the extent to which the mother permits participation. Second, because the paternal role is less well articulated and defined than the maternal role, spousal support may serve to help crystallize the boundaries of appropriate role behavior. The fathers' role, in short, is more discretionary. Third, men have fewer opportunities to acquire and practice skills that are central to caregiving activities during socialization and therefore may benefit more than women from guidance and emotional support. As we will see in Chapter 5, marital quality not only predicts the degree of fathers' involvement, but has a profound impact on the quality of the father-child relationship as well.

Extrafamilial Influences

Informal Social Support

Support from partners or spouses is not the only important source of support that alters men's involvement in child care. Support outside the family can take a variety of forms—informal and formal. Informal support includes extended family members such as parents, siblings, and other relatives as well as friends, co-workers, members of religious organizations, and neighbors. Formal support refers to institutions such as the workplace, social services, and medical centers. Many studies have found that fathers' involvement in child care is linked to the level of extrafamilial support available to them. Although men tend to be less involved in outside kin networks than women, men who are well supported by kin and neighbors tend to be more involved with the care and nurturing of their children in both Euro-American and African American families.[97] Less clear is the relative importance for fathers' involvement of spousal and informal support from outside the family. In African American families with a long tradition of reliance on kinship support for child care and child rearing, this kind of informal extended family aid may be particularly important.

The Dual-Career Family

The relations between the employment patterns of both women and men and their roles in the family are increasingly being recognized.[98] More mothers are working outside the home today than at any earlier time in history. The number of working mothers has increased rapidly in most industrialized nations, particularly since the mid-1950s The rise has been especially dramatic for married women with children. Between 1950 and 1990, the U.S. employment rate for married mothers of children has increased sharply to over 70 percent.[99] How have these shifts affected the quantity and quality of the father's contribution to family tasks such as housework and child care?

Do fathers take more responsibility for child care or simply persist in their traditional pattern when mothers work outside the home? Studies in the United States and other Western industrialized countries suggest that fathers, in general, change their parenting behavior when the mother is employed. One estimate suggests that "men's average contributions to inside housework have roughly doubled since about 1970, whereas women's contributions have decreased by a third . . . [in] the late 1980's men were doing about 5 hours per week or about 20–25 percent of the inside chores."[100] This trend is slightly higher in the case of dual-career families. At the same time, such developments do not negate the fact that the majority of household tasks, including child care, are still performed by women.[101] Moreover, the change in the proportion of time men spend on such tasks often emerges as a result of wives' reducing the amount of time they devote to these duties as well as increases in the absolute amount of time men put in.

Of particular importance for understanding the fathering role is the finding that child care by fathers is most likely to increase when mothers are in the marketplace, while fathers' participation in other household work is less affected.[102] Robinson reports that husbands of women who are employed full time are more involved in child care than husbands of women who are not employed or work only part time. Graeme Russell found similar trends in Australian families. When both parents were employed, fathers doubled their contribution to child care, although mothers still carried most of the burden of routine caretaking.[103] Variables such as the child's age appear to determine whether or not fathers' family work shifts with maternal employment. Walker and Woods found an increase in fathers' family work with maternal employment when the youngest child was one year of age or younger or the couple had five or more children.[104] Similarly, Russell found that maternal employment altered Australian fathers' involvement in family work only when there were children under three years of age. Fathers in this case were slightly more involved when mothers were employed (4.4 hours versus 3.15 hours for employed versus nonemployed, respectively). Russell found further that when mothers are employed, the quality of responsibility that fathers assume shifts: fathers with employed wives spent more time taking sole responsibility for their children compared with fathers with nonemployed wives (4.7 hours versus 1.0 hour). He confirmed that fathers in families where mothers work outside the home are more involved in solo child care with their one-year-old infants than fathers whose wives were homemakers, but the two groups did not differ in their level of leisure involvement with their children.[105] Similar findings are evident in the United States with both infants and older children.[106] Increased involvement by fathers generally means more time in child care, rather than leisure. Adele Gottfried notes: "When mothers are employed, the fathers' increased time involvement concerns the necessities rather than more optional activities."[107] This is well illustrated by a recent survey that found that the percentage of children whose fathers cared for them during their mothers' work hours rose to 20 percent in 1991, after a steady level of around 15 percent since 1977.[108] These modest absolute increases assume greater importance because they directly affect the nature of the father-child relationship. As noted earlier, when total time in child care is considered, including time when mothers are not working, fathers are doing about one-third of the child care in dual-earner couples. In sum, role sharing increases when mother and father both work, but women are still doing the major part of the diaper detail.

Examination of the quantitative shifts in father behavior as a consequence of maternal employment is only one aspect of the problem; the impact of this shift on the quality of the father-child relationship must also be examined. Some evidence from interviews of a sample of fathers of infants seven to fourteen months old suggests that maternal employment is related mainly to the level of fathers' physical involvement in child care and not to fathers' nurturant expressive behavior.[109]

Other evidence, however, suggests that shifts in the style of father-infant interaction may occur as a function of maternal employment. In one study, Pedersen and colleagues assessed the impact of dual-wage-earner families on mothers' and fathers' interaction patterns with their five-month-old infants. Fathers in single-wage-earner families tended to play with their infants more than mothers did, but in the two-wage-earner families, the mothers' rate of social play was higher than the fathers' rate of play. The fathers in these dual-wage-earner families played at a lower rate than even the mothers in the single-wage-earner families. Because the observations took place in the evenings after both parents returned from their jobs, Pedersen and colleagues suggested that the mother used increased play as a way of reestablishing contact with her infant after being away from home for the day. "It is possible that the working mother's special need to interact with the infant inhibited or crowded out the father in his specialty."[110] The result was that fathers in these two-earner families had less playtime with their infants. Family work organization clearly can affect the father's status as primary playmate. Whether or not these mothers continue to be as active play partners as the baby grows older, however, remains unanswered. This behavior of the mother is consistent with studies of maternal employment and infant attachment that found no relation between employment status and the quality of infant-mother attachment but found evidence of insecure infant-father attachment in dual-career families, though only for sons and not daughters.[111]

In an even more stringent test of the modifiability of play styles as a function of family organization, Field compared fathers who act as primary caregivers with fathers who are secondary caregivers.[112] In this reversed family role, Field found that primary caregiver fathers retained the physical component in their interaction styles just as secondary fathers did. In other subtle ways, however, the play styles of primary caregiving fathers were similar to the play styles of mothers. Primary caregivers—both mothers and fathers—exhibited less laughing and more smiling, imitative grimaces, and high-pitched vocalizations than secondary caregiver fathers did. But both primary caregiving and secondary caregiving fathers engaged in less holding of the infants' limbs and in more game playing and poking than mothers. Together with Pedersen's study, these data suggest that both mothers and fathers may exhibit distinctive play styles, even when family role arrangements modify the quantity of their interaction.

Susan McHale, Ann Crouter, and Todd Bartko, in a sample of fourth- and fifth-grade children, found that work status of spouses and role arrangements in families (traditional versus egalitarian) may, in fact, be independent.[113] To understand the effects of fathers' participation on children, it is important to understand both the work status of parents and the family type (traditional versus egalitarian). McHale and colleagues found that an inequitable division of parents' work and family roles relates to poorer socioemotional adjustment of children. Children from traditional dual-earner families were more anxious and depressed and rated themselves lower in terms of both peer social acceptance and school competence than did children from families characterized by an equitable division in parents' work and family role (for example, traditional single-earner and egalitarian dual-earner families).

Even though fathers do less than half the work of child care, their participation can have a positive effect on both the working mother and the child. Michael Lamb and Susan Bronson explain it this way: "By assuming partial responsibility for home and/or child care, such a husband relieves his wife of some of her responsibilities, freeing her time for more unhurried interaction with the child . . . The husband's participation has a beneficial impact on the mother-child relationship and so affects the child's development indirectly." When fathers persist in their traditional ways and refuse to participate, Lamb and Bronson continue, both mother and child may suffer:

> When her husband fails to assume significant domestic responsibilities, the working mother has little time available for unhurried interaction with the child since there are multiple compelling demands on her time. The child of such a mother can clearly be deemed "at risk." Neither of its parents are able or willing to commit much time to it and the interaction that it has with its mother is hurried, insensitive, and dominated by routine activities like feeding and bathing. Father, meanwhile, is not consistently sensitive to child's needs because he does not define this as within his province.[114]

A caveat is in order, because not all women want to go to work nor do all women want help with household and child-care tasks. Although many researchers find that the personal life satisfaction of employed mothers is higher than nonemployed mothers whether they are professional or blue-collar workers, this is not the case for all mothers. A match between their wishes and their employment status works best. The link between dual roles for mothers and their personal happiness is found only for women who want to work outside the home.[115] Mothers of infants who preferred employment but stayed at home, for example, were more depressed than either mothers whose employment status was consistent with their desires or employed women who indicated a preference for nonemployment.[116] The quality of the job and the stability of child-care arrangements can alter the relationship between dual-career status and women's satisfaction as well.[117] Not surprisingly, poor child care and an uninteresting job can make one rethink the advantages of a more traditional lifestyle. Similarly, Catherine Ross has found that fathers' assistance in household tasks and child care has a positive effect on their wives if they want help; if they do not want such assistance, there are negative effects and the father is viewed as interfering in his wife's domain.[118] Congruence between a couple's preferred roles and their actual roles is a major determinant of the impact of maternal employment on children and families as well as on women themselves.

The Demands of Work

Fathers' work demands are another determinant of involvement. As a variety of studies have found, fathers who are highly committed to work and who spend long hours on the job tend to be less involved in fathering activities. A recent cross-cultural comparison between Japanese and American fathers illustrates this issue. In a survey of fathers in the two countries, American fathers reported playing sports, chatting, eating dinner, and reviewing homework with their children more often than Japanese fathers—both routinely and on weekends.[119] In contrast, Japanese fathers are more likely to have break-fast with their children. Workplace demands are one of the major factors that account for this difference across cultures. In Japan, approximately 40 percent of workers work more than forty-eight hours a week and over 90 percent of Japanese firms still have a six-day workweek policy. In the United States, both the number of hours and the days of work per week are considerably lower. Japanese men simply do not have as much time for fathering as American fathers. As we will explore in Chapter 8, a variety of workplace policies, such as flex-time, parental leaves, and on-site daycare, are all aspects of work that could make it easier for men and women to be fathers and mothers as well as workers.

The Quality of Work

Instead of examining whether or not one or both parents are employed, researchers have begun to address the impact of the quality and nature of work on fathers' behavior. Both social scientists and men themselves have viewed work as a central determinant of men's psycho-logical well-being: "According to the view of man-as-worker, the workplace is the arena in which men struggle to establish their identity and by which they measure their success and failure. The home, in contrast, is con-strued as a haven, the place where 'man-the-worker' returns daily to heal the wounds received on the job."[120]

In recognition that both contexts, work and home, are important determinants of fathers' involvement, re-searchers have focused on the ways in which work and home are connected. Ann Crouter has noted that there are two types of linkage.[121] One type of research focuses on work as an "emotional climate," whose effects may carry over to the enactment of roles in home settings. Investigators generally emphasize short-term or transitory effects. A second type of research examines the type of skills, attitudes, and perspectives that adults acquire in their work-based socialization and the ways in which these variations in job experience alter their behavior in family contexts. In contrast to the short-term perspective of the emotional climate research, this type of endeavor considers the more enduring and long-lasting effects of work on family life.

Research in the first tradition has been conducted by Rena Repetti, who studied the impact of working in a high-stress job (air-traffic controller) on family interaction patterns.[122] She found that the male air traffic controllers were more withdrawn and less angry in marital interactions after high-stress shifts and tended to be behaviorally and emotionally withdrawn during interactions with their children as well. Although a high workload is associated with withdrawal, negative social experiences in the workplace have a different effect. Distressing social experiences at work were associated with higher expressions of anger and greater use of discipline during interactions with children later in the day. Repetti views this as a "spillover effect" in which there is transfer of negative feelings across settings. Work patterns have long-term links with fathering as well. Controllers on teams with a poor social climate had a less positive and more negative emotional tone in their interactions with their children.

Positive work experiences can enhance the quality of fathering.[123] Frances Grossman and her co-workers found that men's job satisfaction was associated with higher levels of support for their five-year-old children's autonomy and affiliation in spite of the fact that positive feelings about work were negatively related to the quantity of time spent interacting with their child. This finding draws attention to the importance of distinguishing quantity and quality of involvement.

One caveat: in contrast to the Repetti studies, the Grossman study focused on general job demands and satisfaction rather than daily fluctuations in the level of positivity or negativity experienced in the work setting. Future studies need to assess these two aspects of job-related feelings and involvement separately.

Research in the second tradition of family-work linkage, namely the effects of the nature of men's occupational roles on their fathering behavior, dates back to the classic work of Melvin Kohn and of Donald Miller and Guy Swanson.[124] Men who experience a high degree of occupational autonomy value independence in their children, consider children's intentions when deciding on discipline, and use reasoning and withdrawal of rewards instead of physical punishment. In contrast, men who are in highly supervised jobs with little autonomy value conformity and obedience, focus on consequences rather than intentions, and use more physical forms of discipline. Job-based experiences were thus repeated in parenting roles.

Ellen Greenberger and Robin O'Neil extended Kohn's original work by focusing on the implications of job characteristics not only for the parenting behavior of both mothers and fathers but, in turn, the effects of these variations in parenting for children's development.[125] Fathers with more complex jobs (characterized by mentoring others versus taking instruction or serving others) spend more time alone with sons and more time developing their sons' academic, athletic, mechanical, and interpersonal skills, but this is not the case for daughters. Indeed, fathers spend more time in work and work-related activities if they have daughters. In addition, these fathers tend to behave more warmly and responsively to sons and to use less harsh and less lax control of sons, but report more firm but flexible control with daughters. Fathers who have jobs characterized by a high level of challenge (expected to solve problems; high level of decision making) devote more time to developing sons' skills, give higher-quality explanations to their sons, and use less harsh and more firm but flexible control in their interactions with their boys. Fathers with time urgent jobs (work fast most of the day; find it difficult to take a break) spend more time on work activities, less time interacting, and use less lax control if they have daughters. Overall, when fathers have complex, stimulating, and challenging jobs, boys seem to benefit much more than girls.

In contrast, mothers' job characteristics are in general weaker influences on their parenting than fathers' job attributes, but again when there is a link, boys seem to benefit (higher-quality explanations, warmth, and responsivity) more than girls. Mothers show less interrelationship between work and home in part because of the more heavily scripted nature of maternal roles. According to these researchers, different processes may account for the work-home linkages that result from stimulating or challenging jobs and complexity of occupation. Greenberger and O'Neil argue that "spillover of positive mood" may account for the relationship between stimulating and challenging jobs and good fathering, while "complexity of work with people may increase fathers' intellectual and emotional flexibility in dealing with their sons."[126]

A father's work experience clearly has an impact on his fathering behavior. The process probably operates in both directions, however, so that a man's home experience affects his job performance as well. Neil Bolger and his colleagues, for example, found that arguments at home with wife or a child increased the chance of arguments with co-workers and supervisors the next day.[127] One would expect that a friendly chat with a spouse or a playful romp with a child would create a positive mood and possibly enhance one's workday. Research also underscores the fact that men and fathers reside in the dual worlds of work and home. As a corrective to the view that men's psychological health is primarily determined by their work roles, Rosalind Barnett and her colleagues recently found that men's adjustment in both their family and their job roles are important determinants of their psychological well-being.[128] "As both the job and the family go, so goes men's mental health."[129]

Institutions, such as hospitals, make a difference as well. As we have already seen in Chapter 2, the opportunity to participate in the birth process may alter levels of father involvement. And we will explore the impact of hospital-based training programs on fathers' involvement in Chapter 8.

Cultural Influences

In the final analysis, the culture provides fathers with goals, expectations, and norms. Unless there are shifts in cultural messages to men concerning the appropriateness of their involvement with their children, lasting increases in such activity are unlikely to occur. And the cultural messages begin in childhood, since boys and girls grow up in different worlds of play and work. Contrasting experiences and opportunities afforded children depending on their sex may help shape differences in how men and women approach the task of parenting.

In most societies there is gender differentiation not only in play but also in work. By late preschool boys and girls tend to segregate themselves into same-gender groups.[130] Within these same-sex gender clusters, boys and girls play and act differently.[131] Boys are more competitive, dominant, and turf-protecting. They take more risks and play rougher games than girls—a style of interaction that may foreshadow fathers' more robust physical play in adulthood. Girls, in contrast, are more concerned with maintaining good relationships among group members, more focused on intimate friendships, and, of course, engage in many more activities that are preparation for a later parental caregiving role. While feeding, burping, changing, and dressing baby dolls are a routine part of the nursery school corner for girls, boys are more likely to be building houses out of blocks or playing with trucks or fire engines. Girls take more interest in babies than boys do, which may, in part, account for gender differences in the nature of childhood chores and work.[132] Girls gain much more experience in caring for younger children in many cultures and in the United States as well. Girls also do more cooking, laundry, and general housework, while boys are more involved in "outside work" such as lawn care, snow shoveling, and taking out the garbage.[133]

Clearly the worlds of play and work are different according to a child's gender, and these separate worlds occupied by boys and girls may influence and shape their interests, skills, and competencies as they approach adulthood and parenthood. The fact that boys typically don't babysit may be a prelude to the later finding that men don't do as much caregiving as women. These childhood experiences of boys and girls are so common that this factor is probably more useful in explaining overall differences in levels of fathers' and mothers' involvement than in accounting for individual variations across different fathers. Cultural influences do not end in childhood, of course, but continue to play a formative role as men reach adulthood and assume the role of parent.

What messages does contemporary U.S. culture provide men about fatherhood? Various visions have been offered by television, movies, magazines, and professionals. Most agree that a new version of the involved father is becoming the desired if not the real father. With "Mrs. Doubtfire" and "Kramer vs. Kramer" on the movie screens and numerous articles on new dads, stay-at-home fathers, and the new androgynous fathers, the current culture appears to be sending a clear message to dads about their involvement. Scholars seem to be endorsing the culture's view as well. Anthony Rotundo, author of *American Manhood*, describes a good father as "an active participant in the details of day-to-day child care. He involves himself in a more expressive and intimate way with his children and he plays a larger part in the socialization process that his male forebears had long since abandoned to their wives."[134]

In a similar vein, Furstenberg remarks that "today's father is at least as adept at changing diapers as changing tires."[135] The cultural message heralding the arrival of the new modern father, however, is at odds with the reality of fathers' involvement. There is no doubt that there has been change toward greater involvement by fathers, but the amount of change falls far short of the ideal that has been championed. The prevalence of the "cultural ideal" for contemporary fatherhood has led us to ignore the wide range of fathering styles and types of levels of involvement.[136] The concept of the uninvolved father that was characteristic of the precontemporary era, before the late 1960s, led us to give little weight or credibility to examples of involved fathers, because they were inconsistent with the dominant cultural ideal. In contrast, the uninvolved or disinterested father in the contemporary era receives less recognition because this type of dad violates the current ideal concerning fathers' involvement. In each era a different set of fathers may go unrecognized, depending on the currently dominant ideal. In today's culture, there are really multiple realities rather than a single form of fatherhood. At the same time that many men are moving toward the new cultural ideal for fatherhood, others are moving away from their responsibilities through nonpayment of child support, decreased contact with their children, or even abuse of their offspring. Continued variability is closer to the reality than any single image of the modern father.

Closer scrutiny of cultural messages suggests that there are multiple and conflicting images rather than a clear and coherent vision. The sociologist Scott Coltrane has analyzed the way men and women were depicted in television commercials in the 1950s and 1980s.[137] The portrayals of men showed little change. In the 1950s men were six times more likely to be workers than parents, and in the 1980s they were still four times more likely to be so depicted. While men's portrayals showed little change, women's images moved closer to men's roles. Women in the 1950s were twice as likely to be parents as workers, but in the 1980s women were twice as likely to be workers as parents. One out of three women was pictured parenting in the 1950s, whereas fewer than one out of ten women was so pictured in the 1980s—the same proportion as for men. Interestingly, by the 1980s fathers were twice as likely to be the parent in commercials as mothers, owing to the fact that women were less likely to be stereotyped as mothers in the 1980s than in the 1950s. Coltrane cautions: "Still men were many times more likely to be shown sitting in a board meeting, drinking been in a bar or scaling a mountain than cradling a newborn or diapering a toddler."[138] Moreover, television programs show considerable variation. Although the sensitive and involved fathers in *The Cosby Show* and *Family Ties* are often heralded as part of the new fatherhood, the depictions on *The Simpsons* and *Married With Children* remind us that inept and ineffective father images are still evident as well.[139]

Again, a historical reminder is helpful. Images of fatherhood have fluctuated over the last century and have never been as simple and consistent as we often assume. In spite of the inconsistencies, it is clear that the cultural ideal of the new modern father is at odds with the reality of modern fathers' involvement. Scholars such as Ralph LaRossa have noted the potential negative impact of the asynchrony between the cultural and actual worlds of fatherhood: "Men are being constantly told—and can see for themselves, if they look close enough—that their behavior does not square with the ideal, which means that they are being reminded on a regular basis that they are failing as fathers. Failing not when compared with their own fathers or grandfathers perhaps, but failing when compared with the image of fatherhood which has become part of our culture."[140] Being a parent—a father or a mother—has never been easy, and for fathers the lack of a clear script may make it even more difficult. Cultural ideals, then, present a mixed message. Although they may emphasize the gap between goals and reality, they may nevertheless help promote change and aid in nudging men toward greater involvement as fathers.

The involvement of fathers in the lives of their children is not a simple matter, and no single factor accounts for the variations across individual fathers. Instead, the individual characteristics of both children and men themselves, families, institutions, and culture all play a part in helping us understand why some men are more involved with their children than others.

5 / Socialization and Sociability

Babies begin very early to develop the skills they need for interacting successfully with other people. Sociability begins at home, in the context of the family. Rudolph Schaffer has described three basic steps in the development of social behavior in the first year of life:

> The infant's initial attraction to other human beings that makes him prefer them to inanimate features of the environment.
>
> His learning to distinguish among different human beings so that he can recognize his mother as familiar and strangers as unfamiliar.
>
> His ability, finally, to form a lasting, emotionally meaningful bond with certain specific individuals whose company he actively seeks and whose attention he craves, though he rejects the company and attention of other, strange individuals.[1]

Infants can recognize their mothers by smell, even in the first week of life. Moreover, infants can distinguish their parents from strangers by sight by two months and their mothers from their fathers soon thereafter.[2] Young babies even react differently to mothers and fathers. Infants smile and laugh more at their fathers and gaze more at their mothers.[3]

The next milestone is the development of a preference for a small number of individuals. Often labeled "attachment," this special desire to be near certain persons and to try to keep them from leaving is usually well established at seven or eight months of age. Traditional theorists of social development, including both Freud and Bowlby, believed fathers to be less important attachment figures than mothers.[4] They considered mothers the primary objects of attachment, and there was considerable doubt that infants could initially form attachments to more than one person. The question of whether a baby can form an attachment to its father has fascinated researchers in recent years, and their findings contradict the traditional view.

In the mid-1960s Schaffer and Peggy Emerson published a report entitled "The Development of Social Attachments in Infancy," which challenged the Freud and Bowlby assumptions about the limited role of fathers as attachment figures.[5] In their study of six- to eighteen-month-old infants in Scotland, Schaffer and Emerson used the amount of protest when the infant was separated from a familiar adult as their measure of attachment. They asked mothers whether their infants cried or fussed when left in their crib, outside a shop in their carriage, or in a room by themselves. Young infants did tend to protest more when their mother left than when their father did, but this tendency was short-lived. By eighteen months, most infants protested the departure of father and mother equally. Moreover, in spite of Freud's emphasis on the importance of the feeding context for the development of attachment, these investigators found that infants developed attachments to a wide range of people—many of whom never participated in routine caretaking activities such as feeding and diapering. Even for the mother, the amount of time spent in feeding was not related to the intensity of the infant's attachment. Although feeding appeared not to be critical, Schaffer and Emerson did find that some child-rearing behaviors were associated with the infant's attachment. Social stimulation—talking, touching, and playing—was important, as was the adult's responsiveness to the infant's behavior. The adult who responded quickly and reliably when the infant smiled or cried was preferred over less attentive adults. Fathers, of course, are potentially as capable as mothers of stimulating babies and responding to their signals, and thus both fathers and mothers can provide important ingredients for early social development.

Frank Pedersen and Kenneth Robson, in the United States, used a different approach but came to a similar conclusion.[6] They simply asked mothers how their infants responded when fathers returned home from work. The warm and friendly greetings that the majority of eight-month-old infants showed their fathers were viewed as further evidence of infant-father attachment.

Verbal reports, of course, can be unreliable. Later investigators observed babies and fathers directly, either in the lab or at home. These observational studies provide a better test of whether attachment between infant and father occurs and how father and mother compare as attachment figures for their young babies. Milton Kotelchuck made some important progress in unraveling this puzzle.[7] In a laboratory playroom he compared infants' reactions to the presence, departure, and return of their mother, father, and a stranger. Kotelchuck measured a variety of baby behaviors, such as playing, crying, touching, talking, smiling, and how closely the baby stayed to a person or to the door. Let's look at a familiar measure—crying when an adult leaves. Infants twelve months and older tended to cry when either their mother or their father departed. The difference between their reactions to either parent's leaving was very small, suggesting that the twelve-month-olds had developed attachments to both mother and father. Crying never increased when the stranger left, and the older babies even cried less after the stranger had gone. Other measures tell a similar story. The infants stayed near the door when either parent left, and touched both mother and father when they came back into the room. Neither of these reactions was seen when the stranger left and returned.

Do infants show attachment for both fathers and mothers in the more relaxed and familiar context of the home? Michael Lamb's observation of seven- to thirteen-month-olds provides an answer.[8] When observed at home, infants reacted to naturally occurring separations from their fathers in the same way as to separations from their mothers. Nor were there any clear preferences for one parent over the other. The babies touched, fussed to, asked to be held by, and sought to be near fathers and mothers to about the same extent.

Some lab studies do indicate that infants prefer to stay near their mothers more than their fathers when both parents are available. How can this finding be reconciled with the earlier claim that infants show no preference between their mother and father? The answer lies in the kind of setting in which the observations are made. If the setting is a relaxed or familiar situation, either parent will suffice as an attachment figure. But as we have seen, mothers and fathers appear to play different roles. Mothers are more often the primary caregivers, and babies who are hungry, wet, fatigued, or sick are more likely to seek out their mother than their father. It is not surprising, therefore, that infants look to their mothers for comfort in stressful or upsetting situations. Fathers, by contrast, are more likely to be sought out for play. This more complex picture is more satisfactory. Both mother and father are important attachment objects for their infant, but the circumstances that lead to selecting mom or dad may differ.

Individual Differences in Fathering

All of us know some men who are very involved with their infants and others who are aloof and distant, leaving most of the interaction to their wives. Consider two contrasting fathers:

Warren and Betsy K. are sitting in the living room of their apartment when Roger, their eight-month-old, stirs from his nap and begins to cry. Warren ignores the cries and buries himself deeper in his newspaper. Betty leaves the room, and a few moments later she returns with a quieted Roger nuzzling his head on her shoulder. Warren looks up, nods briefly, and goes back to the sports page.

Jim P. is cradling his four-month-old daughter, Judy, in his arms. He gently strokes her cheek to keep her sucking on the bottle of milk that he is feeding her. A short while later, he sings quietly to Judy and covers her up in her crib. His wife is out for an evening class at the local university. Jim P. does this three nights a week and loves the time alone with his daughter.

Do the different patterns of interaction shown by Warren K. and Jim P. have different effects on their babies? Let's return briefly to the studies of children's reactions to being left alone with a stranger. In addition to observing parents in the playroom, Kotelchuck interviewed the parents to find out how much time they spent with their babies and what kind of things they did with their infants. The infants who interacted most with their fathers and stayed close to them in the laboratory had fathers who were very involved in caretaking at home. In one study in this series, the investigator even found a positive relationship between how close the infant stayed to his father and the number of diapers changed by the father per week.[9]

It is not only the father's involvement in caretaking that matters. Pedersen and Robson found that besides frequency of the father's caretaking, the intensity of the play interactions between father and infant was important for forming infant-father attachment.[10] Recall that these researchers measured attachment by the mother's description of the infant's greeting when its father returned from work. These factors, however, related only to the level of attachment for boys; there was no clear relationship between the father's behavior and attachment by girl babies. This gender difference is not an isolated finding. Other researchers also report that boys, particularly in the second year, show a preference for their father over their mother.

Martha Cox and her colleagues have confirmed these earlier findings, but have also uncovered further predictors of infant-father attachment.[11] Fathers (and mothers) were observed interacting with their infants at three months and at twelve months; attachment was assessed using the strange situation, a laboratory-based paradigm involving brief separations and reunions of parent and infant that is used to assess the quality of infant-parent attachment. Both the quality of interaction and the time spent with the child proved to be important. The more positive, playful, and physically affectionate the father was in his interactions with his infant and, to a lesser degree, the greater the amount of time spent together, the more secure infant-father attachment was observed to be. Fathers' "cognitive models"—as seen in their attitudes toward infants and their parental role—were also important predictors. Fathers were asked about "their delight in the baby," "their acceptance of the baby," and their investment in the parenting role. Infants whose fathers were rated higher on these attitudes had better infant-father attachment scores at one year of age. This work makes clear the importance of considering parents' thoughts about their roles.[12] Because parents' actions are often affected by their attitudes, beliefs, and values, observing behavior may not be sufficient by itself.

I should note that although these patterns suggest that fathers who are more involved *cause* their children to become attached to them, the reverse interpretation cannot be discounted. Perhaps some infants are more inviting, appealing, or interesting. Babies differ in many ways that may affect how involved their parents—both fathers and mothers—will become. In my own research I have found that fathers treat attractive and unattractive babies differently, even in the newborn period.[13] Fathers stimulate attractive infants more than less attractive infants; they touch, kiss, and move highly attractive infants more frequently. Differences in the baby's temperament may have an important effect on a burgeoning relationship between father and infant. If a baby is fussy, irritable, and unresponsive in the first few months, perhaps the father will "turn off" and initiate interaction less often. Studies in both Sweden and the United States suggest that fathers do respond to temperament differences in babies, but that their reactions depend on the gender of the baby.[14] Fathers are apparently more willing to persist in their interaction with difficult boy babies than with difficult girls. The baby's own characteristics thus can affect the development of its relationship with its father.

Another important determinant is the quality of the marital relationship. As we saw in Chapter 4, fathers who are in supportive and satisfying marriages develop more secure attachment relationships with both their infants and their toddlers.[15] Mothers benefit from spousal support as well. Several studies in both the United States and Japan have found that the degree of emotional and social support that fathers provide mothers is related to both maternal competence in caregiving as well as the quality of attachment.[16] Moreover, Cox and her colleagues found that the quality of the marital relationship was related to the quality of both mothers' and fathers' parenting of three- month-old babies even when marital satisfaction was measured prenatally. This suggests that marriage has a powerful impact, one that is, to a degree, independent of the characteristics of the infant or the experience with the infant in the early months of life. In addition, marital quality was important even after taking into account differences in the psychological adjustment of the parents.[17] As others have shown, a supportive marriage can go a long way toward overcoming the negative effects of a parent's poor or disturbed childhood by providing support for alternative views and strategies about parenting and child rearing. This is consistent with the more general finding that "on the whole, marriage provides a protective function for many men. This is shown, for example, by the findings from many studies that married men are physically and mentally healthier than single men, divorced men and widowers."[18]

Many questions remain to be answered. For example, we do not know how much interaction is needed for infants to develop attachment to their fathers, or what kinds of interactions are most important. What role does the mother play in promoting a healthy relationship between father and baby? Researchers will be looking for answers to these questions in future studies.

From Home to the Outside World

As the child gets older it must learn to interact with people outside the family. Unfamiliar adults such as grandparents, aunts and uncles, neighbors, teachers, and store clerks enter the child's world, and the child gets acquainted with other children as well. Developing social skills to interact successfully with new people is an important step. What role do fathers play in helping the child to develop social competence? Does the quality of the early relationship between father and infant affect how well the child can cope with strange adults or with new peers? Can fathers help children to have more fun or more friends?

Very early, even before the infant has developed specific attachments to its father and mother, the quality of the relationship between father and baby seems to affect the baby's social interactions with other adults—perhaps especially if the baby is a boy. Pedersen and his associates tested the reactions of five-month-old infants to a strange but friendly adult.[19] Even at this young age fathers made a difference to their sons: the five-month-old boys who had more contact with their fathers were friendlier to the strange adult. They vocalized more at the examiner, showed more readiness to be picked up, and enjoyed frolic play more than baby boys who had less involved fathers. Baby girls, however, did not show such an effect.

These findings, of course, do not mean that fathers ignore their infant daughters, or that fathers have no effect on the development of their girls' social skills. Perhaps fathers influence their girls indirectly by encouraging mother-daughter interaction, or perhaps, as we shall see, fathers' influence is more evident when their daughters are older.

As children grow, fathers continue to contribute to their boys' and girls' ability to cope with strangers and strange situations. In the same laboratory study described earlier, Kotelchuck and his colleagues investigated how well the one-year-old infant can cope when left alone with a stranger.[20] They compared three groups of infants—one group with very involved fathers, another with indifferent and uninvolved fathers, and the third with fathers who fell between these extremes. The most distress occurred in infants with the lowest paternal involvement, an intermediate amount of distress in infants with medium paternal involvement, and the least distress in the infants with highest paternal involvement. It seems that babies who have more contact with their fathers are better able to handle strange situations.

In a related study, Kotelchuck discovered that the less frequently fathers bathed and dressed their infants at home, the longer the infants cried when left alone with a stranger.[21] In short, children whose fathers are active caretakers are better able to handle the stress of being left alone with a stranger. It is possible that egalitarian families not only share caretaking more but also expose the infant more to other adults, making the infant less likely to be frightened of a strange adult. Also, babies whose parents share child care get used to having one parent leave and be replaced by the other parent. Becoming familiar, in this way, with parental departures may make those babies less afraid of separation from an early age.

Alison Clarke-Stewart showed that fathers (and mothers) are still affecting children's reactions to unfamiliar adults at twenty months of age.[22] She evaluated the reactions of toddlers to a friendly but unfamiliar woman who interacted with the child in specified ways that included looking, smiling, talking, approaching, playing with a toy, and playing a physical-social game. In contrast to early infancy, both boys' and girls' social reactions to the stranger were affected by both their fathers and mothers, but in different ways. When mothers were affectionate and responsive and fathers were available and talkative, girls showed friendly reactions to the strangers. In contrast, boys with an affectionate and responsive mother in combination with a negative or even punitive father were particularly friendly to the female stranger. Perhaps, as Clarke-Stewart suggests, the contrast between an affectionate mother and a punitive father may have made the boys more responsive to women in general. These findings suggest that fathers and mothers may not be interchangeable but may influence their boys' and girls' social development through different kinds of behavior.

These findings are not limited to children in the United States. In some countries fathers have very limited contact with babies. Do these variations in the father's participation affect the infant's ability to cope with strangers? In Guatemala, where paternal caretaking is extremely low, infants protest when left with a stranger at nine months of age—three months ahead of their U.S. counterparts.[23] In Uganda, where fathers also have little to do with infants, infant distress in the presence of a stranger occurs even earlier, at six months.[24] These infants behave much like the U.S. infants whose fathers interacted with them least in the Kotelchuck study. The father's level of involvement, however, is probably not the only factor that accounts for these cross-cultural patterns; maternal interaction patterns likely vary from culture to culture as well.[25]

Evidence gathered by Mary Main and Donna Weston suggests that the relationships that the infant has developed with both mother and father are a better basis for understanding children's social reactions than either the mother-infant or father-infant relationship alone.[26] Main and Weston observed one-year-old infants exploring unfamiliar surroundings in the presence of their mother, father, and a stranger. Some of the infants appeared comfortable in the strange surroundings when either the mother or father was present, became upset when either parent left the room, and were happy when either parent returned. Another researcher, Mary Ainsworth, has characterized these infants as "securely attached."[27] Other infants did not seem to get upset when their parents left the room. Furthermore, when the parents then returned to the room, these babies showed ambivalence, sometimes approaching them and at other times showing little interest or even angrily pushing their parents away. Ainsworth has termed these infants "insecurely attached." Main and Weston observed two other types of relationships as well, in which babies were securely attached to their mother and insecurely attached to their father or vice versa.[28] Even very young children often develop distinctly different relationships with their mothers and fathers. To determine whether the infants' relationships with their mothers and fathers affected their social responsiveness to others, Main and Weston also observed the infants' reactions to a friendly clown. The infants who were securely attached to both parents were more responsive to the clown than those who were securely attached to only one parent and insecurely attached to the other, and the babies who were insecurely attached to both parents were the least sociable with the clown. These results suggest that a less than optimal relationship with one parent can be compensated for by a better relationship with the other parent—and therefore that it is not enough to study just fathers.

A parallel buffering effect can occur in families where

one parent is depressed. Ziarat Hossain, Tiffany Field, and their colleagues have found that young infants (three to six months old) show less optimal interaction (more pouting, less vocalizing, more squirming) while interacting with their depressed mothers. They had more positive interactions with their nondepressed fathers, which suggests that the father may protect the infant, in part, from the negative effects of interacting with a depressed mother.[29] Similarly, in adolescence, the researchers Joan Tannenbaum and Rex Forehand found that a positive father-child relationship can protect children from the negative effects, such as an increase in behavior problems, often associated with depression in their mothers.[30] Viewing the father as part of a family system is the best way of understanding his role in child development.

Fathers (and mothers) serve as emotional guides for infants and young children and help them tell which events or which strangers need to be avoided. Consider the following scenarios:

> Eight-month-old Jennifer was crawling along the floor and encountered a strange object—a rubber spider. She stopped short and looked at her nearby father, who smiled and reassured her. The journey continued as Jennifer reached out and picked up the not-so-scary stranger.
>
> Timothy, another eight-month-old, was sitting in his infant seat playing with a favorite rattle. His mother was sitting at a nearby table preparing dinner. A neighbor unexpectedly dropped by. The mother looked startled and a little upset. Timothy looked at the stranger and at his mother and began to cry.

These examples illustrate social referencing—the way infants systematically rely on emotional cues provided by significant others to help regulate their own behavior in uncertain situations. When infants are confronted by a strange person and object, they look to a trusted figure for guidance; in turn, when provided positive or negative feedback (for example, smiles or frowns), babies use this information as a guide for their behavior and either continue or withdraw. We know that babies form attachments to both fathers and mothers, but do infants learn to use fathers as well as mothers as emotional guides? Laurence Hirshberg and Marilyn Svejda exposed twelve-month-old infants to several scary toys (for example, a hissing alligator, a Star Wars monster, and a plastic robot) in the presence of both their mother and their father.[31] Parents were instructed to show happy or fearful expressions whenever their baby looked at them. Infants were just as likely to reference fathers as mothers, and as expected, babies approached the toy more when parents provided positive rather than negative feedback. Fathers—as well as mothers—are effective emotional guides for their infants in situations of uncertainty.

Just as we have seen that marriage affects other aspects of the father-infant relationship, marital quality is linked with the father's role as a social referencing agent as well. Susan Dickstein and I found that infants referenced less to fathers who were dissatisfied with their marriages than to fathers who were satisfied.[32] Infants referenced equally to happily and unhappily married mothers—a further indication that mother-infant relationship is more buffered than the father-infant relationship. Men in unhappy marriages tend to withdraw emotionally from their spouses and, in turn, may be less available to their offspring as well. Babies may learn not to rely on their unavailable unhappy fathers in times of emotional uncertainty. As these findings indicate, we need to view the marital and parent-child relationships as part of the larger family system.

Fathers, Peers, and Popularity

Does the father's relationship with his children affect their ability to relate to age-mates or to make friends? Two approaches have been taken in trying to answer this question—studying the effects of fathers' absence and direct assessment of the father-child relationship.

The Effects of Fathers' Absence

Studies of older boys whose fathers are absent suggest that fathers do indeed affect how well children are accepted by their peers. Lois Stolz studied children who were infants during World War II, when many of their fathers were away at war. When the children were four to eight years old, Stolz found that those whose fathers had been absent during their infancy had poorer peer relationships. Studies of the sons of Norwegian sailors, who are away for many months at a time, point to the same conclusion: the boys whose fathers are often absent are less popular and have less satisfying peer-group relationships than boys whose fathers are regularly available.[33] But why? Possibly boys who grow up without their fathers have less chance to learn the behavior that other boys in their culture value. They may, for example, tend to be shy, timid, and reluctant to play rough games—traits that may not always make a boy popular with his peers.

More recent and more compelling evidence of the potential detrimental impact of fathers' absence on children's social adjustment comes from the National Longitudinal Survey of Youth. This study involved a nationally representative sample of mothers and children who were between five and nine years of age when they were assessed. The data from this group of over six thousand children and their mothers confirm that children in homes where the father is absent are at higher risk for school and peer problems.[34] But the gender and race of the child qualify the picture. White boys from homes where the father was not there were affected most severely in contrast to white boys from homes where a father was in residence. Only 9 percent of the white boys from father-present homes were rated by their mothers as "not liked by their peers," whereas over 25 percent of the white boys from father-absent homes were unpopular with their age-mates. Similarly, 33 percent of the white boys from father-absent homes "had trouble getting along with other children" in contrast to 19 percent of the white boys in father-present households. Moreover, these father-absent boys were more often disobedient in school (37 percent) than their father-present classmates (16 percent). They were more unhappy, sad, and depressed, more dependent ("clings to adults"), more hyperactive (for example, "has difficulty concentrating"), and more likely to choose deviant peers (for example, "hangs around with kids who get into trouble"). What about white girls? Again, there is some evidence that suggests that white girls from father-absent homes are at a behavioral disadvantage in comparison with white girls in a home with a father. The effects on white girls are much less than on white boys, however, and the problems are different. As is often found, boys tend to act out or externalize while girls tend to display an internalizing pattern. Girls exhibit cheating and lying and "not feeling sorry after misbehaving"—relatively passive behavior problems. They also tend to become overly dependent and have difficulty paying attention, but unlike boys, do not get into trouble at school. Like boys, however, white girls have more trouble getting along with other children if they come from a home where the father is absent. In contrast to the white children, for black boys or girls, there is very little evidence of adverse behavior associated with a father's absence. The patterns for the white children are not due to the early effects of maternal and family background (for example, a mother's education, income, or health) that are present before the father leaves the home. The effects are reduced, however, when factors linked with the disruption of the father's departure—such as family income or long-term maternal health—are taken into account.

What accounts for the marked race differences? Frank Mott, the demographer who conducted this study, suggests that the answer may lie in the pattern of the father's absence in black and white homes:

> Black fathers are much more likely to have been absent from the home very early in the child's life. In contrast . . . white fathers are more likely to leave in the preschool and early school ages and in all likelihood, are more likely to keep leaving in the years ahead. For black children, the biological father, if he is going to leave, is probably gone. For white children, the father leaving process will represent a continuing drama throughout the children's early and mid-school years . . . The departure of parents when children are at the school ages probably represents a greater potential for ongoing psychological damage than does father-leaving at very early ages."[35]

In addition, although there are nearly three times as many black children as white children without father or father figure present, black fathers are more likely to continue to maintain contact with their offspring than white fathers.[36] The traditional reliance of black families on extended kin networks for support may be a further factor in accounting for the lessened impact of fathers' absence on black children.

The Quality of the Father-Child Relationship

Researchers have examined the impact of the quality of the father-child relationship on children's relationships with their peers from two perspectives. First, those in the attachment tradition have explored the connection between the infant-parent attachment and social adaptation in the peer group. The second tradition focuses on the links between the quality of father-child interaction, especially in play, and children's peer relationships.

Attachment and social adaptation. An impressive amount of research suggests that the quality of the child-mother attachment is related to children's later social and emotional development—in preschool, in middle childhood, and even in adolescence. A secure attachment is likely to lead to better social and emotional adjustment. Children are better liked by others, have higher self-esteem, and are more socially skilled.[37] Does the quality of the infant's or child's attachment to the father matter? Suess and his colleagues suggest that the quality of the infant-father relationship at twelve and eighteen months is related to children's later behavior with their preschool age-mates.[38] In this German study, children with more secure infant-father attachments showed fewer negative emotional reactions during play, showed less tension in their interactions with other children, and managed to solve conflicts by themselves rather seeking the teacher's assistance in settling their disputes with classmates. Mothers, of course, were important as well; the infant-mother attachment relationship was an even stronger predictor than the infant-father attachment of children's social adjustment.

Fathers, play, and social adaptation. Other recent work that has focused on fathers' special style of interacting, namely play, suggests that fathers may contribute in unique ways to children's social adjustment. My colleagues and I examined the relation between father-toddler play and children's adaptation to peers. In one study, Kevin MacDonald and I observed fathers and their three- and four-year-old boys and girls in twenty minutes of structured play in their homes.[39] Teachers ranked these children in terms of their popularity among their preschool classmates. For both boys and girls, fathers who exhibited high levels of physical play with their children and elicited high levels of positive feelings during the play sessions had children who received the highest peer popularity ratings. For boys, however, this pattern was qualified by the fathers' level of directiveness. Boys whose fathers were both highly physical and low in directiveness received the highest popularity ratings, and the boys whose fathers were highly directive received lower popularity scores. Girls whose teachers rated them as popular had physically playful and feeling-eliciting but nondirective fathers and directive mothers. Later studies in our lab confirm this general pattern. Popular children have fathers who are able to sustain physical play for longer periods and use less directive or coercive tactics.[40] Joan Barth and I found that fathers who were more effective play partners had children who made a more successful transition to elementary school.[41] Other researchers report that the style of father-child play is important as well. Jacqueline Mize and her colleagues have found that preschool children whose play with their fathers was characterized by mutuality or balance in making play suggestions and following partners' suggestions were less aggressive and more competent and were better liked by their peers.[42] Children's friendships are also influenced by their relationship with their fathers. Lise Youngblade and Jay Belsky found that a positive father-child relationship at three years of age was associated with less negative and less asynchronous friendships at five years of age, while more negative father-child relationships forecast less satisfactory friendships.[43]

What do children learn from playing with their fathers? Being able to read a play partner's emotional signals and to send clear emotional cues is critical for successfully maintaining ongoing play activities. These skills allow partners to modulate their playful behavior so that neither becomes overly aroused or too under-stimulated and play continues at an optimal level of excitement for both. Children learn to recognize others' emotions, improve their own emotional skills, and learn to regulate their emotions in the context of parent-child play.[44] Father-child play may be a particularly important context, because its range of excitement and arousal is higher than in the more modulated play of mothers and children.

Emotion and social adaptation. The quality of the emotions displayed by parents and children during play is an important predictor of social competence with other children as well. Perhaps children model their parent's emotional expressions; children rejected by their peers may have learned to settle their problems in an angry and sometimes aggressive fashion. Emulating their parents' negative and angry tactics and emotions can lead to maladaptive behavior for children with their peers and friends. Popular children and their fathers express more positive emotion during their play and less negative emotion. James Carson and I found that fathers of preschool-aged children who are rejected by their peers show more anger than fathers of well-accepted children.[45] In addition, children who were rated by their teachers as aggressive and/or low in sharing and other prosocial behavior had fathers who were more likely to engage in reciprocal exchanges of negative feelings. In other words, if the child displays an angry or upset expression, the father is likely to reciprocate. Similarly if fathers display negative emotion, children respond in kind. In contrast, parents of popular children tended to respond to children's positive expressions with positive reactions of their own. A similar pattern is evident in observations of families at dinner. Lisa Boyum and I found in a study of kindergarten-aged children that fathers display less anger toward children who are better accepted by their peers.[46] Finally, Sue Isley, Robin O'Neil, and I found that fathers' negative emotion expressed during play with their sons not only was related to how well their five-year-old boys were accepted by their classmates concurrently but also was associated with their sons' social acceptance one year later. Although there is often overlap between mothers and fathers, this study showed that fathers make a unique contribution independent of the mothers' contribution to their children's social development.[47]

It is not only the quality of emotions that fathers display that matters to children's social development, but how fathers deal with children's emotional displays. Are they accepting and helpful when children become distressed, angry, or sad, or are they dismissing and rejecting? Several researchers have found that fathers' comforting and acceptance of their children's emotional distress is linked with more positive peer relationships.[48] For example, John Gottman and his colleagues found that fathers' acceptance of and assistance with their children's sadness and anger at five years of age was related to the children's social competence with their peers three years later at age eight.[49] Girls were less negative with a friend and boys were less aggressive. Mothers' management of children's emotions, in contrast, was generally a less significant predictor of children's later social behavior.

Although fathers' involvement in infancy and childhood is quantitatively less than mothers' involvement, the data suggest that fathers nevertheless have an important impact on their offspring's development. Just as earlier research indicated that quality rather than quantity of mother-child interaction was the important predictor of cognitive and social development, a similar assumption appears to hold for fathers. Together these recent findings lead to a revision in traditional thinking about the ways that mothers and fathers influence their children's development. According to the sociologist Talcott Parsons, mothers were the emotional brokers in the family, and fathers' role was an instrumental one. Instead, this recent work suggests that fathers play a much larger role in the socialization of children's emotion. And it is through the management of their own emotions and their reactions to their children's emotions that fathers may have the greatest impact on their children's social relationships with peers and friends.

Family relationships and social adaptation. Poor parenting and poor marriages often go together, and some fathers' effects are best understood by recognizing this link between parenting and marriage. John Gottman and Lynn Katz found that a poor parenting style, characterized as cold, unresponsive, angry, and low in limit setting and structuring, leads to higher levels of anger and noncompliance on the part of five-year-old children when interacting with their parents.[50] This style is especially likely to be seen in couples with troubled marriages. This combination leads to poor peer outcomes: children from such homes have lower levels of positive play with peers, more negative peer exchanges, and even have poorer physical health. Moreover, marital conflict has lasting effects on children's development. In a follow-up to their study, Gottman and Katz obtained teachers' ratings of internalizing (depression, withdrawal) and externalizing (aggression, disruption) behavior three years later, when the children were eight years old.[51] Couples who in the first study used a mutually hostile style of conflict resolution—one characterized by contempt and belligerence toward each other—had children who exhibited higher levels of externalizing behavior three years later. Families in which the husband exhibited an angry and withdrawn style in resolving marital disputes had children who were higher in internalizing behavior. It is not only the level of conflict in marriages that matters, but *how* conflict is managed that is critical too.

Fathers' own recollections of their early relationship with their own mother and father can help us better understand the paternal impact as well. We all carry memories of our past relationships, and these "internal working models," as Bowlby termed them, serve as guides or templates for our current social relationships. Bowlby commented: "Because children tend unwittingly to identify with parents and therefore to adopt, when they become parents, the same patterns of behavior towards children that they themselves have experienced during their own childhood, patterns of interaction are transmitted, more or less faithfully, from one generation to the next."[52] Main and her co-workers developed an interview to tap mothers' recollections of their relationships with their own mothers during infancy and childhood.[53] Interestingly, the mothers' patterns of memories related to the quality of their current attachment relationships with their own infants. Mothers who had developed secure attachment relationships with their infants revealed in their interviews that they valued close relationships with their parents and others, but at the same time were objective and tended not to idealize their own parents—thus displaying a relatively clear understanding of this important relationship. In contrast, mothers with poor relationships with their infants had different sets of memories; some dismissed and devalued their relationship with their parents or claimed they couldn't recall. Others idealized their parents: "I had the world's best mom." Other mothers with poor attachment relationships with their children tended to recall many conflict-ridden incidents from childhood but could not organize them in a coherent pattern.

Do fathers show similar carry-over effects of early memories? In a German longitudinal study, researchers found that a father's recollections of his own childhood relationship with his parents was indeed linked to his relationship with his own children.[54] Fathers who viewed their own attachment relationship with their parents as secure were more likely to develop a secure attachment relationship with their own infants, more likely to be present at birth, participated more in infant care, and were more supportive of their wives than men with insecure attachment. Moreover, fathers who remembered their childhood attachment experiences, including both positive and negative feelings, and who were open and nondefensive about their recollections, continued to be better fathers as their children developed. They were better play partners to their toddlers. By the time their children reached age six, these fathers served as more sensitive guides during a teaching task and continued to be engaging and tender play partners. Later, when their offspring were ten, these men were more accepting of their children's daily concerns and problems. Remembering both the good and the bad aspects of his own childhood makes a father more sensitive to the needs and feelings of his own child. A recent

American study confirms these European observations.[55] Philip Cowan and his colleagues found that fathers who recalled an earlier attachment relationship with their parents characterized as low in loving and high in expression of anger had children who tended to be rated as more externalizing (for example, aggressive and hyperactive) in kindergarten.[56] Recollections, however, often combine with current conditions—such as the quality of the marriage and parenting competence—to alter children's development. This is the story that emerged from the Cowan study. Although fathers' own attachment memories were important, an even better understanding of children's behavior in kindergarten emerged when contemporary family relationships were considered as well. Fathers with poor attachment histories were often in marriages characterized by high conflict and low satisfaction, and in turn, these men were ineffective parents (low in warmth, responsiveness, and structuring). In combination, these three factors—prior attachment history, current marital relationship, and parenting competence—predicted externalizing behavior two years later when the children were in kindergarten nearly twice as well as the fathers' attachment history alone. Most important, this combination predicted externalizing behavior two times better than these same indices for mothers. Mothers' poor prior attachment history tended to be predictive of children's internalizing behavior in kindergarten. Again, internalizing behavior is better understood when mothers' current marriage and parenting are also considered. The combination of these factors with mothers' recollections was twice as good a predictor of children's internalizing behavior as fathers' scores. The authors note: "Given the fact that men are more implicated in problems of aggression and women in problems of depression, it may not be surprising that fathers and mothers make different contributions to young children's externalizing and internalizing behavior."[57] Not only are both fathers and mothers important to understanding children's development, but each makes distinct contributions to children's social developmental outcomes.

Is the Father-Adolescent Relationship Special?

Our knowledge of fathers' impact on infants and young children far exceeds our understanding of fathers' role in adolescence. Recently, however, researchers have begun to fill this gap. They suggest that, as at other points in a child's life, fathers and mothers play unique roles in adolescent development. One of the major goals of adolescence is the achievement of a balance between intimacy, closeness, and connectedness, on the one hand, and separateness and individuality, on the other hand. As children enter adolescence relationships with family members change; they seek more separation and spend more time with peers or alone than with their family. Men and women, according to Carol Gilligan, relate to others in distinctive ways.[58] Women and mothers focus on connectedness and closeness; men and fathers concentrate on separateness and differentiation. Mothers and fathers, then, may complement each other and provide both models and relationships for adolescents that reflect the two goals of adolescence—connectedness and separateness. Fathers may help adolescents to develop their own sense of identity and autonomy. An Israeli study by Shmuel Shulman and Moshe Klein found support for this distinctive role.[59] In their survey of nearly eighty adolescents ranging in age from twelve to sixteen years, they found that fathers were perceived by their teens as providing more support for autonomy than mothers. Father-adolescent relationships were more "peer-like" and more playful, which is likely to promote more equal and egalitarian exchanges. The authors conclude: "Fathers, more than mothers, conveyed the feeling that they can rely on their adolescents; thus fathers might serve as a 'facilitating environment' for adolescent attainment of differentiation from the family and consolidation of independence."[60]

Others find that fathers share similar views of their role in adolescence. Stuart Hauser and his colleagues found that fathers saw themselves as more encouraging of assertiveness and independence than mothers.[61] Nor are the findings restricted to one culture. Mexican fathers are affectionate with younger children, but shift to a more reserved and distant style during the adolescent years.[62] Fathers clearly play an important role during adolescence and may contribute to children's emerging independence.

Effects on Adult Social Behavior

Most studies focus on short-term effects and assess the impact of fathers on children's socioemotional development at a single point in time or after several years. Do fathers shape children's life outcomes as adults? A follow-up investigation of a classic study of child rearing by Robert Sears, Eleanor Maccoby, and Harry Levin conducted in the 1950s gives us some clues about the long-term impact of fathers on adult lives. Koestner and his colleagues recontacted some of the children in the original study twenty-six years later, when they were thirty-one years old.[63] Empathy—"the tendency to experience feelings of sympathy and compassion for others"—was assessed and related back to the earlier child-rearing information. The most powerful predictor of empathy in adulthood was paternal child-rearing involvement at age five. This factor proved to be a better predictor than several maternal predictors. Moreover, the relationship was evident for both boys and girls. In another follow-up, at age forty-one, men and women who had better social relationships (for example, having a long, happy marriage; having children; engaging in recreational activities with nonfamily members) in mid-life had experienced more paternal warmth as children.[64] As these studies confirm, fathers' relationships with their children have a clear impact on their lives as adults.

Gender-Role Development

Fathers have an important effect on children's gender-role development. In Chapter 3 we saw the beginnings of this influence. Recall that even when the baby is still in the hospital, fathers, especially, treat their boys and girls differently, and that later on fathers play in different ways with their sons and daughters. Fathers, even more than mothers, seem to have a critical part in the development of children's gender roles.

Gender roles for boys and girls, just as for men and women, are in a state of flux. Although stereotypes concerning the "right" behaviors for the sexes still exist, many adults and children today have less rigid views of how boys and girls ought to act. Research findings often show "differences" in behavior that deviate from these stereotypes, but they are just that—differences—and not necessarily deficits or problems.

One of the most common research strategies in this area has been to examine how children develop in homes where no father is present. If fathers play a crucial part in teaching children gender roles, children from homes in which the father is permanently absent or away for long periods might show disruptions in gender-typing. Single-parent families are no longer uncommon. A majority of U.S. children will live in a household with only one parent at some point before they reach age eighteen.[65] What is the effect of this situation on the development of gender roles? Differences in gender-role typing in children from father-present and father-absent homes are most often found in preadolescent boys. These differences depend, however, on how old the boy is when his father leaves. To determine the importance of age of separation, Mavis Hetherington trained male supervisors in a recreation center to observe the behavior of two groups of boys: one group who had been six years old or older when their fathers left, and one group whose fathers had left before they were five years old.[66] The two groups behaved very differently. Boys who had been separated from their fathers before the age of five were more dependent on their peers and less assertive. They played fewer rough physical contact sports such as football, boxing, or soccer. Instead they chose reading, drawing, or working on puzzles—nonphysical and noncompetitive activities. In contrast, if the father was available until his son was six years of age, his later departure did not have this effect. Boys whose fathers left when they were six or older behaved in these areas the same as boys raised in homes with the father present. Although both groups of boys were showing acceptable patterns of behavior, the father-absent boys were exhibiting behaviors that were not stereotypically "masculine."

The effects of a father's absence on older boys are less clear. Some investigators find no differences between boys whose fathers are absent and those whose fathers are present. Others find a pattern known as "compensatory masculinity" in boys separated from their fathers. Such boys sometimes display excessive "masculine" bravado and at other times show "feminine" behavior such as dependency. Delinquents are often found to have this combination of flamboyant swaggering toughness and sexuality along with dependent behaviors. This may be accounted for by the high rates of paternal absence in homes of delinquent children.[67] A father's absence may not be the only reason for heightened aggression and delinquency, of course; among other factors, divorced families are often forced to move to poorer neighborhoods, where they are exposed to more crime and violence.[68] Such influences exacerbate the general problem of learning self-control when fathers are not available as models.

> The male gender role actually requires a delicate difficult-to-learn blend of assertiveness and restraint. For example, a boy has to learn that he should stand up for himself in some situations but also must learn to work with others, for instance as part of a team. A father can be a living illustration of the many facets of the male role including the delay of gratification (going off to work every morning) long-term goal setting (next year we'll build the garage) and co-operating with others toward a common goal (let the quarterback call the plays).[69]

Several studies in both the United States and Trinidad found that boys from homes in which fathers were absent were less able to delay gratification. When asked if they would like a large candy bar in several days or a small one immediately, boys from father-absent families were more likely to settle for the small but immediate gratification. Nor are these differences in self-control inconsequential. Walter Mischel and his colleagues found that four-year-olds who were able to delay gratification were more socially and cognitively competent in adolescence.[70] They were more playful, resourceful, skillful, attentive, and able to deal with frustration and stress—a cluster of traits that are important ingredients for successful coping with the academic and social demands of adolescence.

One reason for the decreasing effect of fathers' absence in older boys is that as boys grow up they encounter a host of other masculine models—teachers, peers, siblings, surrogate fathers, and even television heroes. Many of the lessons in masculinity that they cannot learn from their fathers are learned later from these other figures. Even an older brother can be such a model: in families without fathers, boys who have older brothers show more traditionally masculine behavior patterns than boys without big brothers.[71]

It is important to stress that the effects are not always or necessarily detrimental. In fact, one study found that being from a home without a father had an advantage for boys: they were more knowledgeable about gender-role stereotypes than boys from families with fathers present.[72] Although father-absent boys were less likely to play with masculine toys, they didn't shift to feminine toys; instead they played more with neutral toys. No one has yet shown that playing with blocks and puzzles rather than trucks and cars is harmful to children's development. Carol Beal notes: "In many other cultures both boys and girls often reside exclusively with their mothers until puberty, at which time boys move to live with their father and other adult men. Thus father absence in itself is not necessarily an unusual arrangement for young children nor one that inevitably has detrimental effects on their learning of gender roles."[73]

Just as in the case of boys, fathers' absence can be disruptive to the gender-typing of girls. The most striking evidence of this comes from Mavis Hetherington. She reasoned that earlier studies showed no effects of fathers' absence on girls because they measured the wrong behaviors at the wrong time. According to Marion Johnson's theory of reciprocal role-taking, fathers are particularly important for helping girls learn to interact with males.[74] In Western culture, this process generally doesn't begin until adolescence. So in contrast to earlier studies that examined the behavior of preadolescent girls, Hetherington studied adolescent girls.[75]

Hetherington compared girls who lived with both parents with girls who lived only with their mothers (owing to divorce or the death of their father) on a number of traditional measures (for example, the extent of their "feminine" interests, activities, and behaviors) as well as on less traditional measures (for example, interaction with males). She found that although the groups of girls were, to a large extent, similar in their interests, activities, and behavior, they differed somewhat in their behavior with males. Among the fatherless girls, those whose mothers were divorced and those whose mothers were widowed both reported feeling anxious around males, but the two groups had apparently developed different ways of coping with this anxiety. Daughters of widows appeared shy and uncomfortable when around males, in contrast to daughters of divorced mothers, who were much more assertive with male peers and men than either the daughters of widows or the girls from two-parent families. For example, when the girls were observed at a dance, the daughters of widows stayed with the other girls and frequently hid behind them. Some even spent most of the evening in the ladies' room. The daughters of divorcees behaved very differently, spending more time at the boys' end of the hall, more often initiating encounters, and asking male peers to dance. How do we account for these patterns? All of the mothers were equally "feminine" and reinforced their daughters for gender-appropriate behaviors. Hetherington suggests that daughters of divorced women may have viewed their mothers' lives as unsatisfying and felt that securing a man was essential for happiness. In contrast, daughters of widows may have idealized their fathers and felt that few other men could compare favorably with them, or alternatively may have regarded all men as superior and as objects of deference and apprehension. Widows and divorcees may provide different role models for their daughters as well. The divorced mothers were more likely than the widows to date, which "may function to convey permission by example."[76] Indeed, girls from divorced families do date earlier and more often than girls from either widowed or two-parent families.

A word of caution: the fatherless girls in this study came from a rather extreme and unusual sample. No other males were in the house—either brothers or stepfathers. These girls were deprived of contact with males in general—not just fathers. As divorce becomes increasingly common and, along with it, the rate of remarriage increases, daughters may show less extreme reactions. Also, mothers may react less negatively to divorce today than they did in the 1960s, when Hetherington conducted her study. Attitudes toward marriage and divorce continue to change with the times.

Studying children whose fathers are absent is not the only way to study fathers' effect on children's gender-typing, and it may not be the best way. This is especially true when a father's absence is strongly associated with poverty; it is often unclear whether the effects are due to the stress and anxiety associated with living in poverty or due to the absence of a male figure in the household. Families without fathers may differ from families with fathers in many ways, often making it difficult to tell whether the differences between children from these two types of families are caused only by the father's absence. Pedersen has summarized this problem:

> Children growing up in a single-parent home headed by the mother may be affected by any of the following: the altered family structure and consequent differences in maternal role behavior; the child's diminished or changed quality of interaction with a male adult; proportionally greater interaction with the mother; the presence of surrogate caregivers associated with the mother's employment; or qualitatively different maternal behavior vis-à-vis the child because of the emotional meaning the father's absence has to her. There are many others factors which also may operate either singly or in concert with each other, allowing absolutely no possibility for delineating the "true" causal agents on the child's development.[77]

Because of these problems, researchers have turned to other ways of investigating the father's role in sex-typing, such as by studying the father's influence in two-parent families, particularly the influence of variations in the ways individual fathers interact with their boys and girls. Are fathers warm, supportive, or hostile? Do they encourage their children to use them as role models? Parental warmth and nurturance are particularly important in sex-typing; a number of researchers over the past two decades have found that when the same-sex parent is warm and supportive, learning of sex-role behaviors traditionally viewed as appropriate for boys and girls is enhanced. According to Hetherington, however, whereas both maternal and paternal warmth increase femininity in girls, paternal but not maternal warmth is associated with high traditional masculinity in boys, according to Hetherington. And, of course, the relationship between mother and father is also important. Sex-typing of boys, especially, is affected by whether mother or father is more powerful in family decision making. In families where mothers generally make the decisions while fathers are more passive, boys are less likely to use their fathers as role models. As a result, they exhibit fewer traditionally defined masculine behaviors. Boys who fit the masculine stereotype have fathers who are decisive and dominant in setting limits, and who play an active role in disciplining their sons. These variations in the division of parental power do not seem to affect the development of traditionally defined feminine characteristics in girls.[78]

Fathers also affect the sex-typing of their daughters, but in different ways from the ways they affect boys. Femininity in daughters is related to the father's masculinity, approval of the mother as a model for his daughter, and encouragement of his daughter's participation in feminine activities. And the father's influence does not end in early childhood. Even in adolescence and adulthood, daughters' relationships with males are more influenced by their earlier relations with their fathers than by their relations with their mothers. Fathers who are aloof, uninvolved, or hostile have been linked with problems for women in forming lasting heterosexual relationships.[79]

Researchers have also made more direct observations of interaction between fathers and children. One strategy is to set up situations where fathers' reactions to children's sex-role choices can be observed. Using this approach, Judith Langlois found that fathers enforce sex-role standards even in play situations. Not only do fathers choose different kinds of toys for boys and girls, but they encourage play that they consider sex-appropriate and discourage types of play that they consider sex-inappropriate. Langlois found that this is more true of fathers than of mothers.[80] She observed three- and five-year-old boys and girls with their fathers in a laboratory playroom that included a carefully chosen set of toys that were traditionally considered appropriate either for boys or for girls. The fathers' reaction to their children's play was recorded under two conditions: when the gender-appropriate toys were available and when only sex-inappropriate toys were present. Do fathers react differently when their sons play with toy soldiers and cars than when they play with pots and pans and doll furniture? And do fathers behave in the same way when their daughter plays cowboy as when she plays nurse? Fathers in this study reacted very differently depending on the traditional sex-role appropriateness of the toys. They rewarded their children—by approving, helping, and joining in the play—more often for play with sex-appropriate toys than for play with sex-inappropriate toys, and they discouraged play with sex-inappropriate toys more than play with sex-appropriate toys. In addition, fathers were generally more positive to their girls than to their boys and more punitive to their boys than to their girls. Boys who played with the "feminine" toys (doll furniture, pots and pans) received the lowest amount of reward from their fathers.

In a similar study, Langlois investigated the role that mothers and peers play in teaching children their sex role. Just as in the earlier study, she observed the reactions of mothers and peers to children's play with sex-typed toys in a laboratory playroom. Mother and peers behaved very differently not only from the fathers in the earlier study but also from each other. Mothers encouraged both boys and girls to play with toys traditionally considered appropriate for girls. At the same time, mothers tended to punish both their boys and their girls for playing with "masculine" toys. Peers, who were generally less rewarding than mothers, reacted much the way fathers did, encouraging both boys and girls to play with sex-appropriate toys and actively punishing play with toys considered appropriate for the opposite sex, especially among boys. When boys played with dolls, their peers often interrupted by hitting and ridiculing. Langlois's findings indicate that children learn how persons of their sex are expected to act from a variety of social agents, not just from fathers. But the findings also emphasize the more discriminating role of fathers—in contrast to mothers—in sex-typing.

Another way in which fathers may contribute to their children's learning of sex roles is by the way they treat their children's privacy. Douglas Sawin and I have found that fathers respect their daughters' privacy more than that of their sons; fathers of daughters, especially when their girls reach adolescence, are more likely to knock before entering their daughter's bedroom. Mothers, by contrast, knock less than fathers and appear to make little distinction between sons and daughters in their knocking on bedroom doors.[81] Again, fathers discriminate between boys and girls more than mothers do.

Fathers, then, influence the process of sex-typing in a myriad of ways—through their personalities, by serving as role models, and in their daily interactions with their children. Even more than mothers, they have a striking impact on the development of sex-typed behavior in their boys and girls. Families vary enormously in their organization, their values, and their aspirations for their children, and the particular characteristics that sons and daughters display will depend, in the final analysis, on all of these factors. As our concepts of what behavior is appropriate for boys and girls shift, so may the father's role in this process. Whatever his role in the future, if the past is a reliable guide, it is likely to be a major one.

6 / Intellectual Development

What determines a person's intellectual development? This question has aroused debate for years, and the controversy shows no signs of dying down. Most experts recognize the contribution of genetics to intelligence, but also stress the importance of a variety of environmental influences in shaping children's intellectual development. How do fathers, as one of the environmental factors that influence children's intelligence, contribute to their children's intellectual growth? Fathers can affect how well their children progress in school, which subjects they prefer, and even the kinds of occupations they choose. Whether a child prefers reading and hates math or aspires to be a physicist or an engineer rather than a book critic or a historian is affected by the father's attitudes, encouragement, and other behavior. The intellectual development of both boys and girls is influenced by fathers, but the pathways of influence differ for the two sexes and, in general, the picture is clearer for boys than girls. It is important to remember that both parents contribute to the intellectual development of their children and that often the father-mother relationship is a vital part of the puzzle.

Early Influences

Both fathers and mothers can influence their infant's mental development. One important way is through direct stimulation—touching, talking, and playing. Numerous studies have shown that babies need social stimulation if they are to make adequate cognitive progress. The role of stimulation is dramatically illustrated by classic studies of infants raised in foundling homes or orphanages. Often, in the interest of hygiene, babies were kept in separate cubicles. They had only brief, hurried contacts with adults when they were cleaned or fed. This unstimulating early environment was disastrous for the babies' mental growth: many of them became severely mentally retarded.

Even in a normal home environment, variations in the type and amount of stimulation can affect an infant's intellectual development.[1] Leon Yarrow, Judy Rubinstein, and Frank Pedersen found that the amount and variety of social stimulation—rocking, talking, looking, touching—that five-month-old infants received was positively related to their level of mental ability. And, just as I noted in discussing the development of social responsiveness in babies, the timing of the talking, touching, and other stimulation was important. The parents of the intellectually advanced infants stimulated their infants in response to an infant signal such as a smile or a cry. Adult stimulation is most effective when it is not random, but contingent upon or responsive to the behavior of the infant. Yarrow and his colleagues comment: "It is likely that response to an infant's cries does more than reinforce crying. It reinforces active coping with the environment, reaching out to obtain feedback from people and objects. Moreover, in time, an infant whose parent is quickly responsive to his cries may come to feel that through his own actions he can have an effect on other people and his environment."[2] Rather than spoiling the baby, as parents often fear, being responsive has positive effects on the developing infant. As we have seen, from these early exchanges the infant learns an important lesson: "I can affect other people through my own actions."

As I noted in Chapter 3, infants may acquire a general belief about whether or not they can have an effect on people and events in their environment very early in life. This belief not only is important in infancy but continues to be an important determinant of both cognitive and social progress throughout childhood. For example, children who believe their success in spelling or math is due to their own efforts rather than to luck or some other external factor, such as a nasty teacher, often achieve more and persist longer in the face of failure.[3] These later differences may have their early antecedents in infancy. Moreover, these findings illustrate the bidirectional nature of children's cognitive development: by their behaviors infants and children affect parents' behaviors, just as parents influence them.

Fathers clearly provide the kinds of experiences for their infants that promote cognitive growth, and their impact starts at an early age. According to Pedersen, Rubinstein, and Yarrow, this influence begins as early as five to six months of age. One way to demonstrate that the father's input is helpful to the infant's cognitive progress is to compare infants whose fathers live with them with infants whose fathers are absent. Pedersen and his colleagues made such a comparison using the Bayley Scales of Infant Development—a measure of infant development—and found that boy babies whose fathers were absent got lower scores.[4] At the age of five or six months, the Bayley scales measure sensory-motor behaviors such as reaching, grasping, and following an object, which are thought to be precursors of later intellectual development. For girl babies, the presence or absence of a father made no difference on any of these measures of cognitive development. Another early indication of cognitive progress is the degree of interest babies show in things and events in their environment. Researchers have found that this early form of curiosity is also related to later intellectual development. Pedersen and his colleagues gave the infants a new and unfamiliar toy and recorded how much time they spent manipulating and exploring it. The boy babies who were living without fathers spent less time examining the strange object than those with live-in fathers. Fathers' mere presence in the home during the first few months of life seems to have an impact on male infants' development.

But it is not simply the presence or absence of a father that makes a difference to boys' intellectual development. The amount of stimulation that live-in fathers provide their infant sons is important. Baby boys who have more frequent contact with their fathers score higher on cognitive development measures. For infant girls, neither fathers' absence nor how involved the live-in fathers are seems to affect cognitive progress—at least in early infancy. Fathers do influence their daughters' intellectual growth, but apparently not until later in their development.

These studies of children whose fathers are absent are often difficult to interpret, as was discussed in Chapter 5. Perhaps there are fewer adults present in homes without fathers, and the infants simply receive less total intellectual stimulation because one parent alone cannot possibly spend as much time with the child as two parents can. Fortunately, Pedersen and his colleagues checked and found that there were an equal number of adults in the father-absent and father-present households in their study. A father, it seems, is not just another adult but appears to have "an impact that is qualitatively different from other adults."[5]

Other investigators provide clues concerning behaviors through which fathers contribute to their infants' cognitive growth. Kevin Nugent, in a study of working-class Irish fathers, found that a father's level of caregiving during the first year of life predicted an infant's score on the Bayley Scales of Infant Development at twelve months. As expected, the more the fathers contributed to caregiving, the higher their babies' cognitive development.[6] Alison Clarke-Stewart suggests that both fathers and mothers help the infant develop intellectually, but in different ways: the father through his physical skill as a playmate and the mother through her verbal and teaching talents.[7] Clarke-Stewart observed infants when they were fifteen, twenty, and thirty months of age. To assess "natural" or spontaneous behavior at home, she conducted a series of one-hour observations at each age— when the mother was alone with the infant and when the mother, father, and infant were together. She kept track of parental behavior previously found to relate to children's cognitive development, such as talking, touching, and playing, as well as the level of parental responsiveness. How responsive a parent is to the child's social initiations—a smile, a kiss, showing, or giving—is an important influence on the child's intellectual and language development. Parents were asked to choose among different games that they could play with their child. Some were social/physical activities (such as having a pretend tea party, brushing the child's hair, playing "this little piggy"), others were intellectually stimulating games (reading a story, playing with a stacking toy, building with blocks), and still others were games that the child could play alone. Clarke-Stewart hoped to find differences in the activities that parents prefer and to determine whether parental preferences relate to how the child develops cognitively. Are some parents more skillful playmates than others? To find out, she asked parents to play a series of specific games—to see whether mothers and fathers differed as playmates. The games ranged from coloring and making designs with drinking straws to blowing bubbles and throwing and rolling a ball. Finally, she asked parents to indicate at what age they expected that their child would be able to do certain tasks, such as going next door alone, using a hammer, crossing the street, playing with scissors, or taking a bath without help. Training for independence has been found by other investigators to relate to children's achievement levels.

Clarke-Stewart probed the child's intellectual and social competence, using the Bayley Scales of Infant Development at sixteen and twenty-two months and using a closely related measure of cognitive development that is more suitable for thirty-month-old children at the final testing point. These test situations in combination with the natural observations suggest a great deal about the ways mothers and fathers influence their children's early intellectual development. The most important finding was that mothers and fathers contributed in different ways to their infant's cognitive advancement.

A number of types of behavior by mothers seemed to help infants develop cognitively. Stimulating their infants by talking and showing and demonstrating toys was one effective way. Others were the expression of warmth and affection, and an emphasis on intellectual acceleration—as measured by the mothers' choice of intellectual activities, such as reading. Verbal and toy stimulation in combination with affection thus appear to be the important things that mothers do in helping their infants develop cognitive skills. In earlier work, Clarke-Stewart found this same set of maternal behaviors to be related to infant language and cognitive development. She described this pattern as "optimal maternal care."

Optimal paternal care seems to be different. Fathers could, of course, engage in activities similar to mothers', such as teaching and toy play, but generally they used different ways to influence their young children's cognitive progress. The father's skill as a playmate was one of the main predictors of children's cognitive development. Fathers who were good at peek-a-boo, ball toss, and bouncing bouts had more cognitively advanced children than those who couldn't keep their children interested in their games. A second contributor was the father's anticipation of the child's independence. How early the father expected his child to be able to handle a pair of scissors or take a bath alone was positively related to the child's cognitive development.

We saw earlier that fathers affected the cognitive development of young male infants but not of young female infants. In toddlers and children, however, Clarke-Stewart found that both boys and girls are affected by fathers—as well as by mothers. However, fathers and mothers influence their sons and daughters in different ways. A father's prowess as a playmate—particularly at physically stimulating play—relates to boys' intellectual development more than to that of girls. Fathers affected their daughters' cognitive progress through verbal stimulation, such as talking, praising, and complimenting, and through being responsive to their daughters' social initiatives. Mothers influenced their daughters primarily through verbal and intellectual stimulation; in contrast, mothers affected their sons' cognitive development mainly through physical contact in social play and through being socially responsive to their toddlers' over-tures. The pattern is complex but clear: both parents influence girls through verbal interaction and warmth and boys through physical interaction. As in other areas, fathers and mothers both play influential, but distinctive, roles in encouraging the cognitive development of their infants and young children. And the effects are detectable very early in life. Which specific cognitive skills are affected most by fathers, which by mothers, and when these different effects occur remains to be discovered. Nor is it clear whether parents are reacting to biological differences in the rates at which boys and girls develop. Girls may acquire language earlier than boys, while boys may be more physically active. Possibly the differential parental treatment of boys and girls is in response to these developmental differences. Alternatively, parents may treat boys and girls differently due to gender stereotypes concerning the appropriate ways to interact with sons and daughters.

Parents influence their infants not only through direct interaction but also by the ways they organize their infants' environment. For example, the number, type, and variety of toys that parents make available is one means of "managing" their children's surroundings. Parents set boundaries as well: they limit the areas in the home in which the infant can explore. Being too restrictive can hamper infants' cognitive growth; giving infants the freedom to explore their environment visually and physically can enhance their mental development.[8] One psychologist, Burton White, has made the case very strongly:

> The effective child-rearer makes the living area as safe as possible for the naive newly crawling or walking child and then provides maximum access to the living area for

the child. This immediately sets the process of development off in a manner that will lead naturally to the satisfaction of and the further development of the child's curiosity; the opportunity to learn much about the world at large; and the opportunity to enter into natural useful relationships with people. The child-rearer not only provides maximum access to the living area, but in addition he or she makes kitchen cabinets attractive and available and then keeps a few materials in reserve for those times when the child may become a bit bored.[9]

Fathers and mothers differ in how much exploratory freedom they encourage: fathers tend to allow their infants to explore; mothers are more cautious and tend to put stricter limits on exploration. This pattern is not limited to infancy. As the child develops, fathers generally encourage independent, exploratory behavior more than mothers—both inside and outside the home. Boys, especially, are likely to be trained to be independent and exploratory. Boys are allowed to cross the street alone earlier, to stay away from home more, and to explore a wider area of their neighborhood than are girls.[10] And these opportunities may make a difference. One researcher notes: "The boys' experience in these independent explorations, which girls lack, very likely has considerable importance in the development of independent coping styles, a sense of competence, and even specific skills."[11] Fathers in particular are likely to provide these important opportunities for their developing boys.

Beyond Infancy

The impact of fathers on their children's intellectual development does not end with infancy. Studies of older children have followed the same two approaches as studies of infants: examining the effect of fathers' absence and directly observing the effect of fathers on their children's cognitive development. One finding is clear from both of these approaches: just as in infancy, fathers affect the cognitive development of both boys and girls, but in different ways.

Fathers' Absence and Cognitive Development

Fathers' absence usually refers to a situation in which the father is permanently absent from the home because of death, divorce, or desertion. These are not the only causes of fathers' absence, however. Even fathers who are still members of the family may often be unavailable to their children because of schedules, travel, or just lack of interest. In an important study, Robert Blanchard and Henry Biller demonstrated that fathers' availability, as well as fathers' absence, affects their children's academic performance.[12] Four groups of third-grade boys were compared; all were of average IQ, were from working-class and middle-class backgrounds, and had the same constellation of siblings. Two groups of boys came from homes without fathers: in one group the father had left before the boy was five years old; in the other group, the father had left after the boy's fifth birthday. The other two groups were from two-parent families, but the amount of time that the fathers typically spent interacting with their sons varied: less than six hours per week in one group, more than two hours per day or more than fourteen hours per week in the other. Both the age at which the father had left and the father's availability made a difference. The underachievers, who were working below grade level, came from homes where the father had left before the child was five. The superior academic performers were the boys whose fathers were present and highly available. The boys who had lost their fathers after age five and those whose fathers were generally unavailable were functioning somewhat below grade level. According to Biller, highly available fathers help their sons reach their intellectual potential.

> Highly available fathers can be models of perseverance and achievement motivation. The father can be an example of a male successfully functioning outside of the home atmosphere. Frequent opportunity to observe and imitate an adequate father contributes to the development of the boys' overall instrumental and problem-solving ability. However, having a competent father will not facilitate a boy's intellectual development if the father is not consistently accessible to the boy or if the father-son relationship is negative in quality.[13]

The findings from this study are typical of research using the "father absence" approach to investigate the effect of fathers on children's intellectual development. It is not only boys who are affected by the lack of a father. Although girls are less often included in such studies, when they are examined, their cognitive development seems to be detrimentally affected by the father's absence as well. Marybeth Shinn, in a comprehensive review of the effects of fathers' absence on children's cognitive development, found considerable differences in cognitive performance between children from two-parent families and fatherless families in terms of achievement test scores, IQ scores, and grade-point average.[14]

Several recent sociological and demographic studies using national samples of fathers and children, however, raise questions about these earlier findings. The evidence from these newer reports is clearly mixed. For example, several researchers such as Frank Mott find little evidence that fathers' absence alters children's cognitive development.[15] Yet Lisa Crockett and her colleagues, in contrast, found that fathers' presence during the first three years was positively related to children's cognitive development (verbal functioning) at ages four to six.[16] The effects were particularly evident for Euro-American and Hispanic children born to mothers in their twenties. Fathers' presence or absence had little impact, however, on the verbal functioning of African American children and children of teenage mothers. Instead, maternal IQ and education as well as the economic contributions of fathers accounted for differences in verbal facility for these children.

The most striking evidence of the impact of fathers' absence on intellectual attainment comes from the work of Sara McLanahan and Gary Sandefur.[17] Using several national samples, they estimated that the risk of dropping out of high school was twice as high in one-parent as opposed to two-parent families. Similarly, adolescents from single-parent families had lower test scores, lower grade-point averages, poorer school attendance, and lower college expectations than those from two-parent families. Not surprising was the finding that young adults from single-parent families were less likely to enroll in college and less likely to graduate. In their early to mid-twenties young men from these homes were more likely to be "idle"—out of school and out of work—than men from two-parent homes. Women, especially those with children, show similar trends. Unfortunately, in these analyses single-parent families included stepfamilies as well, making the picture less clear. At the same time, one might expect the effects to be even more dramatic if one assumes that, in some cases, stepfathers contribute positively to children's adjustment and achievement. We will explore the impact of stepfathers in Chapter 7.

Perhaps the frequency and/or quality of nonresident fathers' contact is a more sensitive way to measure the effects of fathering on children's cognitive progress. Although the frequency of nonresident fathers' contact does not seem to be a good predictor of children's cognitive development, in their follow-up study of eighteen- to twenty-one-year-old children of adolescent African American mothers, Frank Furstenberg and Kathleen Harris found clear benefits of fatherhood if the quality of the father-child relationship was taken into account.[18] Those who reported a strong bond or attachment with their father during adolescence had higher educational attainment. The effects were particularly clear in the case of children living with their biological father (or surrogate father figure) and were less evident for nonresidential biological fathers.

Why do children from homes without fathers perform poorly in school and on IQ tests? Attention, encouragement, and stimulation affect a child's cognitive development—especially when they come in response to the child's achievements and emerging abilities and skills. One explanation for the lower level of cognitive ability of children from single-parent households may be that these children receive less adult attention and interact less with adults than do children in two-parent families.[19] Divorced mothers are less likely to read to their children at bedtime, to prolong child-care routines in playful ways, or even to eat with their children. Nor are children in single-parent families as likely to receive help with schoolwork either from mothers or noncustodial fathers.[20] In a single-parent household with a number of children, some of the teaching, playing, and caregiving may be taken over by older brothers and sisters. In some African cultures, studied by Herbert Leiderman and Gloria Leiderman, where siblings and other children give care and stimulation to young children, the level of intellectual growth is lower than in cultures where adults play these roles.[21] Robert Zajonc has offered a similar explanation for why later-born children in large families perform less well on cognitive tasks: their siblings, not their parents, are their teachers.[22] Therefore, it is too simple to attribute these effects entirely to the lack of a father in the home.

Father-Child Interaction and Cognitive Competence

A better way to evaluate the effect of fathers on intellectual development is to directly observe father-child interactions. An example of the observational approach is a series of studies of four-year-olds and their fathers by Norma Radin. She interviewed the father at home while his four-year-old child was present. The ways the father handled his child's interruptions during the interview were systematically observed and recorded. Did he praise the child? Did he ask the child questions? Did he scold or reprimand? Later the children were given an intelligence test and a vocabulary test. Boys of fathers who were nurturant (kind, praising, helpful) scored higher on the tests than boys of fathers who were non-nurturant (cool, aloof). Similarly, restrictive behavior by fathers was associated with low cognitive scores for boys. For girls, Radin found few consistent relationships between cognitive status and how their fathers acted,[23] except that authoritarian paternal behavior tends to be associated with reduced academic competence. There is evidence, however, that proficiency in mathematics in both daughters and sons is related to their fathers' presence.[24] Radin suggests that "one possible explanation is that fathers tend to engage in more physical activities with their children and this appears to enhance the children's comprehension of spatial relations which is related to mathematical ability."[25]

Nor are the effects of fathers' involvement restricted to

Euro-American children. In a study of eight-and-a-half-year-old children, Norma Radin and her colleagues examined this issue in a Native American community (a Chippewa reservation in the midwestern United States).[26] The level of a father's involvement was determined by the percentage of time that he was the child's primary caregiver. As in earlier work, Radin found that a father's involvement was linked with higher cognitive development. Teachers rated children whose fathers were more involved with them as performing better in academic subjects, learning more, and having better grades in social studies. Parental endorsement of traditional Native American values (for example, sharing, harmony with nature, and noninterference), particularly on the part of the mother, was predictive of better cognitive performance as well. Radin concludes: "The overall picture emerging is that relatively high paternal involvement in childrearing, in the context of a maternal belief system which includes traditional American Indian values appear to be the seedbed for successful school performance by the children in this . . . Chippewa community."[27] As this study suggests, both mothers and fathers and their cultural belief systems need to be taken into account in our attempts to understand the impact of fathers on their children's development.

Fathers' interaction style matters at later ages as well. Fathers who praise, compliment, and express pleasure over their offspring's achievements have children who set their educational goals higher. Although mothers' recognition seems to be less important, the education level of both mother and father is associated with children's educational expectations.[28] Others confirm that fathers' style is important. Kathryn Wentzel and Shirley Feldman have found that fathers' style of interaction with their preadolescent sons (daughters were not examined) is linked with their academic achievement.[29] Families were observed at home solving problems and during a family discussion task. Fathers who exercised appropriate control (for example, allowed children autonomy while maintaining appropriate family limits) and were low in hostility (sarcasm, put-downs, mocking) had sons who were higher in achievement. Similarly, boys' achievement was lower if mother-father hostility was high. These marital and fathering effects occur by influencing—not directly, but indirectly—sons' restraint (for example, a boy's ability to follow rules and be considerate rather than losing his temper and being impulsive). Boys' restraint or self-control was evaluated on the basis of teachers' ratings of children's classroom behavior. Fathers' behavior affects how well boys control themselves in the classroom, which in turn alters their level of achievement. Interestingly, mothers' control and level of marital hostility had a direct impact on their sons' achievement attainment. In a subsequent study, fathers' harsh and inconsistent discipline was linked—again through its intermediate effects on sons' emotional adjustment (for example, anxiety, depression, self-esteem, and emotional well-being) and classroom restraint—to poor achievement.[30] Inconsistent fathering even predicted boys' high school achievement four years later, but again the impact was due to the effects on the development of the boys' self-restraint. Across these studies, mothers' consistency in parenting as well as their expectations for their sons' attainment influenced later achievement, also through effects on self-restraint. Other work suggests that achievement and self-control are connected; to achieve in school, the ability to attend to the lessons at hand and avoid distractions is critical. Moreover, teachers may treat misbehaving students more negatively and give them less one-to-one instruction—all of which may lower their levels of achievement.

Marriage and intergenerational relationships between mothers and fathers and their own parents contribute to the academic achievement puzzle. Deborah Cohn and Philip Cowan, as we saw earlier, found that this combination of factors helped to explain children's socioemotional adjustment; it turns out that it is linked to children's academic achievement in kindergarten as well. Early recollections of loving relationships with parents in the family of origin are important and are directly linked to teachers' positive ratings of children's academic competence. The narratives about early attachment bonds of parents with positive memories tend to be more coherent (for example, the recollections are "free flowing, clear, consistent").[31] Their own marriages, in turn, are less conflictual and their interaction style with their three-year-olds is warm and supportive. For fathers (as well as mothers) three predictors—prior family history, current marital satisfaction, and parenting style—are associated with teachers' ratings of academic competence several years later in kindergarten and standard academic achievement test scores in first grade. Although the mothers' model was a stronger predictor than the fathers' model, both parents made important contributions to children's academic outcomes. Unfortunately no separate analyses were available for boys and girls; perhaps fathers had an even more significant impact on the achievement of their sons. Cohn and Cowan note: "The child in this family pattern goes to school with three advantages . . . First, the children in families with more positive grandparent to parent, parent to parent and parent to child relationships may be less distracted and preoccupied with tensions of their lives at home when they are at school. Second, the children have probably experienced more appropriate teaching . . . And third, these children have models of people in their family who can regulate affect and work together to solve problems."[32]

Fathers and Sons, Fathers and Daughters

Fathers contribute to their sons' and daughters' intellectual and educational development in different ways and through different pathways. Fathers may affect their daughters indirectly through their wives, for example. In one California study of children between the ages of twenty-one months and fifteen years, Marjorie Honzik found that the father's friendliness toward the mother fostered the intellectual growth of girls. Possibly girls are more likely to adopt their mother as a role model in a family where the father is supportive of his wife; in turn, as Radin puts it, "the daughters' intellectual growth may be stimulated through their emulation of their mothers' problem solving strategies and thinking processes."[33]

Others have shown that fathers do have a direct impact on their daughters' cognitive development, but that it may not always be positive. Fathers, even more than mothers, tend to respond to their children in gender-stereotyped ways and to encourage masculine pursuits in their sons and feminine ones in their daughters. Since intellectual achievement is still viewed by some parents as a masculine activity, fathers may actually undermine their daughters' intellectual advancement because they view academic success as unfeminine.

This attitude is seen very clearly when a mother and father help their child with a problem-solving task or a complex puzzle under the watchful eye of the videotape camera. These observations show that fathers, more than mothers, treat their sons and daughters differently. In one such study, for example, Jeanne Block found that fathers, especially, are likely to discourage their daughters in subtle ways from achieving. Instead of focusing on their daughters' performance on the task, fathers seemed more concerned with interpersonal aspects of the situation. They spent more time encouraging, supporting, joking, playing, and protecting their daughters than giving helpful hints on how to do better at the task. With their sons, by contrast, fathers concentrated on performance. They might explain the principles of the task to their sons, and they emphasized mastering the task rather than simply enjoying the game. Fathers set higher standards for their sons as well. And they reacted differently when boys and girls asked for help in solving a problem. They answered task-oriented questions and requests for help from boys more than girls. With girls they tended to give help even when it wasn't requested—thus encouraging daughters to be inappropriately dependent, a tendency that prevails throughout the school years. Both fathers and mothers not only appear to discourage independent achievement in their daughters, but, as Block notes, may "devalue their daughters as well. Parents interrupt their daughters more than their sons, thus conveying a message that the ideas of their daughters are considered less important, less worthy of respect."[34] Boys and girls receive very different messages from their parents, especially their fathers: for boys the message is "do well"; for girls it is "have a good time." Just as we saw in infancy, these experiences are likely to undermine the girl's belief that the world is responsive to her actions. The view that through one's own actions the world can be altered is important for developing persistence and a sense of mastery—important ingredients for success in achievement situations.

This same lesson is reflected in the educational and occupational expectations that parents have for their sons and daughters. Both parents, but especially fathers, are more likely to stress the importance of a career and occupational success for their sons than for their daughters. Although one is less likely to be introduced to "Harold, my son the doctor"—who is six months old and sleeping at the time—than in the past, it is still rare to be introduced to Sarah, the lawyer, or Jennifer, the corporation president. These anecdotes are true to some degree, according to Lois Hoffman, who asked more than two thousand mothers and fathers, "What kind of person would you want your son (daughter) to become?"[35] Fathers, even more than mothers, demonstrated the "my son the doctor" syndrome and emphasized occupational success more for their sons than for their daughters. Not only were parents more concerned about career success for their sons, but twice as many parents indicated they wanted their boys to be hard-working and ambitious as opposed to their girls. The other traits that parents desired in their sons, such as being intelligent, self-reliant, responsible, and strong-willed, were all focused on fostering the boys' occupational achievement. There was much less focus on doing well in work and career for girls. Parents hoped their girls would be kind, unselfish, loving, attractive, and well mannered, would have a good marriage, and would be a good mother. These expectations take their toll on girls' later achievement.

There are exceptions to this pattern of differential parental expectations for boys and girls. African American parents, for example, encourage both sons and daughters to do their best and tend not to differentiate between the sexes as much as Anglo or Hispanic American parents.[36]

Fathers can make a difference in their girls' intellectual achievement. Family structure may alter girls' intellectual fate. What happens if girls are reared in father-only households? Recently Douglas Downey and Brian Powell found that girls who lived with their fathers had higher educational expectations and higher scores on standardized achievement tests of science, math, reading, and history than girls in mother-only homes.[37] Boys, in contrast, were not affected as much by the family arrangements. One clue about the advantages for girls of living with their father is that there were more educational aids available in these households. Computers, calculators, dictionaries, and even a place to study were more evident for girls in father-only households. Perhaps a combination of father as model and the availability of tools to help them achieve accounted for these findings. Economics may play a role as well, since it is well known that father-only households are financially better off than mother-only families.[38]

A father's presence is not the only determinant; the way that he interacts with his sons and daughters matters too. In a longitudinal analysis of children's educational mobility, John Snarey studied the father-child relationships of about two hundred twenty-nine-year-old men and women.[39] Fathers who supported their daughters' physical-athletic development in childhood and adolescence had more educationally mobile daughters. In addition, the upwardly mobile women had had a close relationship with their fathers during adolescence. Fathers who provided nurturance as well as support for autonomy and competitiveness had the most educationally mobile daughters in adulthood. Boys were affected by fathers in different ways. Sons' educational mobility was related to their fathers' support of intellectual-academic endeavors in both childhood and adolescence and socioemotional development in childhood, whereas encouragement of physical-athletic development in childhood forecast upward occupational mobility for boys.

As Snarey suggests, fathers contribute in distinctive ways in helping sons and daughters achieve independent and distinctive identities. For boys, the goal is to achieve a degree of independence from their fathers; for girls it is from their mothers. Snarey comments: "For adolescent daughters, it is fathers' active, energetic involvement on life's playing fields that can promote their ability to achieve a significant degree of separation from their mothers and establish a bridge to the outside world."[40]

As social values shift and as women achieve greater advancement in the work force, it is likely that fathers' expectations for their daughters will change and fathers will expect similar levels of achievement from all their children—regardless of their gender. In Radin's words, if the father "sets up a relationship in which his daughter can model his intellectual efforts and achievement motivation and be reinforced for doing so, he can heighten these attributes in his daughter."[41] Research supports this view and suggests that professional women may have had particularly close relationships with fathers who encouraged them in nontraditional roles. In an earlier study, women who were presidents or divisional vice presidents of nationally recognized firms reported extraordinarily close relationships with their fathers.[42] More recently researchers have found that certain professional women (for example, in business) received more encouragement to be competitive ("play to win") from their fathers, while their mothers emphasized traditional feminine values ("look pretty and be ladylike"). For women in the nontraditional professions (for example, medicine, law), however, mothers echoed their fathers' encouragement for their daughters to be assertive ("stand up for your rights"). To break with traditional occupational expectations, women may require encouragement from both fathers and mothers.[43]

Finally, history provides classic examples that illustrate how fathers can enhance their daughters' cognitive and intellectual development. Indira Gandhi, former prime minister of India, was highly influenced by her father, Jawaharlal Nehru. According to her biographer, M. C. Rau, "Indira was not educated on conventional lines but the circumstances and personality of her father combined to give her one of the rarest educations that a person can acquire. Nehru took keen interest in her education and encouraged her to read and think for herself. While he was away; he carried on with the Great Dialogue through letters."[44] Gandhi is not an isolated example. Consider Margaret Mead. In her autobiography, *Blackberry Winter,* she attributes much of her success and values to her father: "He taught me the importance of thinking clearly and of keeping one's premises clear . . . It was proper for women to be committed to pure goodness and purely intellectual activities . . . It was my father, even more than my mother, whose career was limited by the number of her children and her health, who defined for me my place in the world."[45] There are others as well. Margaret Thatcher, the former British prime minister, was strongly encouraged in her early years by her father. And so were a number of other women of achievement such as Congresswoman Shirley Chisolm and the opera star Beverly Sills. Fathers clearly can enhance their daughters' cognitive development.

7/ Divorce, Custody, and Remarriage

Divorce has a profound impact on families, producing changes and stress in fathers, mothers, and children. In many Western nations, divorce rates are increasing. The annual divorce rate in the United States doubled between 1960 and 1986. Today about half of all new marriages are likely to end in divorce. In Denmark, Germany, Sweden, and Switzerland, the rates have doubled and in Canada, France, and the Netherlands, the rates have tripled in the same time period. In Great Britain the rate of marital breakup increased sixfold. Although the divorce rate has stabilized or even dropped slightly in the United States in the early 1990s, it is still at an all-time high. In the United States 60 percent and in Great Britain nearly 75 percent of the divorces involve children. Forty percent of all American children will experience at least one parent's remarriage, and 62 percent of remarriages end in divorce.[1] More parents and children than ever before are undergoing multiple marital transitions and rearrangements in family relationships.

Although attitudes and laws about child custody are changing, in 1990 only 10 percent of children of divorced parents in the United States and 7 percent in Great Britain lived with their fathers—though these proportions had tripled since 1960. Fathers are more likely to get custody of school-aged children than of younger children. Still, in the mid-1980s only 13 percent of thirteen- to fifteen-year-olds resided with their fathers. Boys were slightly more likely to have this arrangement than girls (15 percent as opposed to 11 percent).[2] More recent figures suggest a modest increase during the late 1980s and early 1990s in the percentage of children of divorced families who reside with their fathers. In spite of the increase, paternal custody still represents only a small proportion of custody arrangements. Joint custody has been on the rise, which gives both parents an opportunity to share responsibility for decisions about their children's lives. In California, over 75 percent of divorce decrees provided for some form of joint custody by the late 1980s.[3]

Divorce is often viewed as a single event or a crisis, but this may be too simple. It is more useful to think of it as a "sequence of experiences involving a transition in the lives of children."[4] Often a period of conflict and disagreement among family members precedes the separation. Parental conflict can have serious effects on the developing child, including increased aggression and anger and heightened sensitivity to conflict. Even though children may not be directly involved in marital disputes, the discord can have a marked negative impact on them.[5] Although divorce is a serious step, with consequences for all family members, continual and chronic parental conflict can be a negative influence on children. Boys may be especially vulnerable, because they are more likely than girls to be exposed to parental conflict; parents fight more frequently and longer in the presence of their sons than their daughters.[6] As we shall see, this increased exposure to conflict before the divorce may contribute to the difficulties that mothers and sons experience afterward. Parents are 9 percent less likely to divorce, however, if they have sons than if they have daughters.[7] Perhaps fathers feel closer to sons than daughters or maybe mothers recognize the difficulties of raising boys on their own. Once parents have decided to divorce, however, another series of events is started in motion.

After the separation there is often a lengthy period of family disorganization and disruption and at the same time a search for strategies for handling the different life situation. New schedules are being tried out, moves to new homes and neighborhoods often occur, visitation patterns are being established, and new budget tactics are being explored. Eventually another phase occurs in which the single-parent family settles on a new but stable and organized life style. A variety of factors such as the cause of the divorce, the financial status of the family, the age and gender of the children, the kind of separation settlement, and especially the custody arrangements and the kinds of social support available from relatives, friends, and neighbors can influence how quickly and how successfully families adjust. Fathers—even though they generally do not gain custody of their children— have a significant effect on the course of events.

Maternal Custody

Mothers generally have physical custody of children after the breakup of a marriage, and most of our knowledge of the impact of divorce on children stems from research focusing on families in which the mothers have custody. An ambitious and carefully conducted study of children in homes with maternal custody was carried out by Mavis Hetherington and her colleagues.[8] To explore the impact of divorce on how families function, Hetherington studied ninety-six families over a two-year period. Half of the families were divorced and half were two-parent families. The children were approximately four years old at the time of the divorce, and the families were studied at three points—two months, one year, and two years after the divorce. Hetherington tried to answer a variety of questions about the impact of divorce: How do the parents fare? How do children manage? Does the father affect how well the mother and children cope?

Divorce may cause psychological upset, but it causes practical upset as well. Running a household singlehand-edly is much more difficult than sharing the responsibility with a helpful spouse. In addition to suffering the demands of maintaining a household alone, single parents, especially mothers, encounter financial problems. Lenore Weitzman argues in her book *The Divorce Revolution* that women experience much more economic hardship than men following a breakup.[9] One study estimated that women suffered a 30 percent decline in income in the year after their divorce; in contrast, men's income rose by 15 percent.[10] Because women tend to have lower-paying jobs and work fewer hours than men, these figures are understandable. When two incomes are pooled, couples can manage, but when fathers' wages are dropped from the equation, mothers tend to suffer most. At the same time, although it remains true that women suffer more economic hardship than men after divorce, many studies find that fathers' standard of living usually drops in comparison to that of married men.

Fathers' failure to pay child support contributes to the economic plight of divorced mothers and their children as well. In 1990 about half of divorced women received child support awards, but only half of those awarded support ever received full payment.[11] Moreover, as we shall see later, fathers' contact with children decreases across time, and so do child support payments.[12] Children suffer as a consequence: 10 percent of Euro-American children and 14 percent of African American children slip into poverty in the year after their parents' separation.[13] The demographer Donald Hernandez has estimated that 43 percent of divorced custodial mothers have annual incomes of less than $10,000.[14] Hetherington found that as a result of the divorce, mothers and their children often had to move to smaller homes in less desirable neighborhoods—moves that involve not only the loss of friends and neighbors but possibly poorer schools and more crime and threats to personal safety.[15] The parents' self-concepts suffered: divorced mothers and fathers felt less competent and less able to cope with daily demands. This problem was evident in the degree of household disorganization. Schedules were often missed, meals were often "on the fly" at irregular times, mothers and children ate together less often, bedtime schedules were more erratic, and children were more often late for school. The mothers—who were caring for the children—were more disorganized than the fathers, but fathers suffered disorganization in their lives as well.

In addition, although for some families the conflict that preceded the divorce may subside after the breakup, for others the rancor continues. In combination with the economic, social, and familial strains, it is not surprising that divorce can obviously have serious consequences—at least in the short run—for both mothers and fathers as individuals. The divorced parents in Hetherington's study did not fare too well emotionally; in the first year following divorce, they felt more anxious, depressed, and angry than nondivorced parents. The effects were more severe and lasted longer for divorced mothers than for fathers—particularly mothers of boys. Even after two years they were still feeling less competent, more anxious, and angrier than married mothers or mothers of

girls. Many fathers, however, continue to suffer emotionally from the loss of regular contact with their children.

Just as marital conflict spills over in two-parent families, these practical and emotional disruptions are naturally reflected in the divorced parent–child relationship.
Both mothers and fathers are less effective parents after
divorce, especially in the first year, although they clearly
improve over time. Divorced parents settled for less mature behavior from their children than parents from two-
parent families would accept. The divorced parents expected their children to accept fewer responsibilities—a
factor that may have contributed to the household disorganization.

Divorced mothers and fathers differed in how indulgent and friendly or restrictive and negative they were
with their children. Differences between mothers and
fathers are not surprising, since the mothers had continual access to and responsibility for their children as a
result of receiving custody, while fathers had limited
and less frequent contact. Divorced mothers generally
showed less affection toward their children of either
gender than did married mothers, and especially toward
their sons. Besides being less affectionate, the divorced
mothers treated their sons more harshly and gave them
more threatening commands—though they did not systematically enforce them. "Divorced mothers were bark-
ing out orders like a general in the field, but were not following through and responding appropriately to either
their sons' negative or positive behavior."[16] Divorced
fathers tended to treat every day as Christmas and to be
permissive and indulgent—a pattern that probably made
it even tougher for mothers to control their children. And
the parenting styles had an effect on the children's behavior—especially the boys'. The boys in divorced families didn't obey or attend to their mothers, but they

did whine, nag, and demand. They were also more aggressive than boys in two-parent families. Hetherington notes: "Some desperate divorced mothers described their relationship with their children one year after divorce as 'declared war,' 'a struggle for survival,' 'the old Chinese water torture,' or like getting bitten to death by ducks."[17]

The first year after the breakup appears to be a particularly difficult period for divorced parents and their children; parents seem to have a harder time with their children at one year after divorce than at two months after. The situation was much better after two years, with both parents and children adapting to the situation. Fathers dropped their Santa Claus role and toughened up and became more restrictive with their children; mothers became less restrictive. Even after two years, however, the boys in the divorced families were still more aggressive, more impulsive, and more disobedient with their mothers than either girls in divorced families or children in two-parent families. Clearly, boys suffered more than girls as a result of divorce and the accompanying loss of the father as a live-in parent. This finding highlights our earlier observations concerning the particular importance of the father-son relationship, and it may also reflect mothers' reluctance to raise sons by themselves. As noted earlier, perhaps it is just as well that families with sons are less likely to divorce than are those with daughters.[18]

What happens at home may affect the child's behavior at school, just as conflict at home may disrupt a parent's functioning at work. As I noted in Chapter 5, the quality of social relationships with parents in infancy seems to be associated with making friends in the preschool years. Negative relations among family members often affect a child's relationships with peers.

Hetherington and her colleagues examined the play

and social interactions of preschool children who had recently experienced divorce.[19] They found that the disruption caused by a recent divorce has a substantial effect on children's play and on their ability to get along with their peers. This effect may be important later in the child's life: unsatisfactory relations with peers can have damaging effects on adolescent and adult social and emotional development.

To find out how children play after a divorce, Hetherington and her co-workers watched the children in the classroom and on the playground. Again boys were more affected than girls, and there were marked changes over time in the children's peer relationships. At two months after divorce, boys and girls showed much less imagination in their play than children from two-parent families. "They are less able to free themselves from reality. They need a stick to be a sword or a chair to be a castle. They rarely fantasize completely imaginary objects or people. They also show less reversibility in play. Once a stick is a sword, it is not subsequently transformed into a magic wand or a horse."[20] This deficit in imaginative play may be important for the child's social and cognitive development. According to Jerome Singer, an expert on fantasy and play, "Imaginative play can be viewed as a major resource by which children can cope immediately with the cognitive, affective and social demands of growing up. It is more than a reactive behavior, however, for it provides a practice ground for organizing new schema and for transforming and storing material for more effective later expression in plans, actions, or verbalization."[21] Not only do children of divorce show less imaginative play; they also do less playing and more watching than children from two-parent families.

But the situation changed, at least for girls. By one year after the divorce, the only difference remaining for girls from divorced families was that they still showed lower scores for imaginative play. Two years after the divorce, when the children were six years old, this difference in fantasy play between girls from divorced and nondivorced families had disappeared. In contrast, boys from divorced families still differed in their play patterns, even after two years. They continued to play alone more and showed less cooperative, constructive, imaginative, or game play than boys from two-parent families. They still watched more than they participated in play. When they did play with other children, they played with younger children and girls rather than with boys of their own age. And they appeared to enjoy playing less: boys from divorced homes were more physically aggressive in the first year and were still less happy and more anxious two years after the divorce. By the end of two years, these boys showed low physical and high verbal aggression—a pattern most commonly seen in girls and which may have resulted from their choice of girls and younger peers as playmates. Their aggressive displays tended to be immature, unprovoked, and ineffective.

Not surprisingly, boys their own age did not respond favorably to these boys of divorced parents. In the first year, their peers either ignored them or returned their nastiness. Even after two years, boys from divorced families were still ignored more and isolated more often by their peers. Few boys from single-parent families were selected as best friends by other boys; they were popular only among younger peers or girls. Girls whose parents are divorced fare better and are generally accepted by their peers after two years. These boys from divorced families have as tough a time coping with peers as they have with their mothers at home. As I will discuss below, however, boys whose fathers stay involved with them—even though the dads are not in the home—seem to adjust better with their mothers and with their peers.

Nor is the Hetherington study alone in finding that divorce has short-term negative effects on children. Numerous other studies provide the same general profile of the more lasting impact of divorce on boys than girls.[22]

What about the long-term effects of divorce on children? In a follow-up at six years, Hetherington found that in families in which the mother was still single, the girls who had been relatively well adjusted after two years remained in good social and emotional shape after six years, with a close relationship with their mothers.[23] These girls had both more responsibility and more power within the family. In Robert Weiss's words, "they grow up faster." Although the profile is good for girls in the preschool and elementary school years, adjustment problems are more evident at the onset of adolescence. During the teen years, girls of divorce may show increased conflict with their mothers, increased noncompliance, antisocial behavior, emotional disturbance, loss in self-esteem, and problems in heterosexual relations compared with girls in married two-parent families.[24] Especially if the girls are early maturers, there may be more alienation and disengagement from their families. Although girls do well in the short run, divorce seems to have a long-term "sleeper effect" in their adolescence and young adulthood. In a follow-up study of girls who had experienced divorce early in their lives, Hetherington found that these young women were more likely to have married at a young age, to have been pregnant before marriage, and to have selected husbands who were more psychologically unstable and less educated and economically secure than women in two-parent or widowed families.[25] Moreover, survey studies of nationally representative samples tell a similar story of increased difficulties in heterosexual relationships for young women of divorce. Adult women from divorced families were more likely than those from nondivorced families to have higher rates of divorce themselves.[26]

What about the long-term adjustment of boys? In the Hetherington study, boys remained problematic for their mothers and themselves. Divorced mothers continued to spend less time with their sons and feel less close to them than mothers in nondivorced families. The custodial mothers continued to be ineffective in their control efforts and continued to engage in coercive interactions with their sons. Monitoring was lower in divorced non-remarried households. Mothers knew less about where their children were, who they were with, and what they were doing than mothers in two-parent households. And the situation took a toll on these boys: they engaged in more antisocial behavior and spent more time away from home with peers.

National survey studies suggest that divorce is related to several negative consequences.[27] The risk of dropping out of high school was 31 percent for children of divorced families or over twice as high as for children in two-parent families (13 percent). Similarly, the risk of being a teenage mother increased three times as a result of divorce, from 11 percent in two-parent families to 33 percent in divorced families. Both these outcomes have serious long-term implications and may reduce future employment and educational opportunities.

Perhaps the most dramatic evidence of the long-term effects of divorce comes from a recent study of the predictors of longevity.[28] In a follow-up investigation of a group of gifted children originally studied by Lewis Terman in the 1920s, individuals who experienced parental divorce during childhood were likely to die sooner than those whose parents stayed married. Although these individuals were more likely themselves to divorce as adults, even after taking this into account, parental divorce was still a predictor of premature death. Divorce clearly has long-term consequences, although the mechanisms by which it alters longevity are still not adequately understood. Since divorce is now more common than in the 1920s and 1930s, its impact on longevity may be less than in earlier times.

Divorce and Children's Developmental Status

Hetherington studied children who were four years old when their parents were divorced. What happens to children of other ages? Divorce is traumatic for all children, but those at different developmental stages have different levels of comprehension and different strategies for coping with the changes involved. Preschoolers tend to blame themselves for the divorce: "Daddy left home because I was a bad boy—I didn't put away my toys that day." And they do not understand their parents' emotions, needs, and behavior. Since young children have only poorly formed concepts of families, they often are uncertain about new living arrangements or new patterns of contact between themselves and the departing parent. This often leads to excessive fears of being abandoned and exaggerated hopes of reconciliation.[29]

Children who are older at the time of divorce react differently. Seven- or eight-year-old children are less likely to blame themselves, but fears of abandonment and rejection are common and their interpersonal understanding is still limited. Only by adolescence are children able to understand the divorce process, to assign responsibility for the divorce, to resolve loyalty conflicts with their parents, and to cope with the economic and social changes that often accompany divorce.[30]

Judith Wallerstein and Joan Kelly, in a study of sixty divorcing families in California, found that preschoolers had the most difficulty in adjusting to the divorce.[31] Although the lack of a nondivorced comparison group suggests caution in accepting this finding, a later study by Frank Furstenberg and Paul Allison using a national sample confirmed that children whose parents separated when they were younger than six had more adjustment problems.[32] Adolescents are able to adjust to the trauma of divorce more easily at least in the short run, according to Wallerstein and Kelly.[33] In part this adjustment may stem from the adolescents' greater insight into the divorce process. Other reasons may also be involved, as Hetherington points out: "If the home situation is particularly painful adolescents, more than younger children, do have the option to disengage and seek gratification elsewhere such as in the neighborhood, peer group or school."[34] One-third of older children and adolescents become disengaged from their families, and this involvement in the wider community can have either positive or negative effects. Involvement that translates into more time spent on school issues and closer friendships with well-behaved peers may be all to the good. If weakened family ties lead to joining a gang or drinking and drug use, the results can obviously be damaging.[35]

Children's Maladjustment: An Outcome of Divorce or a Contributor to Marital Dissolution?

Most research on divorce assesses children's functioning after the marriage ends, but children may be having difficulties even before this occurs. In support of this view, Jeanne Block and her colleagues found that the increased aggression in adolescent boys after divorce was evident eleven years prior to the marital breakup.[36] Nor is this an isolated finding. In a study of two large representative samples, a British sample of 14,476 children and an American sample of 2,270 children, Andrew Cherlin and his co-workers examined children's behavior problems before and after divorce.[37] Again there were preexisting behavior problems as well as predivorce family conflict that accounted for the nearly half of the impact of the divorce on children's adjustment. Preexisting problems were especially important for predicting postdivorce adjustment for boys. These studies suggest that although divorce has a negative impact on children, we should be cautious about attributing all postdivorce effects to the divorce itself. Robert Emery and Rex Forehand have argued: "The small differences in psychological adjustment found between children from married and divorced families are at least partially an effect of either pre-divorce family distress or perhaps genetic factors that are linked with both an increased rate of divorce and more behavior problems among children."[38]

Is Divorce Necessarily Negative?

Divorce tends to be disruptive, stressful, and painful for mothers and fathers as well as for children, and it often has a negative effect on children's behavior. But divorce may be the best alternative for some families. Many researchers have found that children in single-parent families are better off than children in conflict-ridden two-parent families.[39] Separation from one parent does not have to have bad effects. Escape from the conflict of an unhappy unbroken home may be a positive outcome of divorce for children. As I noted earlier, marital conflict can have a serious negative impact on children's adjustment.[40] In some families, then, divorce is a well-considered action by a couple to end tension, anguish, and discord. In the words of Margaret Mead, "Every time we emphasize the importance of a happy secure home for children, we are emphasizing the rightfulness of ending marriages when homes become unhappy and insecure."

Father's Role When Mother Has Custody

Even when the mother has custody of the children, the father remains important. Hetherington found that, at first, many divorced fathers had almost as much face-to-face contact with their children as fathers in two-parent homes—a reminder that many fathers in nondivorced families do not spend much time with their children.[41] At two months after the divorce, the fathers' influence was still evident. Fathers in this study were generally less available, however, as time passed. After two years, the fathers had much less contact with their children than they had had immediately after the divorce. Of the forty-eight fathers in the study, nineteen fathers saw their children once a week, twenty-one saw them every two or three weeks, and eight once a month or less.

Other investigators report a similar gradual decline in father-child contact after divorce. In her study of 560 divorced parents, in which nearly 90 percent of the mothers had sole custody of the children, Julie Fulton found that in only one-fifth of the families was there a steady pattern of visitation in the two years after divorce by the noncustodial parent—usually the father.[42] In 50 percent there was a decline in visitation, and in 28 percent of the families, the noncustodial parent never visited.

The sociologists Graham Spanier and Linda Thompson in a large-scale study of families in central Pennsylvania found that only about a third of the fathers saw their children at least once a week, and this figure decreased by the end of the two-and-half-year study.[43] Fathers in the National Survey of Children, a representative sample of children and families studied since the mid-1970s, showed an even lower level of involvement after divorce.[44] Less than 20 percent of the fathers had weekly contact with their offspring and another 20 percent saw them less than once a month. Nearly 50 percent of the fathers in this study had not visited their children in the past twelve months. As time went on, things got worse. Ten years after the divorce, a mere 10 percent of children still had weekly contact with their fathers and nearly two-thirds had had no contact in the past year. More recent studies suggest that the situation may be improving, but only slightly. The demographers Judith Seltzer and Suzanne Bianchi found in their study that 37 percent of fathers saw their children once a month or more and 35 percent never had contact with their children.[45] This is not a marked improvement, and these researchers also found that contact decreases across time. Absence may make the heart grow fonder, but it doesn't seem to translate into action for divorced fathers.

More dramatic evidence of an increase in contact comes from a recent longitudinal study of 1,100 divorcing couples in California, where 64 percent of children reported seeing their fathers during the preceding month after more than three years after separation.[46] Many of these families had legal joint custody arrangements, however, which may have inflated the figures.

Ross Thompson argues that "diminished visitation is neither a necessary nor an inevitable long-term accompaniment of noncustodial parenthood."[47] Mothers who do not have custody, for example, are more likely to maintain contact with their children. While 35 percent of fathers have no contact with their children, the rate for noncustodial mothers is 19 percent, with 46 percent maintaining at least monthly contact with their children.[48] Society defines women as mothers even when they no longer live with their children—another indication of the strong cultural guidelines that shape the definition of motherhood. In contrast, consider Frank Furstenberg and Andrew Cherlin's characterization of divorced fathers: "When these men stop living with their wives and children, they no longer see themselves (or are seen by their former wives) as full-fledged fathers. It is as if their license for parenthood were revoked when their marriage ended."[49]

It is not simply indifference or lack of interest on the part of the fathers that accounts for these visitation patterns. A variety of factors converge in helping us understand fathers' "retreat from parenthood."[50] Most of these factors flow from the circumstances of life after divorce rather than the quality of the father-child relationship before separation. In fact, predivorce parenting is not a good barometer of how involved a father will be with his children after the divorce.[51] What factors do influence noncustodial fathers' involvement? Residential mobility and geographic distance decrease visitation owing to the practical difficulties of maintaining contact. Remarriage—as we shall see shortly—may help some children and wives, but it decreases contact between biological fathers and their children. Nor does it matter who remarries; whether it is mother or father, the result is similar—fathers decrease contact with their biological children. More affluent fathers maintain ties more often than poorer fathers, in part because they can afford to visit and have the funds to make the contact mutually enjoyable. The custodial parent's attitude is important too. Between 25 and 50 percent of mothers may interfere with or make visitation more difficult. Just as we saw in two-parent families, mothers serve as "gatekeepers" in di-

vided families as well. Fulton found that nearly 40 percent of the wives with custody had refused to permit
their ex-husbands to see their children at least once—and
the children's health, safety, or wishes had nothing to do
with the refusal. Fulton notes, "Custodial parents are
attempting to make a new life for themselves and their
children and many of their decisions and actions serve
to keep the other parent at a distance."[52] Nor does the
legal system offer much help, since most states are lax in
enforcing a father's right to spend time with his child or
even in preventing mothers from moving out of state.[53]

Not only does a divorced father's involvement decline
over time, but his financial support drops as well. This
is significant, because child support is one of the major
avenues by which fathers affect the economic well-being
of their children. Of those that are legally awarded child
support, a quarter never receive any payments, a quarter
receive only partial payments, and only half receive full
payments from their former spouses.[54] The amount that
fathers contribute tends to be modest: a 1989 estimate
put the average contribution at $278 a month. Some
estimate that child support payments amount to less
than 15 percent of divorced mothers' income. In view of
the costs of raising a child, these monies constitute only
a small fraction of the real expense.

Many scholars have puzzled over why men don't pay
more. Just as we saw in the case of visitation, the answer
is complex and includes a variety of factors. Fathers who
maintain contact are more likely to pay. Perhaps fathers
who have closer relationships with their children feel
more obligation to support them financially. Alternatively, men who are unable to pay may decrease their
contact with their children and ex-spouses either because
it is too hard to face them or because they fear they will
get caught. Some fathers disappear. In other cases wives

give up trying to squeeze the money out of their former husbands. Some women are willing to forgo the financial support in return for their autonomy: fathers who don't pay probably don't interfere. And in cases where the divorced parents remain in conflict, fathers are less likely to pay.[55] Geography matters too. When postdivorce moves mean that fathers are farther apart from their children, they are less likely to continue to provide financial support. The type of custody arrangement is also important. When joint custody rather than other types of custody is involved, fathers' rate of payment is higher. It is unlikely that these factors operate independently. As Judith Seltzer has recently shown, visitation, child support payments, and a voice in parenting and child-rearing decisions tend to "go together."[56] Fathers who share parenting decisions tend to visit regularly and fulfill their child support obligations. Just as fathers from two-parent families define their role as involving a set of obligations or responsibilities, so apparently do divorced fathers. Seltzer notes: "That some nonresident fathers maintain social, economic and decision-making ties demonstrates that, despite negative press about 'deadbeat dads,' some men take the responsibilities of fatherhood seriously even when they do not live with their children."[57]

Some observers, such as Irwin Garfinkel, have argued that the child support system is unfair and contributes to the low rates of father payments. Fathers do not pay uniform amounts; instead some pay a high proportion of their income and others pay only a small fraction. Moreover, paternal irresponsibility is encouraged because there is no well-functioning system of collecting child support from noncustodial fathers.[58] In light of this system, "it is remarkable that a third of nonresident fathers pay in full on a regular basis! These fathers are a testament to the strong commitment some nonresident parents have to their children."[59]

Noncustodial Fathers' Contact and Children's Development

In her study Hetherington found that as the father's amount of contact declined, so did his influence. Furthermore, the fathers' impact on their children's behavior declined while that of the mothers increased. In two-parent families, mothers' behavior is generally less important in sex-typing than fathers' behavior, but in divorced families, the mother's influence becomes much more important. Single mothers are more influential in teaching their children—especially their sons—what types of behavior are considered appropriate for their sex. Many divorced mothers raise sons who by traditional standards have highly masculine sex-typed behaviors—independence and exploration—by maintaining a positive attitude toward their former husbands. However, as Hetherington and her colleagues note: "Many mothers in single parent families are overprotective, infantalizing, and erratically restrictive with their sons. They are apprehensive when their children indulge in adventurous or boisterous activities . . . in combination with viewing a father as undesirable, these maternal activities may mediate the timorous, dependent behaviors and feminine sex-role typing sometimes found in some of the boys in single parent families."[60] This decline in the father's influence and the accompanying rise in the mother's impact on children's sex-typing is not inevitable when the mother has custody. The fathers in Hetherington's study who maintained frequent contact with their children over the two-year period following their divorce had children who were more stereotypically sex-typed. In other words, by sustaining a regular and continuing relationship with their children, divorced fathers can continue to affect their children's social and emotional development.

Departures from the traditional masculine and feminine stereotypes are, of course, not necessarily problematic; in fact many would view these shifts toward more androgynous sex roles for boys and girls as positive and beneficial. The particular combinations of sex-typed behaviors that boys and girls are likely to exhibit—whether in divorced or two-parent families—depend on the kinds of role models that parents provide and the behaviors that they encourage and value in their children.

The amount of contact between divorced fathers and their children varies widely across families, and may even depend on the sex of the child. Robert Hess and Kathleen Camara found that boys saw their fathers more frequently and for longer periods than did girls and were more often in touch with their fathers between visits.[61] Given the greater difficulty that the boys in the Hetherington study experienced after divorce, it is possible that fathers see their sons more often in an attempt to alleviate some of the problems—a reminder of the bidirectionality of influence among family members. Or maybe fathers place special value on their relationship with their sons—a preference, as we saw in Chapter 3, that is evident even in fathers' earliest interactions with their newborn babies. Moreover, as already noted, families of boys are less likely to divorce than families of girls.[62]

Hess and Camara describe the wide range of patterns of contact that they observed in their families:

Some fathers saw their children every week and talked with them on the phone often. Others visited them infrequently and visits were not predictable. For some, the father's residence was a second home. Visits were for long weekends, holidays or other periods that gave the children the opportunity to become, for a short time, a part of the father's life and household. The children were given responsibilities around the house, not treated as guests. Another pattern was one in which the father picked up the children on an afternoon on the weekend, took them to the park, then to a restaurant, then delivered them to their homes—the "Disneyland father," as two of the parents in our study called it. The routine of the house—preparing meals, fixing items around the home and yard, mowing the lawn, repairing bikes, and such— were not occasions for interaction for these fathers. While the contact between father and children may have been cordial, the children were kept at a distance from the father's new life.[63]

The types of activities that make up a visit with a noncustodial parent are important to children's adjustment and overall well-being. Noncustodial parents who function in a "full service" parental role by including their children in mundane everyday routines such as shopping, reading, visiting, doing homework, or simply watching television together have better-adjusted children than the "Disneyland" mothers and fathers who focus only on social adventures during visits. Spending holiday time with the noncustodial parent was a further factor that was linked with a better outcome for the child. As we have seen so often, the frequency of the contact is less important than the quality of the contact.[64]

Fathers can also affect their children indirectly through their relationship with other family members. This is seen in divorced fathers who affect their children indirectly by the support they give their former wife in her parenting role. Hetherington and her colleagues found that the mother's effectiveness in parenting was related to support from her ex-husband in child rearing and agreement with her ex-husband in disciplining the child. When divorced couples agreed with and supported each other, the disruption in family functioning appeared to be less extreme and the restabilizing of family functioning occurred earlier—by the end of the first year as opposed to two years later.[65]

The effects of fathers' contact are not short-lived. Wallerstein and Kelly found that even five years after divorce, "the most crucial factor influencing a good readjustment was a stable, loving relationship with *both* parents between whom friction had largely dissipated, leaving regular dependable visiting patterns that the parent with custody encouraged . . . The contribution that the out of home parent could make emerged with a clarity at five years. Frequent, flexible visiting patterns remained important to the majority of children."[66] Nearly one-quarter of the children in this study continued to see their fathers weekly, while another 20 percent saw their fathers two to three times a month. The 17 percent who saw their fathers less than once a month continued to be anguished by their fathers' inattentiveness; even after five years these children still wished for more contact with their fathers. Overall Wallerstein and Kelly "found that 30 percent of the children had an emotionally nurturant relationship with their fathers five years after the marital separation and that this sense of a continuing close relationship was critical to the good adjustment of both boys and girls." These investigators explain it this way: "The father's presence kept the child from a worrisome concern with abandonment and total rejection and from the nagging self-doubts that follow such worry.

The father's presence, however limited, also diminished the child's vulnerability and aloneness and total dependency on one parent."[67] Again, the Wallerstein and Kelly study, though suggestive, needs to be viewed with some skepticism, since there was no control group of nondivorced families. The impact of fathers' contact in children's adjustment, while potentially positive, remains a controversial issue.

In fact, contact between a father and his children following divorce is not always helpful. In some cases such contact can be harmful. According to Hetherington, when a divorced father disagrees with his former wife about child rearing, when he has a negative attitude toward her, and when he is emotionally immature, it is better that he have little contact with the family.[68] In this case, frequent visits by the father are associated with poor relations between the mother and child and with disruptions in the child's behavior. Wallerstein and Kelly confirm these observations. They found that almost one-fifth of the children in such situations did not find the visits pleasurable or gratifying. A number resented being used to carry hostile messages between parents. As one thirteen-year-old put it, "My father has to understand that when he shoots arrows at my mother, they first have to go through our bodies before they reach her." The father who visits erratically can cause his child to feel "rejected, rebuffed, and unloved and unlovable."[69]

The message of these studies is clear: quality of contact between fathers and their children is more important than amount of contact. Hess and Camara conclude: "The child's confidence in the tie with the father apparently depended less on frequency of scheduling than it did on the quality of interaction that took place when they did meet."[70]

The best situation for children of divorce is one in which they maintain close relationships with both parents—not just with the father or the mother. A good relationship with one parent helps, but keeping close ties to both mother and father is even better. Hess and Camara compared three groups of children of divorce: children who had positive relationships with both parents, children who had negative relationships with both, and children who had a positive relationship with one parent and a negative relationship with the other. These three patterns of relationship had strikingly different impacts on the children. Those who maintained positive relationships with both parents had the lowest scores on measures of stress and aggression and were rated more highly on work effectiveness and social interaction with peers. Where both relationships were unsatisfactory, the negative effects of divorce were most severe. However, recall from Chapter 5 that Mary Main found that for infants a good relationship with one parent could compensate, at least in part, for a poor relationship with the other parent. Hess and Camara found a similar effect among their children of divorced families. The children who had a positive relationship with one parent were nearly identical to children who had good relationships with both parents on measures of aggression and stress and were between the groups of children who had either positive or negative relationships with both parents in their work effectiveness and their ability to get along with their peers. Relationships with *both* parents thus need to be considered. Unfortunately Hess and Camara did not investigate whether the mother-child or father-child relationship is more important or, more critically, whether it is better for the child to have a positive relationship with the parent who has custody. A situation in which a child lives with one parent but wishes to be with the other obviously is not ideal. Unraveling the complexities of the impact of fathers' contact after divorce has only begun, and many questions about the issue remain unanswered.

Paternal Custody

Sometimes fathers gain custody following divorce, and children are raised in a home with a father as the single caregiver. What effect does this reversal of the usual child-care arrangement have on the child? Although we tend to take maternal custody in divorce cases for granted, it is a twentieth-century phenomenon. Before this century, under English law, children (and wives) were viewed as the property of the husband, and fathers were nearly always granted custody of their children. A father had to be grossly unfit before an exception was made. In 1817, for example, the poet Shelley was denied custody of his children on the grounds of his "vicious and immoral" atheistic beliefs. In our century, by contrast, until very recently fathers were typically awarded custody only if the mother was viewed as exceptionally incompetent.

The view that mothers are uniquely suited—both biologically and psychologically—to raise children has prevailed. And this attitude is generally held by the courts, which "have long paid lip service to a 'best interest' doctrine when child custody is at issue, but in practice, . . . have been guided by the generalization that the mother should be awarded custody except in extreme circumstances."[71] By the 1970s the situation had shifted, and the inevitability of maternal custody was being challenged. Consider this legal opinion from a judge of the New York Family Court:

The simple fact of being a mother does not by itself indicate a capacity or willingness to render a quality of care different from that which the father can provide. The traditional and romantic view, at least since the turn of the century, has been that nothing can be an adequate substitute for mother love . . . Later decisions have recognized that this view is inconsistent with informed application of the best interests of the child doctrine and out of touch with contemporary thought about child development and male and female stereotypes.[72]

At the same time that our conceptions of gender roles for mothers and fathers are changing and the father's competence as a parent and caretaker is being documented and recognized, more fathers are seeking and gaining custody of their children. As indicated earlier, in 1990 approximately 10 percent of divorced fathers had custody of their children in the United States and about 7 percent in Great Britain. These trends toward increased paternal custody should not be exaggerated. Many more fathers indicate that they would like physical custody than actually seek this arrangement. In one study in California, of the 33 percent of fathers who indicated they desired physical custody of their children, more than half either failed to request custody or requested maternal custody in their court documents.[73] Women have a higher interest in retaining custody than men— in spite of the legal and ideological shifts that our society has undergone over the last two decades. Paternal custody remains a relatively rare arrangement in most Western countries, and most fathers still have a tough time gaining custody of their children.[74] In spite of recent changes in attitudes about fathers' competence as a caregiver and parent, it remains true that fathers are most likely to gain sole custody when the mother is unfit or suffering from some psychological problem. Sara McLanahan and Gary Sandefur have noted: "The average child in a single-father family is more likely to have a 'problem nonresident parent' than is the average child in a single-mother home."[75]

Because paternal custody is a new and still relatively rare phenomenon, our understanding of its effects is limited. The results from the handful of studies that are available are consistent and help to set aside some myths and prejudices. Who are the divorced men who receive custody of their children? To find out, Kelin Gersick studied forty recently divorced fathers, half of whom were awarded custody of their children and half of whom were not. Contrary to popular expectation, the men who sought and gained custody were not a younger, more radical group with unusual life styles. Instead they were older, more established, and in a higher socioeconomic position. Possibly they could afford better legal aid, and perhaps they were viewed more favorably by the judges. And these men were not more likely to come from divorced homes themselves; there was no difference between the custodial and noncustodial fathers in the percentage of one-parent and two-parent families of origin. Interestingly, the men who had custody of their children had more intense relationships with their own mothers and more distance from their fathers than the men who did not have custody, who were close to both parents. The mothers of the custodial fathers generally had assumed more complete responsibility for child care and had not worked outside the home. These men may have patterned themselves after their mothers, who provided a child-oriented model of parenting. One father who had custody commented: "I guess I'm more similar to my mother. We certainly share an interest in child rearing." The intriguing aspect of this pattern, in Gersick's words, is that "men from traditional families are more likely to make the extremely nontraditional decision to seek custody."[76]

In spite of their increasing numbers, fathers with custody of their children are still viewed as "brave explorers of the new sex role frontier."[77] Consequently people often treat them differently from the way they treat divorced mothers who have custody. Fathers with custody receive more offers of help, say, in the form of babysitting or dinner invitations. And they generally get more credit: "Isn't George a terrific father, and he does it alone!" How often do single mothers get extra credit for managing on their own? For fathers, raising children singlehandedly is considered a special role; for single mothers, it's expected that they should and can do it.

Men who do gain custody generally manage to handle the tasks associated with caring for children effectively. Fathers with custody are not bumbling and ineffectual characters who can't change a diaper, fry an egg, or vacuum a carpet. Divorced fathers can raise their children competently and effectively, and research supports this claim. Helen Mendes asked single fathers, the majority of whom had received custody following divorce, how they coped with the daily chores of homemaking: "Twenty-eight of the thirty-two fathers regularly cooked, cleaned, shopped, and managed their homes. None of the fathers acknowledged that he had any feeling of lack of masculinity because he had to perform these functions. Most of the fathers knew how to cook prior to becoming single fathers."[78] Although many single fathers—just like single mothers—experience considerable stress as they try to coordinate the multiple tasks of caring for their home and their children, they do master these new tasks. Single fathers and mothers may differ, however, in the kinds of problems that they encounter. Fathers have more difficulty than mothers with monitoring their children's whereabouts, activities, and progress in school. In contrast, single mothers report more problems in remaining firm and patient. These differences reflect predivorce roles, in which mothers tend to assume more managerial responsibilities and fathers often act as disciplinarians.[79]

How do fathers with custody affect their children's development? As we saw in the Hetherington project, boys do not fare as well as girls do following divorce—at least when mothers have custody. Do boys in their fathers' custody show less disruption? Custodial fathers themselves believe that their children are less likely to be adversely affected by divorce than do noncustodial fathers. But do objective reports support fathers' perceptions? The tentative answer is that the fathers appear to be correct—children, especially boys, suffer from fewer problems in their father's than in their mother's custody. In an early influential study, John Santrock and Richard Warshak investigated the impact of maternal versus paternal custody on the social development of boys and girls.[80] Their results suggest that children who live with the opposite-sex parent are less well adjusted than children living with the same-sex parent. Their conclusion is based on a careful evaluation of how fathers and mothers with custody relate to their six- to eleven-year-old children in a problem-solving task in the laboratory. The families were videotaped while parent and child planned an activity together and discussed the main problems of the family. On the basis of these videotaped observations, Santrock and Warshak found a variety of differences in the children—depending on the custody arrangement. For boys, paternal custody appeared to be beneficial: the boys who lived with their fathers were more mature and more sociable and displayed higher levels of self-esteem than boys who were in their mother's custody. For girls, the opposite was the case: they were less demanding, more independent, and more mature when in the custody of their mothers. A similar picture emerges from ratings that were made when the children were interviewed. Girls who lived with their father were seen as less cooperative and less honest than girls in their mother's custody. Similarly, the boys in paternal custody were more honest and more cooperative than the boys in maternal custody. These findings suggest that paternal custody may be a better arrangement for boys—but not for girls—when a divorce does occur. We need to be careful about drawing strong conclusions from this study, however, because only twenty paternal custody and twenty maternal custody families were involved and the range of outcomes that were assessed was limited.

A more ambitious evaluation of the impact of paternal custody on children's development was recently completed by Alison Clarke-Stewart and Craig Hayward.[81] A substantial sample of 187 five- to thirteen-year-old children, 72 in their father's custody and 115 in their mother's custody, were assessed using both parental and child reports of psychological well-being. Children in paternal custody were doing better than children in maternal custody in terms of overall psychological well-being: they had higher self-esteem, less anxiety and depression, and fewer "difficult" behaviors. Although both boys and girls did better in paternal than maternal custody, the effects were stronger for boys, just as in Santrock and Warshak's study. Other factors made a difference, as we saw earlier. Clarke-Stewart and Hayward found that children did best when they were in paternal custody *and* the custodial parent was happier and more affluent, and when they also spent holidays and engaged in a broad range of activities with the noncustodial parent. Again, boys were more likely to benefit from this set of factors, while girls appeared to be mainly affected by contact with the mother—the nonresidential parent.

Nor are these findings evident in only small-scale studies or in young children.[82] James Peterson and Nicholas Zill in a study of a 1981 national sample of 1,400 children, aged twelve to sixteen, found similar beneficial effects of living with a same-sex parent after a divorce.[83] Antisocial behavior, depression, and impulsive or hyperactive behavior were all lower for children residing with a same-sex parent following the family breakup. Others report that high school students living with their same-sex parent were less likely to drop out of school than were students living with the opposite-sex parent— unless the custodial parent had remarried.[84] Santrock and Warshak note the implication of these types of findings:

> There appears to be something drastically important about the ongoing, continuous relationship of a child with the same-sex parent. For example, when fathers are given the major role in rearing both boys and girls, they may sense what the psychologically healthy needs of boys are more so than girls. Similarly, when mothers are given virtually sole responsibility for rearing their children, as in a mother custody divorce arrangement, they too may bring to the situation a better sense of girls' needs more so than boys'.[85]

We need to be cautious in interpreting these findings or in generalizing from these studies to all divorced fathers. A recent study of over four hundred eighth graders living in mother-only or father-only homes failed to find *any* evidence that boys and girls benefit significantly from living with their same-sex parent.[86] In view of the inconclusive nature of our understanding of maternal versus paternal custody, the courts ought to be cautious about basing decisions on the evidence currently available.

Moreover, men who do receive custody may be unusual in some ways, since the awarding of custody to fathers is still uncommon. These fathers may have been unusually talented and devoted parents, or possibly had already developed particularly close relations with their children—which may have been one reason for awarding them custody in the first place.[87] Their success as single parents therefore tells us less about what to expect from custodial fathers whose ties to their children are more typical. In addition, children in paternal and maternal custody have different kinds of lives and experiences. Fathers tend to use additional caretakers, such as the mother, babysitters, relatives, daycare centers, and friends more than do mothers. Just as do single mothers, single fathers with children tend to have more involvement with their parents than married fathers; for nondivorced men their wives are more likely to be the "kin keepers" in the family.[88] Children whose fathers have custody also are enrolled in daycare for more hours a week (twenty-four hours versus eleven hours). Although some research indicates that children in paternal custody see their mothers more often than children in maternal custody see their fathers, other studies find that the frequency of contact does not differ across custody arrangements. Children in paternal custody, however, are more likely to continue to think of their nonresidential parent as part of the family than children in maternal custody.[89] Petersen and Zill found that only 33 percent of adolescents maintained a positive relationship with their absent (nonresidential) father compared with 57 percent of the children who maintained relationships with their absent mother.[90]

Whether fathers seek those social supports more often or whether friends, relatives, and neighbors feel that fathers need more help than mothers in rearing their children has not been determined. Because men are typically perceived as less capable caregivers than women— research evidence aside—fathers who raise children by themselves may receive more unsolicited help. These social support systems appear to be important: regardless of the type of custody, the total amount of contact with additional adult caretakers is directly linked to the child's warmth, sociability, and social conformity, at least as these characteristics show up in the laboratory.[91] It is less clear why these social supports are beneficial. Perhaps they enable children to receive more and higher-quality adult involvement both from the added caretakers and from the parent they live with, whose resources are less depleted. Possibly children in general benefit from contact with a richer and expanded social network of people who can offer additional support at well as alternative role models. Fathers, mothers, and children are best understood when their ties to people and institutions outside the family are considered.

Regardless of the custody arrangements, fathers themselves may learn from the experience of caring for their children that may result from a divorce. Kristine Rosenthal and Harry Keshet, who studied 129 separated or divorced men, suggest that "men who have separated from or divorced their wives and have taken on some major responsibility for their children's care find that the demands of that responsibility can become an important focus for their own growth."[92] They conclude that children not only need their fathers, but "men need their children . . . In learning to take care of his children's needs, a man learns to take care of his own."[93]

Is Joint Custody a Solution?

In view of the fact that men are competent caregivers and women are more active participants in the outside work force, it is not surprising that the doctrine of sole custody has been reexamined. Perhaps children and ex-spouses would all benefit if joint custody were an option in most cases of divorcing adults with children. "At its best," Ross Thompson writes, "joint custody presents the possibility that each family member can 'win' in postdivorce life rather than insisting that a custody decision identify 'winners' and 'losers': mothers and fathers each win a significant future role in the lives of offspring and children win as a consequence."[94]

Joint custody can take two main forms. Joint legal custody refers to an arrangement by which both mother and father retain and share responsibility for decisions concerning their children's lives, but the children generally physically reside with just one of their parents. Under a joint physical custody arrangement, the children live with each parent for certain periods of time throughout the year. Although the length and timing of these periods vary, it is expected that children will have physical access to both parents on a regular basis. In 1979 California became the first in the United States to adopt a statute that explicitly authorized joint custody arrangements following divorce. When both parents requested it, the law supported the awarding of joint custody. The law has resulted in a sharp increase in joint custody arrangement. In 1979, 4 percent requested joint legal and physical custody, while 21 percent opted for joint legal custody. By the mid-1980s, 19 percent requested joint legal and physical custody and another 39 percent requested joint legal custody. Since that ruling, thirty-four states have adopted a similar set of legal guidelines.[95]

Does it help or hurt children's development when joint

custody is in place? Does it have advantages over sole custody arrangements? The most ambitious investigation of these issues is a Stanford University study directed by the psychologist Eleanor Maccoby and the legal scholar Robert Mnookin.[96] They followed 1,100 families beginning with the parents' separation, through their divorce, and for another two and a half for a total of three and a half years. In their study, these researchers found that a large portion—nearly 80 percent—of the families had joint legal custody. Mothers received sole physical custody in over 67 percent of the cases, however, and fathers received sole physical custody less than 10 percent of the time. As noted earlier, fathers are less likely than mothers to seek physical custody and are less likely to succeed in the effort. Maccoby and Mnookin point out: "Although gender stereotypes are no longer embedded in the statute books themselves, . . . the actual custodial outcomes still reflect profound gender differentiation between parents: the decree typically provides that the children live with the mother."[97] Even when joint physical custody is the legal decision, only about half of the children actually live in dual-residence arrangements, while a third live with their mothers. Overall, more than two-thirds of the families opted for the children to live with their mother and continued with this residence plan for the three-year period. Boys, however, were more likely to live with their fathers or in dual residence than girls, who more often lived with their mothers. Moreover, older children were more likely to live with their fathers and children between three and eight in dual-residence arrangements. Arrangements were not static; many children changed their residential arrangements over the course of the study. Over one quarter (28 percent) of the children had changed houses during the three years of the study. And nearly half

(45 percent) of the children living with their mothers changed—either increased or decreased—the amount of contact that they had with their fathers. Dual residential arrangements increase the degree to which parents engage in joint decision making; and they increase the chance that both fathers and mothers will participate in decisions concerning religion, school choices, or medical care. Surprisingly, joint legal custody does not enhance joint decision making. In spite of the expectation that this law would maintain fathers' contact and increase their involvement in decision making, there were no differences between nonresidential fathers who did and who did not have joint legal custody in their degree of participation in either day-to-day or major decisions.

To understand the impact of differing custody arrangements on children, we first need to consider parenting patterns. In the Maccoby and Mnookin study, children in a large proportion of the families spent considerable time in both households—either in dual-residence arrangements or in visitation to the other parent during regular portions of the year. The authors observe:

> It is clear from the experience of these families that it is not an easy matter for separated parents to do business with each other in carrying out joint parental responsibilities. With the best will in the world, a parent may still find it onerous to drive children back and forth between households, to negotiate with the other parent about schedules or child-related decisions, or to adapt his or her own schedule to the comings and goings of the children.[98]

What patterns of co-parenting emerge? Unfortunately, only about a quarter of the families were able to cooperate. Another 25 to 30 percent of the parents were conflicted. The largest group (30 to 40 percent) were "disengaged," with the parents avoiding contact with each other and practicing "parallel" uncoordinated parenting in the two residences. Whenever circumstances such as young children or multiple offspring make parenting more difficult, it is tougher to maintain a cooperative parenting relationship. Over time conflicted parenting decreased, and disengagement increased. Parents learn to ignore each other and "run their own show" as time passes. Maccoby and Mnookin regard these shifts as "good news that conflicted co-parenting gives way to disengaged parallel parenting."[99] And the good news is for the children as well as the parents.

In a follow-up, four and a half years after separation, adolescents (ten- to eighteen-year-olds) were interviewed to assess their feelings about their parenting arrangements and their own adjustment.[100] "Feeling caught" between parents was more likely to occur in high conflict/low cooperation families. Feeling caught was measured by questions about whether parents "ask children to carry messages" and ask questions "you wish they wouldn't ask." Adolescents "of parents who had disengaged from one another were less likely to feel this way than adolescents whose parents were still 'at war' but more likely to 'feel caught' than adolescents of parents who were cooperating."[101] Dual-residence arrangements were particularly harmful when parents continued to be in conflict. At the same time, adolescents in dual residence seem to benefit from interparental cooperation more than do adolescents in sole-residence arrangements. Feeling close to one's parents helps too. In fact, adolescents who felt close to both parents were least likely to feel caught between them. Concerns about conflicting loyalties appear not to be warranted. Of those surveyed, older adolescents and girls were more likely to feel caught between their parents. And this reaction is linked to children's adjustment. Adolescents with higher feelings of "being caught" were more likely to experience depression and anxiety and engage in deviant behavior (for example, smoking, drugs, fighting, cheating, stealing).

These findings, indicating that it is the degree of parental conflict rather than custody arrangements themselves that seem to be the best predictor of children's adjustment, are consistent with earlier smaller studies.[102] Although some studies report that self-esteem is higher and emotional and behavioral problems—as viewed by family members (mothers) and outsiders (teachers)—are lower with joint custody, such conclusions must be interpreted cautiously in light of the variability among families.[103]

Joint custody is clearly not a panacea for divorced families or for divorced fathers in particular. Fathers' influence and contact with their children seems governed less by custody arrangements than by other factors such as geographic distance and their relationship with their ex-spouses. Regardless of the type of custody arrangements, fathers can remain part of their children's lives after divorce. In the long run, the advantage of joint custody may be its "symbolic value to parents and children"[104]—a sign to the father that he retains rights and obligations as a parent and a message to his children that their father is still part of their larger family and a significant figure in their lives. For the time being, no final word on the long-term impact of joint custody on mothers, fathers, and children is available.

Fathers as Stepparents

Another role is emerging for men as a result of the increasing number of divorces and remarriages—the role of stepfather. Some estimate that 75 percent of women and 80 percent of men will remarry after a divorce. About 40 percent of American children will spend some time in a stepparent family before they are eighteen.[105] Having a stepparent in the family has some clear advantages, of course. The economic stress that often accompanies single parenthood is reduced with another paycheck to help pay the bills. A stepparent can assist and support the biological parent in caring for the children. But there are drawbacks as well. Ties with biological fathers may wane when either the father or mother remarries.[106] Consider this observation about a remarried father: "He used to have [his children] come visit him, but he just has no room for them anymore now that he's remarried."[107] When the mother remarries, some fathers feel that they are no longer needed or feel hurt by being replaced by another father.[108]

Of particular significance for some children is that remarriage may be only temporary, a "waystation rather than a destination,"[109] since the rate of divorce in remarried families is even higher than in first marriages. The differences are not dramatic—only about 10 percent of couples in second marriages are more likely to divorce than those married for the first time.[110] One study found that 37 percent of remarriages end in a separation or a divorce within ten years, compared with 30 percent of first marriages.[111] Divorce is most likely to occur in remarried families in the first five years—the period in which the new stepfamily is trying to work out an acceptable organizational system.

Achieving this goal is not easy. As Furstenberg and Cherlin note:

> Step-families are a curious example of an organizational merger; they join two family cultures into a single household . . . Couples in first marriages generally have a

chance to work out their differences before children come along . . . Stepparents, on the other hand, are not afforded the same amount of time to build a family identity; rather it is frequently imposed upon them. Step-families must blend subcultures that have been established for years. Children, steeped in the habits of an existing family culture, are often sensitive to the imposition of new family values, rules and routines.[112]

Because most women have custody of their children, men assume the stepparent role in most cases. How fathers navigate the stepfather terrain will affect not only their satisfaction in their new marriage but their new partner's adjustment and the development of the children as well. As expected from a family systems perspective, the children themselves contribute to the degree of success or failure that the new stepfamily achieves.

Let us first examine how a father's behavior affects life in a stepfamily. The Hetherington study discussed earlier in the chapter provides some clues. A number of the divorced families in the original study had remarried when Hetherington recontacted the participants six years after the divorce. Men had a tough time making the transition to stepfatherhood. Stepfathers, in contrast to biological fathers, tended to be disengaged and less likely to have an optimal parenting style—involving warm, responsive but firm discipline and good communication. Over time, however, stepfathers' approach improved—at least in the case of boys. For girls, disengagement remained the main parenting style. Many stepfathers tend to act like polite strangers with their stepchildren. Gradually building a relationship is preferable, suggests Hetherington: "The best strategy of a stepfather to gain acceptance by stepchildren seems to be one where there is no initial active attempt to take over and/or actively control the child's behavior. Instead the

new father should first work at establishing a relationship with the child and support the mother in her parenting."[113] Does the parenting style of a stepfather matter? Authoritative, but not authoritarian, parenting is
associated with more positive outcomes for children
in remarried families—just as is true in nondivorced
families.

Focusing only on fathers is too simple. The characteristics of the children need to be considered too. Both
age and gender contribute to how successfully children
accept a stepfather. In her study of more than 21,000
remarriages Jessie Bernard found that very young children and postadolescent children tend to accept a stepparent more easily than adolescents.[114] Other research
tells a similar story. Adolescence is a particularly difficult
age period for children to undergo the changes associated with remarriage. In a recent longitudinal study of
remarriage, Hetherington and Glenn Clingempeel examined how well nine- to thirteen-year-olds cope with this
type of transition. Although remarriage improves the
adjustment of younger children, especially boys, in comparison with living only with their mothers, the introduction of a stepfather does not alleviate the adjustment
problems in adolescents. Adolescents in remarried families demonstrated a variety of problems—both externalizing disorders, such as acting out and disruptive behavior, and internalizing problems, such as depression and
withdrawal. Nor did they fare well in school. They were
less competent socially and academically than children
from nondivorced families. At a twenty-six-month follow-up, there was little improvement for adolescents in
remarried families.[115] Henry Biller and Dennis Meredith
explain this phenomenon: "Becoming a stepfather to a
teenager is particularly difficult. The young person has
already done a lot of maturing emotionally and has

established his ties elsewhere. He is also fighting for his own independence from the family and is not in a position to establish close ties with a new family member."[116]

Gender matters too. Although boys seem to more adjustment problems in single mother–headed households than girls, when remarriage occurs the gender picture is reversed. Boys who often have been involved in coercive relationships with their custodial mothers may have little to lose and much to gain from the addition of a caring stepfather. Daughters, in contrast, may feel the intrusion of stepfathers into their close relationship with their mothers as more threatening and disruptive. In preadolescent children, divorce seems to have more adverse consequences for boys and remarriage for girls. Sociologists and demographers agree that these gender differences should be viewed cautiously, since large-scale national studies have generally not found clear differences in boys' and girls' adaptation to remarriage.[117] Recent studies of remarriage when children were in adolescence, moreover, have found few gender differences.[118]

Even with younger children, the arrival of a stepfather can create tensions in the family—especially in the early stages. One of the main problems, according to Judith Wallerstein and Joan Kelly, is timing: "Only a few men appeared sensitive to the need to cultivate a relationship with stepchildren gradually and to make due allowance for suspiciousness and resistance in the initial stages." Instead, Wallerstein and Kelly found, most of the stepfathers moved too quickly into the parent role and assumed "the prerogatives and authority that this position traditionally conveys."[119] In spite of difficult beginnings, however, these investigators found that the relationship between the preadolescent children and their stepfathers became "happy and gratifying to both child and adult."

One of the problems that children face when their

mother remarries is how to maintain relationships with two fathers—their biological father and their stepfather. Wallerstein and Kelly investigated this issue as well. Contrary to some expectations, they found that in happily remarried families children do not experience serious problems or conflicts, nor do biological fathers fade out of their children's lives. A great many of the fathers in their study continued to visit their children after their ex-wives remarried, much as they had earlier. And the children accommodated by enlarging their view of the family to make room for three parents—mother, father, and stepfather. As ten-year-old Jerry said when asked how often he saw his father, "Which Dad do you mean?"

Wallerstein and Kelly did find some problems in families of remarriage: "The most tragic situations for the child were those in which mother and stepfather demanded that the child renounce his or her love for the father as the price for acceptance and affection within the remarried family. Such children were severely troubled and depressed, too preoccupied with the chronic unresolvable conflict to learn to develop at a normal pace."[120] Thus it is important that the mother and stepfather allow and even encourage the child's love for the biological father. If neither father nor stepfather tries to monopolize the children's affection, the children have room in their lives for close relationships with both their fathers—and both fathers can help the children develop.

What are the long-term effects of growing up in a home with a stepfather? Are children better off living with just one parent, or does remarriage benefit the children? Of course the answers to these questions vary from family to family. As for overall trends, the evidence is mixed. Some investigators report that the presence of a stepfather has beneficial effects—especially for teaching boys the behaviors traditionally considered masculine.

Others are not so positive about the impact of "reconstituted" families and argue that "remarriage and the presence of a stepfather tend to create more problems than they solve."[121] In a national survey of children, Nicholas Zill found that children living with mothers and stepfathers were significantly more likely to be seen as "needing help" than were children in mother-father or single-parent homes.[122] Divorce and the subsequent adjustments that children must make are certainly difficult, and remarriage may bring new problems and require even further new adjustments. However, parents and stepparents who are sensitive to the child's needs can develop good family relationships. We should bear in mind that only about 25 percent of children in remarried families experience any long-term adverse effects. Although this is not an insignificant proportion, the vast majority of children in remarried families are doing quite well. Remarriage is no easy answer for children of divorce, but neither is it necessarily or permanently problematic.

Social scientists are much better at describing the complexities of divorce, custody, and remarriage than they are at prescribing solutions for individual children and families. We can describe the impact of divorce and remarriage on children and their parents in general, but the best path for individual children, mothers, and fathers can be guided only in part by these findings. In the final analysis decisions about divorce, custody, and remarriage need to be informed by the unique circumstances of individual lives and the values, priorities, and prospects of individual families.

8/ Innovations in Fathering

The traditional division of labor between father and mother is being challenged and changed in many two-parent families. Various social changes, such as paternity leaves, shorter workweeks, and flexible working hours, allow men more time to be with their children. In families where both mother and father work outside the home, the father often shares more in child care. In some families the traditional economic roles are reversed: the mother goes off to work each day and the father is the homemaker. What do these innovative ways of organizing the family mean for children?

Time for Fathering

In most industrialized countries it is usual for a woman to take time off from her job—maternity leave—after she delivers her baby. What about fathers? Paternity leave gives a father a chance to learn about and to enjoy his new baby from the beginning. Instead of a brief visit at feeding time in the hospital on a lunch hour and fleeting glimpses into the sleeping baby's crib at home after a full day on the job, leaves for fathers permit a more leisurely introduction to fatherhood. Paternity leave is gaining acceptance slowly in the United States; in some other countries it is already common. In Sweden, for example, government legislation in 1974 allowed all men a period of paid leave from their usual work schedules after their infants are born. Parents receive at least 90 percent of their former pay, and since 1991 fathers and mothers have been able to take up to twelve months of paid leave, three additional months of low-paid leave (for example, $10 a day) and three months of unpaid leave. Fathers (and mothers) are also granted up to 120 days each year to care for children or relatives. Parents are even given two days a year to visit their children's school or daycare or to attend children's school events.[1] Although only 3 percent of eligible fathers took leaves in the early years of the program, recent evidence suggests that more than 44 percent of Swedish fathers take some advantage of these opportunities. Swedish fathers take an average of 53 days, while mothers take four times as much time off after the birth of a baby (225 days). Parents choose to be absent from work sequentially rather than simultaneously, with the mother generally staying at home for the first five or six months followed by the father, who takes off a month or more to allow his spouse to reenter the work force. The high rate of breastfeeding in Sweden accounts, in part, for this pattern. Although men appear to take later and less frequent leaves than women even in Sweden, nearly 85 percent of Swedish fathers take a special ten-day leave upon the birth of the child.

What about the United States? Despite the heated national discussion of family values in the political arena, the United States has less organized family policy than any other industrialized country. Formal paternity leave is generally less available in the United States than in Sweden and other European countries, such as West Germany, Denmark, Portugal, France, and Norway.[2] A major breakthrough in U.S. government policy for families occurred with the passage of the Family and Medical Leave Act in 1993. This legislation allows workers to take up to twelve weeks of unpaid leave for the birth or adoption of a child or to care for an ill family member. This was an important policy advance, since prior to this new law only a minority of employers offered paternity leave in the United States. In one recent survey of workers in companies with at least one hundred employees, only 18 percent of full-time males were allowed unpaid paternity leaves and a mere 1 percent had paid leave. In contrast, 37 percent of women were permitted paid leave and 3 percent had unpaid leave. Other surveys of large companies have found that 44 percent offer unpaid paternity leave. Government employees fare reasonably well; a third of full-time male workers in state and local governments had unpaid paternity leave available in 1990.[3] Yet in spite of the fact that some men do work in jobs that permit parental leave, most do not make formal use of them. One study discovered that in only 9 of 119 companies offering unpaid leaves did fathers actually take the leaves,[4] while another study puts the rate at 1 percent of eligible fathers.[5]

Recently Joseph Pleck, a close observer of shifting policies for men, has found that fathers' use of parental leave is increasing. For example, about 10 percent of the workers at IBM who took family leave when their child was born are men. Moreover, in 1990, the Equal Employment Opportunity Commission argued that child-care leave ought to be available to both men and women on an equal basis.[6] Men seem to be responding to companies' policy changes: in a study of four states in which recent laws have granted parental leave, 75 percent of fathers took off some time after the birth of a child—a modest but clear 5 percent increase from prestatute levels.[7] Men were out for four days on average. Other researchers confirm these findings. Pleck interviewed 142 fathers of preschool children and found that 87 percent had taken some time off when their infant was born.[8] On average, dads took off 5.3 days, but generally did not view this time as "paternity leave." In fact, about half of the "leave" was vacation or sick days.

Do paternal leaves make a difference to fathers' involvement? The more days that fathers took off from work, the higher their current involvement in child care. Pleck cautions: "Although these associations do not necessarily show that taking time off from work at birth causes higher levels of later paternal involvement, they do indicate that leave taking is consistent with a broader pattern of greater paternal involvement."[9] Perhaps more involved fathers take more time off so that they can spend time with their children. The direction of influence is far from established. What determines whether men will take leave? As Linda Haas suggests, a variety of factors contribute to the decision. Those that influence a man against a leave include men's belief in their breadwinning role, lack of support for male caregiving roles, insufficient social support from co-workers, relatives, and friends, and, of course, economic hardship.[10] Nevertheless, Maureen Green notes, "an allotted span of time for a young father to be around the house and enjoy the first weeks of his son's or daughter's life is beginning to be thought of less as an eccentricity, and more as a personal necessity."[11]

Flexible working hours may also give men more time for fathering. Flexible hours, for example, may permit fathers to stay home later in the morning and get their children ready for school; or alternatively, to be at home to greet the children after their day at school. Relationships between children and their fathers might be very different if fathers were available for these daily child-care routines. Evidence from Europe and the United States indicates that this type of arrangement has positive benefits for fathers and families. A recent report from a Volvo factory in Sweden indicates that flexible working hours are economically feasible and may have positive benefits for both families and employers. A British study of male scientific workers found that flextime fathers spent more time in socializing and caring for their children when their wives were also employed.[12] U.S. evidence also points to flextime's positive effects. R. A. Winett and M. S. Neale found that government workers in Washington, D.C., increased their family time by over thirty minutes a day after the introduction of flextime. Workers who did not participate in the program showed no change. And most of the new "found" time was spent with children.[13] But other evidence suggests that flextime may not make much difference in family relations. In a study of seven hundred employees in two U.S. government agencies, one of which was on flextime and the other on a regular schedule, Halcy Bohen and Anemaria Viveros-Long asked how workers allocated their time between work and home.[14] Neither mothers nor fathers on flextime reported spending more time with their children than did workers on regular schedules. The people on flextime did, however, report less conflict between their home and work responsibilities than those on regular schedules. Perhaps under such circumstances the quality of the relationship between parent and child may improve—even if the amount of time does not shift. It is clear that merely making more time available to parents does not guarantee that the time will be devoted to children. James Levine points out: "Free time won't and can't be used by all men or women to attend to their children; there is shopping, community, and church work, bowling, and so forth. In many cases, free time will mean a second job in order to meet family expenses in an inflationary economy. What's important here, however, is not only the possibility for new relationships, but recognition of the fact that men too have a family stake in job restructuring."[15] Although the final word concerning the value of flextime for fathers and families is not yet in, flextime is a growing trend in the United States; between 1990 and 1995, the percentage of companies offering flexible scheduling rose from 54 percent to 67 percent.[16]

Other changes in the work world are offering even greater possibilities for men to share in the care and rearing of their children. Although most men still hold full-time jobs, "part time work for full time parents," in Levine's phrase, is becoming more common in both the United States and Europe. One type of part-time work arrangement is the split job, whereby a husband and wife share the same job, but each person works only part time. On some U.S. college campuses, for example, some Ph.D.s have shared a single faculty position. In Norway, Erik Gronseth studied sixteen couples who either shared a single job or both held part-time jobs, and found that most were motivated to try this arrangement by a desire for better relationships with their children. In these families, most of whom had preschoolers, the mother and father shared equally in child care but the wife still did most of the housework. Many aspects of family life improved as a result of these shifts in work and child-care responsibilities. Fathers reported that they had "better and more open contact" with their children, felt closer to them, and understood them better. Mothers benefited too, and enjoyed their children more—because of their reprieve from full-time child care. Nearly everyone in the study thought that "the children are the ones whose interests are best served by the work sharing pattern."[17]

The marital relationship of these work-sharing couples improved as well. Couples reported less conflict, improved solidarity, and more mutual understanding. This effect may have been good for the children too, of course, since the way parents feel about each other can influence their relationships with the children. Recall from Chapter 1 that Frank Pedersen showed that the husband-wife relationship influenced how effectively the mother fed her baby. In general, Gronseth found that the work-sharing families experienced "less strain and stress and better marital and parent-child relations than they did prior to the adoption of the pattern."[18] This way of organizing work and family life is likely to remain rare, but its advantages for both parents and children may make it attractive to more couples in the future, especially during the years when their children are small.

The shorter workweek is another innovation that may affect relationships between fathers and children. Do fathers who work longer days but fewer days spend more time with their families? David Maklan compared men who worked four ten-hour days a week with men who worked five eight-hour days.[19] The men who worked four days a week devoted nearly four more hours a week to child care, but there were no differences in the amount of time devoted to housework. Possibly men do want to spend time with their children but do not usually have the chance to do so—and evidently they have no similar craving to do more housework. The father's assumption of a larger share of child-care tasks may improve his relationship with his children and may also, by relieving the mother of some of the routine of child care, make her relationship with the children more enjoyable as well. It is not yet clear just how giving fathers more uninterrupted time at home affects their children. It is apparent, however, that this reorganization of work schedules allows more contact between father and child. Thus it appears to be a promising way to "make time for fathering."

Role-Sharing Families

Most mothers work outside the home, whether part time or full time, but fathers who assume an equal role in child care are still rare. Even less common are fathers who reverse roles with mothers and become full-time caregivers to their children. In spite of their rarity, families in which mothers and fathers have radically departed from traditional roles are well worth examining. They can tell us a good deal about the possible roles that fathers can play in the family and the possible ways in which families can reorganize themselves to provide more flexibility for both parents and children.

Graeme Russell studied fifty Australian families in which fathers took major or equal responsibility for child care.[20] In these families, fathers and mothers shared about equally (55 percent for mothers, 45 percent for fathers) the full range of child-care tasks such as feeding, diapering, and bathing. In traditional families, by comparison, fathers performed these tasks only about 12 percent of the time.

More time was devoted to play in nontraditional families—mostly because fathers were interacting more with their children. Just as in traditional families, nontraditional fathers play more than mothers, while mothers spend more time reading to the children and helping with schoolwork—but the differences were much less evident than in traditional families. As we saw in earlier chapters, fathers and mothers in traditional families tend to have different styles of play, with fathers being more physical and engaging in more outdoor games. When fathers share caregiving, however, play styles change: the stereotyped roles of father as football coach and mother as storyteller are less evident. In some of Russell's role-sharing families both mothers and fathers engaged in both indoor and outdoor activities; in others fathers spent more time talking, singing, and drawing with their children than roughhousing or playing football. We saw in Chapter 3 that this same kind of shift in parents' style of play begins in infancy. Fathers who are full-time caregivers for their young babies show some of the same play styles as full-time mothers.

These nontraditional role-sharing families have different attitudes toward sex roles than conventional families. Not surprisingly, fewer of the role-sharing fathers feel that a mother's place is in the home. And the parents in nontraditional families have greater faith in the father's ability to care for children. More than 80 percent of the fathers and 90 percent of the mothers in nontraditional families believed that fathers could be capable caregivers—although some felt that fathers were still not as good as mothers. In contrast, only 49 percent of the fathers and 65 percent of the mothers in the traditional families felt that fathers were capable of taking care of children. Why do parents decide that the mother will be the breadwinner and the father, the homemaker? Although some parents reported that they simply believed that they should share the care of their children, a majority of families adopted this lifestyle for economic reasons. Interestingly, the reasons for choosing this arrangement and the reasons for continuing it may be different. One father described the process: "We started out doing it because of money . . . we wanted to buy a house. When we got the house, Sally wanted to stop working . . . she wanted me to go back to a 9 to 5 job. I didn't want to because that would have meant that I wouldn't have seen the kids as much. I felt I had as much right to see the kids as she did. The way we were meant we both take care of them for about equal time. I want it to stay like that."

Sharing or switching roles has distinct benefits for both mothers and fathers. Mothers report increased self-esteem and greater independence as a result of the opportunity to return to work. One mother commented: "After going back to work I started to value myself more . . . I have also become more pleasant." And fathers benefit too. Seventy percent of fathers who take care of their children report that their relationships with the children improved: "I think it has increased the amount of pleasure I get from them." "Being with them all the time has helped cement my relationship with them." "I became a lot more involved, understood her a lot better, and got on a lot better with her." Besides understanding their children better, these primary caretaking fathers showed greater awareness of the mother-house-wife roles—and an appreciation of the pressures and demands that are involved in this set of roles usually assumed by women. And some fathers felt the relief from career pressures. One reflected: "I enjoy the freedom from the routine, pressures and hassles of work."

As is the case with any social change that disrupts traditional roles and routines, there is a down side too. Sixty percent of the mothers who were working and sharing caregiving experience difficulties associated with the physical and time demands of a dual role.[21] Even when dads take more responsibility, mothers still feel the strain of doing a "second shift"—as Arlie Hochschild has called it.[22] Nor is the experience all positive for fathers either. Nearly half of the fathers found the demands—the constancy, the physical work, and the boredom—associated with child care and housework to be difficult to manage.[23] Over a two-year period, in fact, tension and conflict in the father-child relationship increased—part of the realities of assuming an increased caregiving role. "When I first stayed home I found it hard . . . All the nappy [diaper] changing and just the constancy of it." A small percentage (11 percent) of the dads adapted easily to the change in lifestyle: "It just comes naturally to me." But other fathers missed their jobs and the loss of status associated with the shift away from full-time employment: "I had a lot of difficulty adjusting to the idea of not having a job. I didn't realize how important that was to me."

In spite of the mixed reactions of parents to the effects that role reversal had on them, the majority of mothers and fathers in Russell's study did not believe that their children suffered as a result of this unorthodox family arrangement. According to one father, "There doesn't seem to be any bad side of it from Luke's [the child's] point of view. He has adjusted well." In a two-year follow-up, nearly two-thirds of the parents continued to view improved father-child relationships as the major advantage of this sharing arrangement.[24]

Researchers have investigated how children are affected by having their father as primary caretaker, and the father in Russell's study was right. There do not seem to be any major negative effects, and there are apparently some positive effects for both parents and children. In a study by the psychiatrist Kyle Pruett, seventeen families in which the father was the primary caregiver were tracked. Consistent with earlier findings, Pruett found that the positive effects of the father's increased availability were evident even in infancy.[25] Toddlers scored higher than average on standardized tests of development, including problem-solving skills as well as personal and social skills, during the first two years of life.

Follow-up measures two and four years later revealed no negative impact on gender identity and clear evidence of a heightened appetite for novel experience and stimuli. Pruett suggests that the robust and stimulating style of father-child interaction may contribute to this outcome. Men as primary caregivers not only do an adequate job of rearing children, but may benefit their children's development as well.

Even more striking evidence that role reversal can have clear benefits for the children comes from an Israeli study of primary caregiver fathers and their three- to six-year-old children. Over half of the fathers were either equally or more involved in child care than mothers. Abraham Sagi and his colleagues found that children of fathers with intermediate and high involvement exhibited more internal locus of control (a belief that you, rather than some external source, are responsible for your outcomes) than children of fathers with low involvement. Moreover, the intermediate- and high-involvement fathers had higher expectations for independence and achievement and offered more encouragement than low-involvement fathers. Empathy increased with involvement as well, with the children of the highly involved fathers showing the highest empathy scores. In addition, there was evidence of more androgynous gender-role orientation on the part of girls—probably as a result of being reared by more nurturant, involved fathers who were not sex-stereotyped themselves and who did not respond to girls in a sex-stereotyped fashion.[26]

In the United States, Norma Radin studied families with preschool children in which the father was the primary caregiver. These fathers were responsible for their preschooler about 60 percent of the time; in comparison, traditional fathers in Radin's study cared for their children only 22 percent of the time.[27] What kinds of men take on the nontraditional role of caregiver? The traditional and nontraditional fathers did not differ in terms of their own self-reported masculinity; men who were raising their children were just as masculine, assertive, and forceful as men whose wives were primarily responsible for child care. Both traditional and nontraditional fathers in this study had grown up in homes with traditional fathers. Both mothers and fathers who chose this nontraditional arrangement, however, came from homes with working mothers—a pattern that may have helped to influence their choice of family organization. The wives in the nontraditional families had enjoyed their interaction with their own fathers, even though their fathers had been relatively uninvolved in child rearing.

When fathers were primary caretakers both boys and girls showed greater internality—a higher belief in their own ability to control their fate and to determine what happens to them—than did children in traditional families. As noted in Chapter 6, this belief in one's ability to control external events is important for children's later achievement. Radin suggests that "creators of new roles particularly in defiance of social norms would perceive themselves as masters of the major outcomes in their lives" and, in turn, would provide models of self-determination for their developing children.[28]

Although boys usually profit from their father's involvement more than girls, in the case of the highly involved fathers, Radin, like other researchers, found that daughters benefited as well. Both boys and girls who were primarily raised by their fathers scored higher on verbal ability than the children raised in traditional families in this study. Child-rearing fathers set higher educational and career expectations for their sons *and* their daughters than traditional fathers. And these highly involved fathers worked harder at producing their future high achievers by stimulating their children's cognitive growth more. Girls, in particular, benefited, and the child-rearing fathers tried hardest with their daughters, "perhaps to combat sexist influences they will experience in the larger society."[29]

Some areas of development were unaffected by these role reversals. The preschoolers' sex-role identification is unaffected by this type of family structure. Not surprisingly, however, some of their sex-role expectations about who takes on household duties are different. When asked who generally uses common household objects, such as a dishwasher or a vacuum cleaner, children give less stereotyped answers in the families where the father is the primary caregiver.

An eleven-year follow-up showed that these arrangements had long-term effects on children. Radin and her colleagues found that a greater amount of paternal involvement in the preschool years was associated with adolescents' support for nontraditional employment arrangements. This included greater approval of both spouses working full time and sharing child care and less approval of the husbands working full time with wives not working and caring for the children on a full-time basis. Second, children who experienced high paternal involvement at seven to nine years were supportive of more nontraditional child-rearing arrangements (that is, high father involvement or shared child care). Radin and her colleagues conclude: "Norm-violating parental socialization practices do appear to have an impact on children's gender-related attitudes although it may take a decade to become evident."[30]

Radin and Williams found no long-term impact of fathers' early involvement in child rearing, however, on academic grades or expectations for higher education.

Perhaps the seeming tendency of involved fathers to be less oriented toward achievement has diluted their impact on their children's academic aspirations.[31] Radin notes: "A mixed message regarding education and occupational advancement may have been conveyed by the caregiving fathers. The message to get good grades and an advanced degree . . . may have been counterbalanced by the fact that the father put his own career on the back burner to become a more involved caregiver."[32] At the same time, these fathers' unusual commitment to the parenting role may mean that their children will become highly involved parents too. Future follow-ups will tell us more.

Parents who reverse roles are a recent phenomenon, and evidence suggesting that children from these families fare better is not conclusive. Such parents may be different in other ways from parents who maintain traditional roles, and might have influenced their children differently from "traditional" parents, no matter which parent stayed home with the children. However, it is likely that parents who reverse roles are significantly affected by their choice, and that therefore the nontraditional environment in which their children develop is at least partially responsible for differences between children from traditional and nontraditional families. As new family role arrangements become more common and are more intensively studied, the effects of role reversal and other innovations will be better understood.

It seems that few couples persist in sharing child care. In a sobering follow-up investigation two years after his first Australian study, Graeme Russell found that only about one-fourth of his role-sharing families were continuing with this arrangement.[33] A number of factors may account for the small number of families that choose this alternative and persist in it. For example, in general men are still paid more than women, so that most families may find that it makes better economic sense for the father to be the breadwinner. Men may be reluctant to request leaves of absence that may jeopardize their job security—particularly in times of scarce jobs and inflation. In some cases, such as when the mother is breast-feeding a child, these role reversals may be difficult to implement. The basic problem, however, may be one of attitude. In spite of recent changes, many individuals in Western cultures still hold fixed views about the appropriate roles for mothers and fathers, especially in the area of child care. Until there is some change in the traditional view about the roles that men and women can or should play in rearing their children and more economic support (including paid leaves, child care, equal wages for women and men), few families will either try alternative patterns or persist in them for extended periods of time.

Societal Support for Fathering

Girls have opportunities and encouragement to learn "how to mother" as they grow up. Boys, in contrast, receive little clear information about how to be fathers. One researcher notes:

> Almost nothing in the prefatherhood learning of most males is oriented in any way to training them for this role. Males are actively discouraged as children from play activities involving baby surrogates, and, except in rare instances of large families with few or no older sisters, they are not usually required to help much in the daily care of young siblings. In short, a new father has only the vaguest idea of what he is expected to do and how he out to do it.[34]

We need to give future fathers opportunities to acquire and practice fathering skills. Developing the attitudes and skills to become an effective and competent father is a life-long process.[35] It is shaped not only by childhood experiences and the kinds of roles and opportunities provided for boys and girls in our culture, but also by the kinds of relationships that children develop with their own mothers and fathers. Boys have fewer chances than girls to learn the nurturing skills during childhood that are central to fathering in contemporary society. As I noted in Chapter 4, they are given fewer dolls to cuddle and provided fewer chances to take care of infants or younger children.[36] Moreover, for many modern men, their own fathers provided models that are not well suited to the demands of the new nurturant and involved father role. Learning to be an effective father is thus often a "catch-up" process that involves a good deal of on-the-job training. Fortunately, neither fathers nor mothers exist in a social vacuum. As I have stressed throughout this book, families should be viewed as existing within a wider social network of relatives, friends, neighbors, and institutions. These individuals and groups that are outside the immediate family can play an important part in supporting fathers and in helping them become wise and effective parents.

As early as 1925, the Parent-Teacher Association advocated that education for parenthood begin during adolescence, in high school. Today there are many pre-parent programs across the United States aimed at preparing girls and boys for the day when they will become parents.[37] In these programs future fathers and mothers learn about such subjects as child development and basic child-care skills, as well as the economics of raising a family and the impact of children on a couple's social life. For the adolescent boys who take them, such courses provide an opportunity to acquire caretaking skills and realistic expectations about fatherhood. Yet few boys sign up for these classes. To many boys and young men, fatherhood seems too remote to worry about.

Men's interest in parenthood, as we saw in Chapter 2, increases during pregnancy, and men get another chance to learn if they accompany their wives to childbirth preparation classes. In one assessment of the effect of Lamaze childbirth classes, however, "many men said they were pleased with their training for childbirth, but felt totally unprepared for what comes after."[38] These classes do well at what they intend to accomplish—preparing fathers and mothers for the experience of childbirth; but they focus little on postpartum caretaking or relationship skills. At the same time, there is no reason why there could not be interventions designed to address these issues and provide parents with the skills that they are going to need to navigate the postpartum period.

A better time to teach fathering may be right after birth, during the mother's postpartum hospital stay or immediately thereafter, when the father may be both accessible and highly motivated to learn parenting skills. Evidence from studies in Sweden and the United States suggests that men can learn a great deal about fathering during this period. In Sweden, John Lind let fathers feed their infants, undress them, and change their diapers while they were still in the hospital. This chance to learn was effective: these fathers were more involved in infant care and household tasks three months later than fathers who had not cared for their infants in the hospital.[39]

My colleagues and I tried a somewhat similar experiment in the United States.[40] We showed fathers a videotape on fathering soon after their babies' birth, while mother and baby were still in the hospital. The videotape provided information about the newborn infant's perceptual and social competence, about play techniques, and about caretaking skills. Then we observed fathers who had watched the videotape and fathers who had not while they fed and played with their infants. We also questioned them about their attitudes toward child care and their knowledge about infant development, and three months later we checked how often they fed and diapered their babies at home. The men who had viewed the videotape knew more about infant perceptual capacities, were more responsive to their infants during feeding and play, and fed and diapered their babies more often at three months than fathers who had not seen the videotape. The videotape increased the fathers' involvement, however, only if their babies were boys; fathers of girls were unaffected. This selective effect is similar to earlier findings that fathers are more involved with sons than with daughters.

More recently Brent McBride designed a more intensive parent-education program aimed at new fathers.[41] New fathers attended two-hour sessions on ten consecutive Saturday mornings. The sessions included group discussions with other fathers and instruction on normal child development and infant care as well as opportunities for father-child play. And the program did positively affect the fathers. In comparison with nonparticipating fathers, the fathers in the group scored higher on tests of parental competence and in accessibility to their children on nonworkdays. Although they did not increase their accessibility or the amount of time that they spent in interaction with their infants on workdays, they did increase the degree of interaction with their children on days off. This underscores once again the critical importance of work as a significant barrier to fathers' involvement. Finally, even though fathers increased in their involvement with their children, they were still far from equal to the mother's level of care and involvement.

Learning to be an active and involved father need not be restricted to this early period just after the baby is born. Men can learn fathering skills at a variety of times.

Furthermore, different men need support at different times. Some fathers may be good at the early chores of feeding and diapering, but be at a loss when it comes to playing with their active two-year-old. Others will do just fine when their kids are old enough for math problems and football, but will have difficulty with those early feedings in the middle of the night. In the case of parents who adopt their children, learning to parent may begin when the child is three months or three years old. There is no clear evidence that the period right after birth is in any sense a "critical" time for men to learn fathering skills or to develop emotional ties to their infants and children.

To further illustrate that fathers (and mothers) can learn new skills, consider a study by Jane Dickie and Sharon Gerber.[42] They selected nineteen families who were interested in learning more about their four- to twelve-month-old infants. Ten families—mothers and fathers—attended eight weekly classes that taught them how to interpret and respond to infant signals appropriately and that focused on differences in infant temperament. Nine other families received no training. To assess the effects of the training, the investigators observed mother, father, and infant in the home. The training had its greatest impact on the fathers, who increased their interactions with their infants. The mothers who participated in the training sessions, however, decreased their interactions. Perhaps as fathers' competence increases, mothers are more willing to relinquish some of the child-rearing tasks to their spouses. These "trained" parents—both mothers and fathers—were rated overall as more competent than the untrained parents, and not just by the observers: trained mothers and fathers thought their spouses were more competent than did untrained parents. In contrast to the untrained fathers, the trained fathers touched, held, and looked at their infants more and were more likely to smile and talk in response to the baby's behavior. And the infants seemed to appreciate their trained parents' new skills: those with trained fathers sought to interact more than those with untrained fathers. Mothers were selected by their infants for play and interaction less in the trained families than in the untrained families—in part because the fathers in trained families were receiving a large share of the infants' attention. The babies benefited from the training too—and were rated as more responsive than infants of families who did not receive training.

In another study, Philip Zelazo and his colleagues showed that fathering skills can be improved even in families where fathers do very little playing or caretaking.[43] They selected twenty fathers with year-old sons and "tutored" twelve of these fathers by demonstrating a variety of games, toys, and play strategies that could be used with their infants. After the tutoring, the fathers played with their infants for half an hour each day for four weeks at home. The other eight fathers received no tutoring. The infants whose fathers had learned and practiced new playing skills showed more interest in their fathers than the infants whose fathers had not been tutored. In addition, the infants of the tutored fathers looked at their dads more often and initiated play more frequently. Improving fathers' interaction skills thus seemed to make the relationship between father and infant closer.

Nor are interventions effective only with infants. Alan Hawkins and his colleagues recently conducted a program aimed at increasing men's involvement in housework as well as in child care with preschool children.[44] After six weekly two-hour sessions, they found that wives reported a significant increase in paternal involvement in child care and housework shortly after the end of the program, and it was still present six months later. Husbands, in contrast, did not report themselves as changing very much. However, women were generally more satisfied with family work arrangements as a result of the intervention.

Similarly, Ronald Levant has developed the "Fatherhood Course," aimed at improving fathers' communication skills—particularly learning to listen and respond to children's feelings and to express their own feelings in a constructive manner.[45] In addition, the course—which meets one evening a week for eight weeks—teaches fathers about normal child development and child management. A skill-training format involving role playing and videotape playback techniques is combined with home exercises for fathers and their children. Laborers and lawyers from their late twenties to their mid-fifties, with children from infants to young adults, have participated in this program, and it works. In comparison with nontrained fathers, the fathers in the program improve their communication skills, including increased sensitivity and increased acceptance of the child's expression of feelings. Interestingly, children perceive their relationships with their fathers as more positive after the "Fatherhood Course" as well. Moreover, fathers' views of the ideal family changed, which suggests that fathers underwent a cognitive restructuring as a result of the program. In view of the important role that fathers play in children's emotional development, the program's focus on communication and sensitivity to emotions may be one of the keys to the its effectiveness. Helping men focus on emotions may legitimize the expression of the "softer side" of themselves and aid them in becoming more sensitive fathers and perhaps spouses as well.

Although many studies have focused on fathers alone,

fathering is a family affair and perhaps should focus on the couple rather than on the individual. This view is consistent with our family systems view of fathering and is the approach adopted by Carolyn and Philip Cowan in their "Becoming a Family" project.[46] Couples were recruited during pregnancy and some participated in a couples' intervention group; others merely completed the researchers' questionnaires without any special treatment. Couples in the intervention group met for six months beginning in the seventh month of pregnancy until the baby was three months old. The weekly meetings of four couples and a leader couple focused on issues surrounding the transition to parenthood—marital, home, and work adjustments. How effective was this couple-based approach? Fathers in the couples' groups did not immediately become more involved in housework or caring for their infant than fathers without the intervention. By eighteen months after the birth of their infant, however, both fathers and mothers in the intervention groups were more satisfied with their division of family labor arrangements than parents who had not participated in these groups. Marital satisfaction was also higher for fathers in the intervention group—even though marital satisfaction dropped for both groups following the birth of the baby. Two years after the transition to parenthood, the marriages of all the couples in the intervention were still intact. In contrast, 12 percent of the couples who had become parents but did not receive intervention were separated or divorced. The long-term effects of intervention are rarely examined, but the Cowans followed their families through the children's completion of kindergarten. Five and a half years after the intervention ended, the couples in the intervention and no-intervention groups did not differ on role arrangements, marital quality or stability, or in their relationships with the children. Perhaps, as the Cowans argue, "it is not realistic to expect the effects of a six month intervention to be evident four or six years later . . . By then couples have been dealing with the effects of having more children, job changes, moves, births in their extended families and the strain of working and rearing young children."[47] Just as booster shots help maintain children's health, programs for fathers and families may need to consider booster interventions in the form of periodic brief retraining sessions after the main dose program. This type of approach may improve the long-term effectiveness of early intervention efforts aimed at increasing fathers' involvement.

Many Programs, Many Fathers: Recognizing the Diversity of Fathers

One of the promising trends in fatherhood education is the recognition that different fathers have different needs and that programs, to be successful, need to be tailored to fit the characteristics of the group of men being addressed. Urban teenage fathers need different programs than suburban married dads. Similarly, Latino men may require a different intervention approach than African American or Asian American men. In his book *Getting Men Involved*, James Levine and his colleagues recount this story illustrating the need for cultural sensitivity in approaching fatherhood issues.[48]

Consider the situation of two Head Start trainers trying to promote male involvement to Inuit tribes in remote villages of Alaska . . . According to one Inuit custom, a man cannot take the risk of holding a young child who is not toilet trained or who might have an "accident" on him. The reason: the scent of urine will spoil the hunt since it lets animals smell the hunter approaching. The

fact that most Inuit men hunt for sport rather than sub-
sistence does not seem to matter very much. The men in
these villages don't expect to have much direct contact
with their children—typically their sons—until they are
old enough to join in the hunt . . . The trainers were
outraged that Eskimo women were being put in a position of having to do all the child care because of the
antiquated hunting myth. They sincerely wanted to promote male involvement for children and their fathers.
And they had to be taught just how important it is to
respect cultural differences, not to automatically impose
their values.[49]

A variety of programs in the United States are currently
available that are especially designed for fathers of different ethnic backgrounds.[50] For example, the Nueva
Family Initiative—a parent-education program aimed at
immigrant Latino fathers in Los Angeles—illustrates that
men are willing to participate in parenting programs,
especially if they are organized in ways that recognize
cultural differences.[51] This successful program gave fathers roles in program routines such as leading group
singing at the end of the session, in recognition of men's
leadership roles in the Latino culture. In addition, husbands and wives in Latino families often serve as informal gatekeepers of their spouses' or partners' involvement in programs, and in this program, care was taken
to ensure that spousal support for participation was obtained. In fact, this Los Angeles initiative found that
fathers' participation was higher when couples—both
mother and father—rather than just fathers were included. Finally, program success was enhanced when
nonparenting issues such as survival strategies for low-
income immigrants in an often hostile U.S. culture were

included as part of the program agenda. Although the success of such new programs remains unclear, cultural sensitivity is probably critical in attracting and retaining participants.

Teen fathers who are often unwed also require special programs to meet their needs if their potential contributions as fathers are to be realized. As noted earlier, teenage dads are often unemployed, uneducated, and unprepared for the fathering role. One of the most ambitious programs directed at young fathers was the Teen Father Collaboration—a national project serving 395 teen fathers and fathers-to-be at eight sites.[52] This program provided a comprehensive range of services to males of a variety of backgrounds—African Americans, Euro-Americans, Hispanic Americans, Asian Americans, and Native Americans. Services included counseling, vocational training, employment placement, educational services, parenting skills classes, family planning services, and prenatal education. Joelle Sander, one of the program organizers, summarized: "The overall goals of all services to the young men were to keep them involved in their children's lives. This was best done by teaching them the rudiments of child care so they did not feel irrelevant as caretakers, by counseling them about their desires and fears and by assisting them to become financially supporting parents at the appropriate time."[53] The program produced positive effects. These teen fathers developed closer ties to their families, learned how to take care of their children, and increased their knowledge of developmental milestones—knowledge that helped reduce abusive behavior and increased control and patience. One father spoke of learning "even how to hold my baby, put on diapers and fix formula." Another benefited from "different viewpoints on how to properly raise my child." One teen dad spoke for many when he said he learned "to be a better father to my child than my father was to me."[54]

Simply learning how to be a better father is not enough to sustain young men's involvement with their children. Teen fathers are often marginal figures in the lives of their partners and their children owing to their inability to contribute to the family's economic well-being. Many drop out of high school; many more are either unemployed or in minimum wage jobs. The Teen Fathers Collaboration helped improve their educational and job prospects. Nearly half of the nongraduated either returned to school or worked on obtaining a a high school equivalency certificate. Similarly, nearly 40 percent of those unemployed at the beginning of the program obtained jobs, which permitted them to contribute to their family and probably enhanced their own sense of competence as a provider.

Although Teen Fathers Collaboration was helpful, it aided only a proportion of the young men who initially enrolled. Many dropped out or attended only sporadically, and many were not changed. Interventions alone cannot alter the underlying cultural and economic factors that promote and sustain teenage fatherhood in the United States. Frank Furstenberg, one longtime observer of adolescent parenthood, recently commented: "Men can be brought back into the family only when they have more resources—material and emotional—to invest in their children. Only then will they be admitted into the family by women and their kin and only then will they have confidence that they have a rightful claim. Currently too many men discover a painful revelation after they become parents: They are in no better position to assume fatherhood than their fathers were when they became parents."[55]

Changing Men's Level of Involvement: A Word of Caution

Although these studies and others report modest success, the intensive efforts also reveal how difficult it is to change men's level of involvement. As I have noted throughout, individual, familial, institutional, and cultural factors operate together in determining fathers' roles in contemporary society. Focusing on only one or two of these factors is unlikely to result in large or very lasting changes. In addition, it is important to bear in mind the difference between competence and performance. Programs can improve men's competence or capacity for adequate caregiving; it may be a lot harder to modify their level of participation in these tasks.

The intervention efforts I have described suggest that fathering skills can be learned and that this learning can take place at a variety of times in the father's life. Learning to father effectively is a continuing process, in any case, as the child's development requires new skills on the part of the parent to meet the child's changing needs. At present, we have only begun to explore the ways that fathers (and mothers) can be aided in this task.

Is Intervention Always Justified?

Considerable care must be taken with the implementation of family services and support systems. Parents' rights are important, and need to be considered. An implicit model of many intervention programs for fathers, for example, is the egalitarian rather than the more traditional family organization. Yet the goal should not be to shift all families toward an egalitarian family arrangement, but to provide the quality and quantity of support that will enable family members to enact their roles competently within their own ideological framework. For some families this may mean modest levels of participation by the father, while in other families it may mean shared responsibility between spouses. Too often "more" is equated with "improvement"; in some families, however, a father's increased participation may cause conflict and disruption by threatening well-established and satisfying role definitions. Intervention, therefore, should be sensitively geared to the needs of individual families, and the dynamics and ideology of the couple should be given primary recognition. At the same time, as we have seen, fathers' participation—especially when it is sensitive and responsive—can have clearly beneficial effects on children's development. In this sense, the child's right to receive the benefits of an involved and available father needs to be considered in this debate as well. As more women continue to enter the work force or increase their level of work involvement, greater equity of participation on the part of men and women in the care and nurturing of children is likely to become the ideological goal for many families.

Beyond Children: Fathering and Men's Own Development

Although I have focused on the impact of fathers on children's development throughout this book, I want to close with a reminder that children influence their fathers just as fathers influence their children. The transition to fatherhood has both positive and negative short-term effects on fathers' identity, marriage, and work. Is there a long-term impact as well, especially for involved fathers? A life course perspective on development suggests that men's investment in being a parent has implications for their own psychological development and well-being.

The most comprehensive effort to address the link between fathering and men's own development comes from a study by John Snarey—*How Fathers Care for the Next Generation.*[56] In a unique follow-up to a longitudinal study of men who were originally studied in the 1940s and 1950s, Snarey examined the impact of the men's involvement in child rearing on their own development as adults. Work and marriage were positively related to being an involved father. Snarey notes: "Fathers who provided high levels of social-emotional support for their offspring during the childhood decade (0–10 years) and high levels of intellectual, academic and social emotional support during the adolescent decade (11–21 years) were themselves as men at mid-life, more likely to be happily married."[57] Similarly, Snarey found that fathers' involvement in child rearing across the first two decades of the child's life moderately predicted fathers' occupational mobility (at age forty-seven) above and beyond other background variables (for example, parents' occupations, his IQ, current maternal employment). In sum, men who are involved fathers tend to have happier marriages and more successful careers.

Fathering is not limited to one's own family and children but may extend to the next generation of children or younger adults in one's work organization, neighborhood, or community.[58] This kind of mentoring through which men nurture and guide younger people has been called "generativity"—a term used by Erik Erikson. Snarey offers this succinct summary:

> The psychosocial task of middle adulthood, Stage 7 [in Erikson's Stage theory], is the attainment of a favorable balance of generativity over stagnation and self-absorp-

> tion . . . Most broadly, Erikson . . . considers generativity
> to mean any caring activity that contributes to the spirit
> of future generations, such as the generation of new or
> more mature persons, products, ideas, or works of art . . .
> Generativity's psychosocial challenge to adults is to cre-
> ate, care for, and promote the development of others,
> from nurturing the growth of another person to shep-
> herding the development of a broader community.[59]

Subsequent theorists have distinguished among different types of generativity.[60] Snarey describes three types
that apply to fathers, namely biological generativity (indicated by the birth of a child), parental generativity
(indicated by child-rearing activities), and societal generativity (indicated by caring for other younger adults:
serving as a mentor, providing leadership, and contributing to generational continuity). Although serious questions have been raised about the utility of Erikson's notion of stages, especially the inevitability of their order
and their universal applicability, the concept of generativity is nonetheless a useful marker for assessing the
long-term relation between fathering behavior and other
aspects of mature men's lives.

A series of studies has examined the relations between
fatherhood, especially paternal competence and involvement, and social generativity. D. H. Heath and H. E.
Heath noted a link between satisfaction with fatherhood
and community participation; fathers who reported
higher satisfaction in parenting were more likely to be
active participants in community organizations or professions in the prior decade.[61] Similarly, George Vaillant
found a positive relation between paternal competence
and the combination of societal generativity and social
adjustment.[62] Men who held positions of responsibility
for other adults and who were well adjusted socially
were rated higher in terms of their psychological close-

ness to their children. Is men's societal generativity at mid-life related to the level of care and support they provide their children? Snarey rated a father's social generativity on a three-point scale and tapped whether "he demonstrated a clear capacity for establishing, guiding, or caring for the next generation through sustained responsibility for the growth, well-being, or leadership of younger adults or of the larger society . . . beyond the sphere of the nuclear family."[63] Snarey found that men who nurtured their offspring's social-emotional development during childhood and who also contributed to both social-emotional and intellectual-academic development during the the child's second decade were, in addition to being happier in their marriages at mid-life as already noted, more likely to become generative in areas outside their family.

Snarey offered several interpretations of his findings. First, a disequilibrium explanation suggests that paternal child-rearing responsibilities result in demands that are difficult to meet and that, in turn, promote "increased complexity in the fathers' cognitive, emotional, and behavioral repertoire . . . This commitment beyond the self . . . prepares the way for societal generativity which involves a commitment beyond the family."[64] Second, perhaps a nurturing predisposition may underlie both parenting and societal generativity and account for the continuity across time. Third, the arrival of children often leads to increases in men's participation in neighborhood and community organizations on behalf of children, which may continue into the mid-life years. It should be noted that the direction of causation may work the opposite way—men who are in happier marriages and who have more successful careers may become more involved fathers. At this point we cannot unravel the direction of causality. Although the processes are not yet well understood, active involvement in fathering is clearly related in positive ways to other aspects of men's lives. Snarey notes: "Men who are parentally generative during early adulthood usually turn out to be good spouses, workers, and citizens at midlife."[65] Encouraging fathers' participation may thus have benefits not only for children and mothers, but for men themselves. The investment in enhancing fathers' involvement could yield important social dividends for us all.

There is no "average" father. Family organization and gender roles are changing rapidly in our society, and the definition of fathering is no longer rigid or restricted. Although in many families the father is the breadwinner and the mother has primary responsibility for the children, many other families are part of society's transition—families in which fathers share more in child care or even reverse roles with their wives, and families in which the father or mother is a single parent. This book is a progress report of what we know today about how fathers act and how they influence their children.

One thing is clear: fathers are perfectly capable of caring for children, even very young babies. They are not simply substitute mothers; mothers and fathers have distinct styles of parenting. Fathers tend to spend more of their available time playing with their children than mothers do, and to play differently. Their physical and robust approach complements and contrasts with mothers' verbal, paced style. Children profit from this diversity of experience. These patterns are not fixed, however, and they are likely to evolve as social and work roles for men and women continue to change.

Fathers and families do not exist in isolation. They are embedded in wider communities and cultures, and the support they get from friends, relatives, neighbors, and institutions is important. I have mentioned ways that society can adjust the demands of work, for example, to make fathering more possible and more satisfying. Institutions, too, such as hospitals and schools and mental health clinics, can help fathers learn to be effective parents and can provide advice and assistance when families have problems.

Fathers are no longer, if they ever were, merely a biological necessity—a social accident. They are an important influence on children's development. And a close relationship between father and child benefits the father as well as the child. Children need their fathers, but fathers need their children, too.

Notes

1 / FATHERHOOD

1. P. Stearns, "Fatherhood in Historical Perspective: The Role of Social Change," in F. W. Bozett and S. M. H. Hanson, eds., *Fatherhood and Families in Cultural Context* (New York: Springer, 1991); R. D. Parke and P. Stearns, "Father and Child-Rearing," in G. Elder, J. Modell, and R. D. Parke, eds., *Children in Time and Place* (New York: Cambridge University Press, 1993); R. L. Griswold, *Fatherhood in America* (New York: Basic Books, 1993); E. A. Rotundo, *American Manhood* (New York: Basic Books, 1993).
2. R. R. Sears, E. E. Maccoby, and H. Levin, *Patterns of Child Rearing* (Evanston, Ill.: Row, Peterson, 1956); J. M. W. Whiting and I. L. Child, *Child Training and Personality* (New Haven: Yale University Press, 1953).
3. M. Ribble, *Rights of Infants* (New York: Columbia University Press, 1943); R. A. Spitz, "Hospitalism: An Inquiry into the Genesis of Psychiatric Conditions in Childhood," *Psychoanalytic Study of the Child,* 1945, 1, 53–74. For a review of these early studies, see L. J. Yarrow, "Separation from Parents during Early Childhood," in M. L. Hoffman and L. W. Hoffman, eds., *Review of Child Development Research,* vol. 1 (New York: Russell Sage Foundation, 1964).
4. J. Bowlby, *Maternal Care and Mental Health* (Geneva: World Health Organization, 1951); J. Bowlby, *Attachment and Loss,* vol. 1, *Attachment* (New York: Basic Books, 1969).

5. M. M. Katz and M. J. Konner, "The Role of the Father: An Anthropological Perspective," in M. Lamb, ed., *The Role of the Father in Child Development* (New York: Wiley, 1981); B. S. Hewlett, ed., *Father-Child Relations: Cultural and Biosocial Contexts* (New York: Aldine, 1992).

6. I. DeVore, "Mother-Infant Relations in Free-Ranging Baboons," in H. L. Rheingold, ed., *Maternal Behavior in Mammals* (New York: Wiley, 1963).

7. A. Chamove, H. J. Harlow, and G. D. Mitchell, "Sex Differences in the Infant-Directed Behavior of Preadolescent Rhesus Monkeys," *Child Development*, 1967, *38*, 329–335.

8. G. D. Mitchell, "Paternalistic Behavior in Primates," *Psychological Bulletin*, 1969, *71*, 399–417; G. D. Mitchell, W. K. Redican, and J. Gomber, "Males Can Raise Babies," *Psychology Today*, 1974, *7*, 63–67; W. K. Redican and D. M. Taug, "Male Parental Care in Monkeys and Apes," in Lamb, *The Role of the Father in Child Development*; J. J. McKenna, "Parental Supplements and Surrogates among Primates: Cross-Species and Cross-Cultural Comparisons," in J. B. Lancaster, J. Altmann, A. S. Rossi, and L. R. Sherrod, eds., *Parenting across the Life Span: Biosocial Dimensions* (New York: Aldine DeGruyter, 1987).

9. R. D. Parke and S. J. Suomi, "Adult Male–Infant Relationships: Human and Nonhuman Primate Evidence," in K. Immelmann, G. Barlow, M. Main, and L. Petrinovitch, eds., *Behavioral Development: The Bielefeld Interdisciplinary Project* (New York: Cambridge University Press, 1981), pp. 700–725, at 707.

10. J. S. Rosenblatt, "The Development of Maternal Responsiveness in the Rat," *American Journal of Orthopsychiatry*, 1969, *39*, 36–56; J. S. Rosenblatt, "Hormonal Basis of Parenting in Mammals," in M. Bornstein, ed., *Handbook of Parenting*, vol. 2 (Hillsdale, N.J.: Erlbaum, 1995), pp. 3–25; A. S. Fleming and C. M. Corter, "Psychobiology of Maternal Behavior in Nonhuman Mammals," in ibid., pp. 59–85.

11. A. S. Rossi, "Gender and Parenthood," *American Sociological Review*, 1984, *49*, 1–19; Rossi, "Parenthood in Transi-

tion: From Lineage to Child to Self-Orientation," in Lancaster, Altman, Rossi, and Sherrod, *Parenting across the Life Span.*

12. R. D. Parke and B. J. Tinsley, "Parent-Infant Interaction," in J. Osofsky, ed., *Handbook of Infancy* (New York: Wiley, 1987); R. D. Parke and B. J. Tinsley, "The Father's Role in Infancy: Determinants of Involvement in Caregiving and Play," in Lamb, *The Role of the Father in Child Development.*

13. M. Kotelchuck, "The Infant's Relationship to the Father: Experimental Evidence," in Lamb, *The Role of the Father in Child Development.*

14. M. P. M. Richards, J. F. Dunn, and B. Antonis, "Caretaking in the First Year of Life: The Role of Fathers and Mothers' Social Isolation," *Child: Care, Health, and Development,* 1977, *3,* 23–26; S. Jackson, "Great Britain," in M. E. Lamb, ed., *The Father's Role: Cross-Cultural Perspective* (Hillsdale, N.J.: Erlbaum, 1987), pp. 29–57.

15. A. Szalai, ed., *The Use of Time: Daily Activities of Urban and Suburban Populations in Twelve Countries* (The Hague: Mouton, 1972); J. P. Robinson, V. G. Andreyenkov, and V. D. Patrushev, eds., *The Rhythm of Everyday Life* (Boulder: Westview Press, 1989).

16. A. E. Gottfried and A. W. Gottfried, eds., *Maternal Employment and Children's Development: Longitudinal Research* (New York: Plenum, 1988); L. W. Hoffman, "Effects of Maternal Employment in the Two-Parent Family," *American Psychologist,* 1989, *44,* 283–292; A. E. Gottfried, A. W. Gottfried, and K. Bathurst, "Maternal and Dual-Earner Employment Status and Parenting," in Bornstein, *Handbook of Parenting,* vol. 2, pp. 139–160.

17. F. A. Pedersen, "Mother, Father, and Infant as an Interactive System" (paper presented to the American Psychological Association, Chicago, September 1974); F. A. Pedersen, B. J. Anderson, and R. L. Cain, "An Approach to Understanding Linkages between the Parent-Infant and Spouse Relationships" (paper presented at the Society for Research in Child Development, New Orleans, March 1977).

18. Pedersen, "Mother, Father, and Infant," p. 4.
19. Ibid., p. 6.
20. E. M. Cummings and P. Davies, *Children and Marital Conflict* (New York: Guilford Press, 1994); B. J. Wilson and J. M. Gottman, "Marital Interaction and Parenting," in Bornstein, *Handbook of Parenting*, vol. 4 (1995), pp. 33–56.
21. J. Belsky and B. L. Volling, "Mothering, Fathering, and Marital Interaction in the Family Triad during Infancy: Exploring Family System's Processes," in P. Berman and F. Pedersen, eds., *Men's Transition to Parenthood* (Hillsdale, N.J.: Erlbaum, 1987).
22. See U. Bronfenbrenner, *The Ecology of Human Development* (Cambridge, Mass.: Harvard University Press, 1979); U. Bronfenbrenner, "Ecological Systems Theory," in R. Vasta, ed., *Annals of Child Development*, vol. 6 (Greenwich, Conn.: JAI Press, 1989); P. Moen, G. H. Elder, and K. Lüscher, eds., *Examining Lives in Context* (Washington, D.C.: American Psychological Association, 1995).
23. R. D. Parke and B. R. Tinsley, "Fatherhood: Historical and Contemporary Perspectives," in K. A. McCluskey and H. W. Reese, eds., *Life-Span Developmental Psychology: Historical and Generational Effects* (Orlando, Fla.: Academic Press, 1984), pp. 203–248; R. D. Parke, "Families in Life-Span Perspective: A Multilevel Developmental Approach," in E. M. Hetherington, R. M. Lerner, and M. Perlmutter, eds., *Child Development in Life-Span Development* (Hillsdale, N.J.: Erlbaum, 1988).
24. F. W. Bozett and S. M. H. Hanson, eds., *Fatherhood and Families in Cultural Context* (New York: Springer, 1991); Lamb, *The Father's Role: Cross-Cultural Perspectives*.
25. A. Mirandé, "Ethnicity and Fatherhood," in Bozett and Hanson, *Fatherhood and Families in Cultural Context*.
26. P. Cowan, "Becoming a Father: A Time of Change, an Opportunity for Development," in M. Bornstein and P. Cowan, eds., *Fatherhood Today: Men's Changing Role in the Family* (New York: Wiley, 1988).
27. E. Erikson, *Life History and the Historical Moment* (New York: Norton, 1975); Erikson, *The Life Cycle Completed* (New York: Norton, 1982).

28. J. Snarey, *How Fathers Care for the Next Generation* (Cambridge, Mass.: Harvard University Press, 1993), p. 18.
29. M. Green, *Fathering* (New York: McGraw-Hill, 1976).

2 / THE TRANSITION TO FATHERHOOD

1. J. L. Shapiro, *The Measure of a Man* (New York: Delocorte Press, 1993).
2. P. M. Shereshefsky and L. J. Yarrow, *Psychological Aspects of a First Pregnancy and Early Postnatal Adaptation* (New York: Raven Press, 1973).
3. J. L. Shapiro, *When Men Are Pregnant* (New York: Dell, 1987), p. 98.
4. D. R. Entwisle and S. G. Doering, *The First Birth* (Baltimore: Johns Hopkins University Press, 1981); B. Py-Liberman, "Mom, Meet Your Baby," *Psychology Today*, June 1989, p. 18.
5. C. L. Kohn, A. Nelson, and S. Weiner, "Gravidas' Responses to Realtime Ultrasound Fetal Image," *Journal of Obstetric, Gynecologic, and Neonatal Nursing*, 1980, *9*, 77–79.
6. R. T. Mercer, S. Ferketich, K. May, J. DeJoseph, and D. Sollid, "Further Exploration of Maternal and Paternal Fetal Attachment," *Research in Nursing and Health*, 1988, *11*, 83–95.
7. T. Field, D. Sanberg, T. A. Quetel, R. Garcia, and M. Rosario, "Effects of Ultrasound Feedback on Pregnancy, Anxiety, Fetal Activity, and Neonatal Outcome," *Obstetrics and Gynecology*, 1985, *66*, 525–528.
8. J. Cain, "The Couvade or 'Hatching,' " *Indian Antiquary*, 1874, *3*, 151, cited in J. H. Wapner, "An Empirical Approach to the Attitudes, Feelings, and Behaviors of Expectant Fathers" (Ph.D. diss., Northwestern University).
9. W. H. Trethowan and M. F. Conolon, "The Couvade Syndrome," *British Journal of Psychiatry*, 1965, *111*, 57–66; B. Liebenberg, "Expectant Fathers," *American Journal of Orthopsychiatry*, 1967, *37*, 358–359; B. Liebenberg, "Expectant Fathers," *Child and Family*, 1969, *8*, 265–277.
10. J. F. Clinton, "Expectant Fathers at Risk for Couvade," *Nursing Research*, 1986, *35*, 290–295.

11. C. P. Cowan and P. A. Cowan, *When Partners Become Parents* (New York: Basic, 1992).

12. Ibid.; Entwisle and Doering, *The First Birth.*

13. H. Osofsky and R. Culp, "Risk Factors in the Transition to Fatherhood," in S. H. Cath, A. Gurwitt, and L. Gunsberg, eds., *Fathers and Their Families* (Hillsdale, N.J.: Analytic Press, 1989).

14. Ibid.

15. D. G. Dutton, *The Domestic Assault of Women* (Boston: Allyn and Bacon, 1988).

16. D. Rush and P. Cassano, "Relationship between Cigarette Smoking and Social Class to Birthweight and Perinatal Mortality among Births in Britain," *Journal of Epidemiological Community Health,* 1983, *37,* 249–255.

17. F. D. Martinez, A. L. Wright, and L. M. Taussig, "The Effect of Paternal Smoking on the Birthweight of Newborns Whose Mothers Do Not Smoke," *American Journal of Public Health,* 1994, *84,* 1489–1491.

18. H. W. Bernard, *Human Development in Western Culture* (Boston: Allyn and Bacon, 1962), p. 43.

19. S. Bittman and S. R. Zalk, *Expectant Fathers* (New York: Hawthorn Books, 1978).

20. W. Masters and V. Johnson, *Human Sexual Response* (Boston: Little, Brown, 1966).

21. Cowan and Cowan, *When Partners Become Parents.*

22. K. A. May, "Factors Contributing to First-Time Fathers' Readiness for Fatherhood," *Family Relations,* 1982, *31,* 353–361.

23. H. L. Raush, W. A. Barry, R. K. Hertel, and M. A. Swain, *Communication, Conflict, and Marriage* (San Francisco: Jossey Bass, 1974).

24. J. D. Gladieux, "Pregnancy—The Transition to Parenthood: Satisfaction with the Pregnancy Experience as a Function of Sex-Role Conceptions, Marital Relationship, and Social Network," in W. B. Miller and L. F. Newman, eds., *The First Child and Family Formation* (Chapel Hill, N.C.: Carolina Population Center, 1978).

25. Ibid., p. 292.

26. Cowan and Cowan, *When Partners Become Parents*.
27. Bittman and Zalk, *Expectant Fathers*, (New York: Hawthorn Books, 1978), p. 166.
28. F. K. Grossman, L. S. Eichler, S. A. Winickoff, M. K. Anzalone, M. Gofseyeff, and S. P. Sargent, *Pregnancy, Birth, and Parenthood* (San Francisco: Jossey Bass, 1980).
29. Entwisle and Doering, *The First Birth*.
30. C. Legg, I. Sherick, and W. Wadland, "Reaction of Preschool Children to the Birth of a Sibling," *Child Psychiatry and Human Development*, 1974, *5*, 3–39.
31. A. L. Baldwin, "Changes in Parent Behavior during Pregnancy: An Experiment in Longitudinal Analysis," *Child Development*, 1947, *18*, 29–39.
32. J. L. Shapiro, *When Men Are Pregnant: Needs and Concerns of Expectant Fathers* (New York: Delta, 1993).
33. Bittman and Zalk, *Expectant Fathers*.
34. C. R. Phillips and J. T. Anzalone, *Fathering: Participation in Labor and Birth* (St. Louis: Mosby, 1978), pp. 46–47.
35. S. Duncan and H. J. Markman, "Intervention Program for the Transition to Parenthood: Current Status from a Prevention Perspective," in G. Y. Michaels and W. A. Goldberg, *The Transition to Parenthood: Current Theory and Research* (New York: Cambridge University Press, 1988), pp. 270–310.
36. R. Fein, "Men's Experiences before and after the Birth of a First Child" (Ph.D. diss., Harvard University, 1974).
37. W. J. Hennenborn and R. Cogan, "The Effect of Husband Participation on Reported Pain and the Probability of Medication during Labor and Birth," *Journal of Psychosomatic Research*, 1975, *19*, 215–222.
38. Entwisle and Doering, *The First Birth*.
39. R. P. Klein, N. F. Gist, J. Nicholson, and K. Standley, "A Study of Father and Nurse Support during Labor," *Birth and the Family Journal*, 1981, *8*, 161–164.
40. J. D. Bertsch, L. Nagashima Whalen, S. Dykeman, J. H. Kennell, and S. McGrath, "Labor Support by First-Time Fathers: Direct Observations with a Comparison to Experienced Doulas," *Journal of Psychosomatic Obstetrics and*

Gynaecology, 1990, *11*, 251–260.

41. Entwisle and Doering, *The First Birth.*
42. Ibid.
43. J. Shapiro, cited in L. Mosedale, "Fathers in the Delivery Room," *Self*, April 1991, pp. 104–108.
44. J. Kennell, M. Klaus, S. McGrath, S. Robertson, and C. Hinkley, "Continuous Emotional Support during Labor in a U.S. Hospital," *Journal of the American Medical Association*, 1991, *265*, 2197–2201.
45. J. H. Kennell and S. K. McGrath, "Labor Support by a Doula plus Father vs. Father Alone for Middle-Class Couples: The Effect on Perinatal Outcomes" (paper presented at the meeting of the Society for Behavioral Pediatrics, Providence, R.I., September 1993).
46. M. Levine and R. Block, unpublished study, cited in J. C. McCullagh, *Baby Talk*, 1980, p. 3.
47. Shapiro, *The Measure of a Man.*
48. M. Gainer and P. Van Bonn, "Two Factors Affecting the Caesarean Section Delivered Mother: Father's Presence at the Delivery and Postpartum Teaching" (master's thesis, University of Michigan School of Nursing, 1977).
49. F. Pederson, M. T. Zazlow, R. L. Cain, and B. J. Anderson, "Caesarean Birth: The Importance of a Family Perspective" (paper presented at the International Conference on Infant Studies, April 1980).
50. J. Lind, "Observations after Delivery of Communication between Mother-Infant-Father" (paper presented at the International Congress of Pediatrics, Buenos Aires, October 1974).
51. M. H. Klaus and J. H. Kennell, *Maternal-Infant Bonding* (St. Louis: Mosby, 1976); M. H. Klaus and J. H. Kennell, *Parent-Infant Bonding* (St. Louis: Mosby, 1981).
52. W. D. Keller, K. A. Hildebrand, and M. E. Richards, "Effects of Extended Father-Infant Contact during the Newborn Period" (paper presented at the biennial meeting of the Society for Research in Child Development, April 1981).
53. S. Goldberg, "Parent-Infant Bonding: Another Look,"

Child Development, 1983, *54*, 1355–1382; M. E. Lamb and C. P. Hwang, "Maternal Attachment and Mother-Infant Bonding: A Critical Review," in M. E. Lamb and A. L. Brown, eds., *Advances in Developmental Psychology*, vol. 2 (Hillsdale, N.J.: Erlbaum, 1982); R. Paklowitz, "Father's Birth Attendance, Early Contact, and Extended Contact with Their Newborns: A Critical Review," *Child Development*, 1985, *56*, 392–406.

54. K. May, cited in Mosedale, "Fathers in the Delivery Room."

55. H. Osofsky, "Expectant and New Fatherhood as a Developmental Crisis," *Bulletin of the Menninger Clinic*, 1982, *46*, 209–230, at 226.

56. P. A. Cowan, "Becoming a Father," in P. Bronstein and C. P. Cowan, eds., *Fatherhood Today: Men's Changing Role in the Family* (New York: Wiley, 1988), pp. 13–35.

57. A. Rossi, "Transition to Parenthood," *Journal of Marriage and the Family*, 1968, *30*, 26–39.

58. Cowan and Cowan, *When Partners Become Parents.*

59. F. K. Grossman, "Separate and Together: Men's Autonomy and Affiliation in the Transition to Parenthood," in Berman and Pedersen, *Men's Transition to Parenthood*, pp. 89–112.

60. D. H. Heath, "Competent Fathers: Their Personalities and Marriages," *Human Development*, 1976, *19*, 26–39.

61. J. Belsky, M. Rovine, and M. Fish, "The Developing Family System," in M. Gunnar and E. Thelen, eds., *Systems and Development*, vol. 22, Minnesota Symposia on Child Psychology (Hillsdale, N.J.: Erlbaum, 1989), pp. 119–166.

62. Cowan and Cowan, *When Partners Become Parents.*

63. Ibid., p. 110.

64. C. P. Cowan, "Working with Men Becoming Fathers: The Impact of Couples Group Intervention," in Bronstein and Cowan, *Fatherhood Today*, pp. 176–198.

65. Belsky, Rovine, and Fish, "The Developing Family System"; J. Belsky, H. J. Ward, and M. Levine, "Prenatal Expectations, Postnatal Experiences, and the Transition to Parenthood," in R. Ashmore and D. Brodinsky, eds., *Per-*

spectives on the Family (Hillsdale, N.J.: Erlbaum, 1986), pp. 111–146.

66. Belsky, Rovine, and Fish, "The Developing Family System"; Cowan and Cowan, *When Partners Become Parents.*
67. P. A. Cowan, "Becoming a Father," p. 14.
68. Cowan and Cowan, *When Partners Become Parents.*
69. M. Rutter, "Psychosocial Resilience and Protective Mechanisms," *American Journal of Orthopsychiatry,* 1987, *51,* 316–331.
70. Cowan and Cowan, *When Partners Become Parents.*
71. S. M. McDermid, T. Huston, and S. McHale, "Changes in Marriage Associated with the Transition to Parenthood: Individual Differences as a Function of Sex-Role Attitudes and Changes in the Division of Household Labor," *Journal of Marriage and the Family,* 1990, *52,* 475–486; B. A. McBride, "Stress and Fathers' Parental Competence: Implications for Family Life and Parent Educators," *Family Relations,* 1989, *38,* 385–389.
72. H. Osofsky and R. Cupp, "Risk Factors in the Transition to Fatherhood," in S. Cath, A. R. Gurwitt, and L. Gunsberg, eds., *Fathers and Their Families* (Hillsdale, N.J.: Analytic Press, 1989), pp. 145–165.
73. Cowan and Cowan, *When Partners Become Parents.*
74. P. A. Cowan, "Becoming a Father," p. 14.
75. Ibid.
76. Cowan and Cowan, *When Partners Become Parents,* p. 118.

3 / FATHERS' INVOLVEMENT

1. M. Greenberg and N. Morris, "Engrossment: The Newborn's Impact upon the Father," *American Journal of Orthopsychiatry,* 1974, *44,* 526.
2. R. D. Parke and S. E. O'Leary, "Father-Mother-Infant Interaction in the Newborn Period: Some Findings, Some Observations and Some Unresolved Issues," in K. Riegel and J. Meacham, eds., *The Developing Individual in a Changing World,* vol. 2, *Social and Environmental Issues* (The Hague: Mouton, 1976), pp. 653–663.

3. Ibid.
4. D. Phillips and R. D. Parke, "Father and Mother Speech to Prelinguistic Infants" (University of Illinois, 1981).
5. J. Sachs, "The Adaptive Significance of Linguistic Input to Prelinguistic Infants," in C. E. Snow and C. A. Ferguson, eds., *Talking to Children* (Cambridge: Cambridge University Press, 1977); A. Fernald, "Meaningful Melodies in Mothers' Speech to Infants," in H. Papousek, U. Jürgens, and M. Papousek, eds., *Non-Verbal Communication: Comparative and Developmental Approaches* (Cambridge: Cambridge University Press, 1992).
6. A. Fernald and P. K. Kuhl, "Acoustical Determinants of Infant Preference for Motherese Speech," *Infant Behavior and Development,* 1987, *10,* 279–293; J. F. Werker and P. J. McLeod, "Infant Preference for Both Male and Female Infant-Directed Talk: A Developmental Study of Attentional and Affective Responsiveness," *Canadian Journal of Psychology,* 1989, *43,* 230–246; Fernald, "Meaningful Melodies in Mothers' Speech to Infants."
7. A. M. Frodi, M. E. Lamb, L. A. Leavitt, and W. L. Donovan, "Fathers' and Mothers' Responses to Infant Smiles and Cries," *Infant Behavior and Development,* 1978, *1,* 197.
8. A. M. Frodi, M. E. Lamb, L. A. Leavitt, W. L. Donovan, C. Neff, and D. Sherry, "Fathers' and Mothers' Responses to the Faces and Cries of Normal and Premature Infants," *Developmental Psychology,* 1978, *14,* 490–498.
9. P. H. Wolff, "The Natural History of Crying and Other Vocalizations in Early Infancy," in B. Foss, ed., *Determinants of Infant Behavior,* vol. 4 (London: Metheun, 1969); O. Wasz-Hockert, J. Lind, V. Vuorenkoski, T. Partanen, and E. Valanne, *The Infant Cry: A Spectrographic and Auditory Analysis* (Suffolk: Lavenham Press, 1968); A. Wiesenfeld, C. Malatesta, and L. DeLoach, "Differential Parental Response to Familiar and Unfamiliar Infant Distress Signals," *Infant Behavior and Development,* 1981, *4,* 281–295.
10. G. W. Holden, "Adults' Thinking about a Child-Rearing Problem: Effects of Experience, Parental Status, and Gender," *Child Development,* 1988, *59,* 1623–1632.

11. R. D. Parke and D. B. Sawin, "Infant Characteristics and Behavior as Elicitors of Maternal and Paternal Responsivity in the Newborn Period" (paper presented at the biennial meeting of the Society for Research in Child Development, Denver, 1975); R. D. Parke and D. B. Sawin, "The Father's Role in Infancy: A Reevaluation," *The Family Coordinator*, 1976, *25*, 365–371.

12. R. D. Parke and D. B. Sawin, "The Family in Early Infancy: Social Interactional and Attitudinal Analyses," in F. A. Pedersen, ed., *The Father-Infant Relationship: Observational Studies in the Family Setting* (New York: Praeger, 1980).

13. M. E. Lamb, J. Pleck, and E. L. Charnov, "Paternal Behavior in Humans," *American Zoologist*, 1985, *25*, 883–894.

14. J. Pleck, *Working Wives, Working Husbands* (Newbury Park, Calif.: Sage, 1985).

15. F. F. Furstenberg, "Good Dads, Bad Dads: Two Faces of Fatherhood," in A. J. Cherlin, ed., *The Changing American Family and Public Policy* (Washington, D.C.: Urban Institute Press, 1988), pp. 193–218.

16. Parke and Sawin, "The Father's Role in Infancy: A Reevaluation."

17. C. P. Cowan, P. A. Cowan, L. Coie, and J. D. Coie, "Becoming a Family: The Impact of a First Child's Birth on the Couple's Relationship," in Miller and Newman, *The First Child and Family Formation*; Cowan and Cowan, *When Partners Become Parents*.

18. M. Kotelchuck, "The Infant's Relationship to the Father: Experimental Evidence," in Lamb, *The Role of the Father in Child Development*.

19. B. Volling and J. Belsky, "Multiple Determinants of Father Involvement during Infancy in Dual Earner and Single Earner Families," *Journal of Marriage and the Family*, 1991, *53*, 461–474.

20. Pleck, *Working Wives, Working Husbands*.

21. Z. Hossain and J. L. Roopnarine, "African-American Fathers' Involvement with Infants: Relationship to Their Functioning Style, Support, Education and Income," *Infant Behavior and Development*, 1994, *17*, 175–184.

22. Z. Hossain, T. Field, J. Malphurs, C. Valle, and J. Pickens, "Fathers' Caregiving in Low Income African-American and Hispanic-American Families" (University of Miami Medical School, 1995).

23. Ibid.

24. Ibid.

25. S. Ortiz-Archilla, "Families in Puerto-Rico: An Analysis of the Socialization Process from a Macro-Structural Perspective," in J. L. Roopnarine and D. B. Carter, eds., *Parent-Child Socialization in Diverse Cultures* (Norwood, N.J.: Ablex, 1992), pp. 159–171; Mirandé, "Ethnicity and Fatherhood," in Bozett and Hanson, *Fatherhood and Families in Cultural Context*; J. L. McAdoo, "The Roles of Black Fathers in the Socialization of Black Children," in H. P. McAdoo, ed., *Black Families* (Newbury Park, Calif.: Sage, 1988), pp. 257–269; J. L. McAdoo, "The Roles of African-American Fathers: An Ecological Perspective," *Families in Society: The Journal of Contemporary Human Services*, 1993, 74, 28–34.

26. M. P. M. Richards, J. F. Dunn, and B. Antonis, "Caretaking in the First Year of Life: The Role of Fathers, and Mothers' Social Isolation," *Child: Care, Health, and Development*, 1977, 3, 23–26;

27. M. E. Lamb, A. M. Frodi, C. P. Hwang, and M. Frodi, "Varying Degrees of Paternal Involvement in Infant Care: Attitudinal and Behavioral Correlates," in M. E. Lamb, ed., *Nontraditional Families: Parenting and Child Development* (Hillsdale, N.J.: Erlbaum, 1982); M. E. Lamb, A. M. Frodi, C. P. Hwang, M. Frodi, and J. Steinberg, "Effects of Gender and Caretaking Role on Parent-Infant Interaction," in R. M. Emde and R. J. Harmon, eds., *Attachment and Affiliative Systems* (New York: Plenum, 1982).

28. C. W. Greenbaum and R. Landau, "The Infant's Exposure to Talk by Familiar People: Mothers, Fathers, and Siblings in Different Environments," in M. Lewis and L. Rosenblum, eds., *The Social Network of the Developing Infant* (New York: Plenum, 1982), pp. 229–247.

29. A. Sagi, "Antecedents and Consequences of Various Degrees of Paternal Involvement in Childrearing: The Israeli

Project," in Lamb, *Nontraditional Families*, pp. 205–232; A. Sagi, N. Koren, and M. Weinberg, "Fathers in Israel," in Lamb, *The Father's Role: Cross-Cultural Perspectives*, pp. 197–226; A. Sagi, M. E. Lamb, R. Shoham, R. Dvir, and K. S. Lewkowicz, "Parent-Infant Interaction in Families on Israeli Kibbutzim," *International Journal of Behavioral Development*, 1985, *8*, 273–284.

30. Sagi, Lamb, Shoham, Dvir, and Lewkowicz, "Parent-Infant Interaction in Families on Israeli Kibbutzim," p. 282.

31. Cowan and Cowan, *When Partners Become Parents*.

32. Cowan, Cowan, Coie, and Coie, "Becoming a Family."

33. G. Russell and A. Russell, "Mother-Child and Father-Child Relationships in Middle Childhood," *Child Development*, 1987, *58*, 1573–1585.

34. R. Montemayor, "The Relationship between Parent-Adolescent Conflict and the Amount of Time Adolescents Spend Alone with Parents and Peers," *Child Development*, 1982, *53*, 1512–1519.

35. W. W. Hartup, "The Social Worlds of Childhood," *American Psychologist*, 1979, *34*, 944–950.

36. B. L. White, B. Kaban, B. Shapiro, and J. Attonucci, "Competence and Experience," in I. C. Uzgiris and F. Weizmann, eds., *The Structuring of Experience* (New York: Plenum, 1976), pp. 115–152.

37. T. G. Power and R. D. Parke, "Play as a Context for Early Learning: Lab and Home Analyses," in I. E. Sigel and L. M. Loasa, eds., *The Family as a Learning Environment* (New York: Plenum, 1982); A. Clarke-Stewart, *Daycare* (Cambridge, Mass.: Harvard University Press, 1993).

38. Russell and Russell, "Mother-Child and Father-Child Relationships in Middle Childhood."

39. N. Bhavnagri and R. D. Parke, "Parents as Direct Facilitators of Children's Peer Relationships: Effects of Age of Child and Sex of Parent," *Journal of Social and Personal Relationships*, 1991, *8*, 423–440; R. D. Parke and N. Bhavnagri, "Parents as Managers of Children's Peer Relationships," in D. Belle, ed., *Children's Social Networks and Social Supports* (New York: Wiley, 1989); G. W. Ladd, S. M.

Profilet, and C. H. Hart, "Parents' Management of Children's Peer Relations: Facilitating and Supervising Children's Activities in the Peer Culture," in R. D. Parke and G. W. Ladd, eds., *Family-Peer Relationships: Modes of Linkage* (Hillsdale, N.J.: Erlbaum, 1992), pp. 215–254.

40. S. Coltrane, *Family Man* (New York: Oxford, 1996).

41. Parke and Sawin, "Infant Characteristics and Behavior as Elicitors of Maternal and Paternal Responsivity"; Parke and Sawin, "The Father's Role in Infancy."

42. Entwisle and Doering, *The First Birth.*

43. J. T. Hawthorne, M. P. M. Richards, and M. Callon, "A Study of Parental Visiting of Babies in a Special Care Unit," in F. S. W. Brimble-Come, M. P. M. Richards, and N. R. C. Roberton, eds., *Early Separation and Special Care Nurseries* (London: Simp/Heinemann Medical Books, 1978); M. W. Yogman, "Development of the Father-Infant Relationship," in H. Fitzgerald, B. Lester, and M. W. Yogman, eds., *Theory and Research in Behavioral Pediatrics*, vol. 1 (New York: Plenum Press);

44. J. V. Brown and R. Bakeman, "Relationships of Human Mothers with Their Infants during the First Year of Life: Effects of Prematurity," in R. W. Bell and W. P. Smotherman, eds., *Maternal Influences and Early Behavior* (Holliswood, N.Y.: Spectrum, 1980); S. Goldberg, "Premature Birth: Consequences for the Parent-Infant Relationship," *American Scientist*, 1979, *67*, 214–222; S. Goldberg and B. DeVitto, *Born Too Soon: Preterm Birth and Early Development* (San Francisco: Freeman, 1983).

45. K. Minde, S. Trehub, C. Corter, C. Boukydis, B. Celhoffer, and P. Marton, "Mother-Child Relationships in the Premature Nursery: An Observational Study" (Department of Psychiatry, The Hospital for Sick Children, Toronto, 1977).

46. R. Schaffer, *Mothering* (Cambridge, Mass.: Harvard University Press, 1977), p. 37.

47. Kotelchuck, "The Infant's Relationship to the Father"; Hossain and Roopnarine, "African-American Fathers' Involvement with Infants."

48. See M. E. Lamb, "Father-Infant and Mother-Infant Interaction in the First Year of Life," *Child Development*, 1977, *48*, 167–181; M. E. Lamb, "The Development of Mother-Infant and Father-Infant Attachments in the Second Year of Life," *Developmental Psychology*, 1977, *13*, 637–648; and M. E. Lamb, "The Father's Role in the Infant's Social World," in J. H. Stevens, Jr., and M. Mathews, eds., *Mother-Child, Father-Child Relations* (Washington, D.C.: National Association for the Education of Young Children, 1978), p. 42.

49. Hossain and Roopnarine, "African-American Fathers' Involvement with Infants."

50. Hossain, Field, Malphurs, Valle, and Pickens, "Fathers' Caregiving in Low Income African-American and Hispanic-American Families."

51. Richards, Dunn, and Antonis, "Caretaking in the First Year of Life"; Lamb, "Father-Infant and Mother-Infant Interaction."

52. M. Yogman, S. Dixon, E. Tronick, H. Als, and T. B. Brazelton, "The Goals and Structure of Face-to-Face Interaction between Infants and Fathers" (paper presented at the biennial meeting of the Society for Research in Child Development, New Orleans, March, 1977).

53. T. B. Brazelton, "Behavioral Competence of the Newborn Infant," *Seminars in Perinatology*, 1979, *3*, 42.

54. J. Bruner, "Early Social Interaction and Language Acquisition," in H. R. Schaffer, ed., *Studies in Mother-Infant Interaction* (London: Academic Press, 1977).

55. Power and Parke, "Play as a Context for Early Learning."

56. Lamb, "The Father's Role in the Infant's Social World."

57. K. MacDonald and R. D. Parke, "Bridging the Gap: Parent-Child Play Interaction and Peer Interactive Competence," *Child Development*, 1984, *55*, 1265–1277.

58. K. MacDonald and R. D. Parke, "Parent-Child Physical Play: The Effects of Sex and Age of Children and Parents," *Sex Roles*, 1986, *7–8*, 367–379.

59. R. Larson and M. H. Richards, *Divergent Realities: The Emotional Lives of Mothers, Fathers, and Adolescents* (New York: Basic Books, 1994).

60. Ibid., p. 170.
61. R. Larson, "Finding Time for Fatherhood: The Emotional Ecology of Adolescent-Father Interactions," in S. Shulman and W. A. Collins, eds., *Father-Adolescent Relationships* (San Francisco: Jossey-Bass, 1993), pp. 16–17.
62. Ibid.
63. K. A. Clarke-Stewart, "The Father's Contribution to Children's Cognitive and Social Development in Early Childhood," in F. A. Pedersen, ed., *The Father-Infant Relationship: Observational Studies in the Family Setting* (New York: Praeger, 1980); K. A. Clarke-Stewart, "And Daddy Makes Three: The Father's Impact on Mother and Young Child," *Child Development,* 1978, *49,* 466–478.
64. H. Ross and H. Taylor, "Do Boys Prefer Daddy or His Physical Style of Play?" *Sex Roles,* 1989, *20,* 23–33.
65. D. B. Lynn and A. R. Cross, "Parent Preference of Preschool Children," *Journal of Marriage and the Family,* 1974, *36,* 555–559.
66. See Lamb, *The Father's Role: Cross-Cultural Perspectives;* Roopnarine and Carter, *Parent-Child Socialization in Diverse Cultures,* p. 174; B. S. Hewlett, *Intimate Fathers: The Nature and Context of Aka Pygmy Paternal Infant Care* (Ann Arbor: University of Michigan Press, 1991); R. New and L. Benigni, "Italian Fathers and Infants: Cultural Constraints on Paternal Behavior," in Lamb, *The Father's Role: Cross-Cultural Perspectives;* J. L. Roopnarine, F. H. Hooper, M. Ahmeduzzaman, and B. Pollock, "Gentle Play Partners: Mother-Child and Father-Child Play in New Delhi, India," in K. MacDonald, ed., *Parent-Child Play: Descriptions and Implications* (Albany: State University of New York Press, 1993).
67. R. D. Parke and E. Anderson, "Fathers and High Risk Infants: Empirical and Conceptual Analyses," in Berman and Pedersen, *Men's Transition to Parenthood.*
68. T. Field, "Fathers' Interactions With Their High Risk Infants," *Infant Mental Health Journal,* 1981, *4,* 249–256.
69. T. Field, "Interaction Behaviors of Primary versus Secondary Caretaker Fathers," *Developmental Psychology,* 1978, *14,* 183–185.

70. F. A. Pedersen, R. Cain, M. Zaslow, and B. Anderson, "Variation in Infant Experience Associated with Alternative Family Organization" (paper presented at the International Conference on Infant Studies, New Haven, Conn., April 1980).

71. Parke and Suomi, "Adult Male–Infant Relationships."

72. M. J. Meany, J. Stewart, and W. W. Beatty, "Sex Differences in Social Play: The Socialization of Sex Roles," in J. S. Rosenblatt et al., eds., *Advances in Study of Behavior,* 15 (New York: Academic Press, 1985), pp. 1–58.

73. E. E. Maccoby, "Gender as a Social Category," *Developmental Psychology,* 1988, 24, 755–765, at 761.

74. M. Zuckerman, "Sensation-Seeking: The Balance between Risk and Reward," in L. Lipsitt and L. Mitnick, eds., *Self-Regulatory Behavior and Risk-Taking: Causes and Consequences* (Norwood, N.J.: Ablex, 1991), pp. 143–152.

75. E. Aries, "Interaction Patterns and Themes of Male, Female and Mixed Groups," *Small Group Behavior,* 1976, 7, 7–18; W. R. Charlesworth and C. Dzur, "Gender Comparisons of Preschoolers' Behavior and Resource Utilization in Group Problem Solving," *Child Development,* 1987, 58, 191–200.

4 / WHAT DETERMINES FATHERS' INVOLVEMENT?

1. T. Caplow and P. Chadwick, "Inequality and Lifestyles in Middletown, 1920–1978," *Social Science Quarterly,* 1979, 60, 367–385.

2. Pleck, *Working Wives, Working Husbands.*

3. J. Robinson, *How Americans Use Time* (New York: Praeger, 1977).

4. P. Daniels and K. Weingarten, *Sooner or Later: The Timing of Parenthood in Adult Lives* (New York: Norton, 1981).

5. J. Robinson, "Who's Doing the Housework," *American Demographics,* 1988, 12, 24ff.

6. J. Pleck, "Are 'Family Supportive' Employer Policies Relevant to Men?" In J. Hood, ed., *Men, Work, and Family* (Newbury Park, Calif.: Sage, 1993), pp. 221–222; Coltrane, *Family Man.*

7. Lamb, *The Father's Role: Cross-Cultural Perspectives.*

8. M. Ishii-Kuntz, "Paternal Involvement and Perception toward Family Roles," *Journal of Family Issues,* 1994, *15,* 30–48.

9. K. Daly, "Reshaping Fatherhood: Finding the Models," *Journal of Family Issues,* 1993, *14,* 510–530; W. Marsiglio, "Contemporary Scholarship on Fatherhood: Culture, Identity, and Conduct," *Journal of Family Issues,* 1993, *14,* 484–509.

10. J. Belsky, "The Determinants of Parenting: A Process Model," *Child Development,* 1984, *55,* 83–96; Cowan and Cowan, *When Partners Become Parents;* R. D. Parke and B. R. Tinsley, "The Early Environment of the At-Risk Infant: Expanding the Social Context," in D. Bricker, ed., *Intervention with At-Risk and Handicapped Infants: From Research to Application* (Baltimore: University Parke Press, 1982), pp. 153–177; R. D. Parke, "Determinants of Father Involvement" (Cynthia Longfellow Memorial Lecture, Sarah Lawrence College, May 1989).

11. J. A. Levine, *Who Will Raise the Children: New Options for Fathers (and Mothers)* (New York: Lippincott, 1976).

12. G. Russell, "Primary Caretaking and Role-Sharing Fathers," in M. E. Lamb, ed., *The Father's Role: Applied Perspectives* (New York: Wiley, 1986), pp. 29–57; Snarey, *How Fathers Care for the Next Generation.*

13. A. Bandura, "Cognitive Social Learning Theory," in R. Vasta, ed., *Six Theories of Child Development* (Greenwich, Conn.: JAI Press, 1989).

14. C. P. Cowan and P. A. Cowan, "Men's Involvement in Parenthood," in Berman and Pedersen, *Men's Transition to Parenthood,* pp. 145–174; Cowan and Cowan, *When Partners Become Parents;* A. Sagi, "Antecedents and Consequences of Various Degrees of Paternal Involvement in Childrearing."

15. H. B. Biller, "The Mother-Child Relationship and the Father-Absent Boy's Personality Development," *Merrill-Palmer Quarterly,* 1971, *17,* 227–241; E. M. Hetherington, "The Effects of Familial Variables on Sex Typing, on Parent-Child Similarity, and on Imitation in Children," in J. P.

Hill, ed., *Minnesota Symposia on Child Psychology*, vol. 1 (Minneapolis: University of Minnesota Press, 1967), pp. 82–107; G. Russell, "Primary Caretaking and Role-Sharing Fathers," in Lamb, *The Father's Role: Applied Perspectives.*

16. G. K. Baruch and R. C. Barnett, "Fathers' Participation in Family Work and Children's Sex-Role Attitudes," *Child Development*, 1986, *57*, 1210–1223.

17. J. Belsky, "Parental and Nonparental Child Care and Children's Socioemotional Development," in A. Booth, ed., *Contemporary Families: Looking Forward, Looking Back* (Minneapolis: National Council on Family Relations, 1991), pp. 122–140; Snarey, *How Fathers Care for the Next Generation.*

18. K. Daly, "Reshaping Fatherhood: Finding the Models," *Journal of Family Issues*, 1993, *14*, 510–530.

19. Ibid., p. 521.

20. Ibid., p. 518.

21. Ibid.

22. Ibid.

23. Ibid., p. 522.

24. Ibid.

25. S. L. Bem and E. Lenney, "Sex Typing and the Avoidance of Cross-Sex Behavior," *Journal of Personality and Social Psychology*, 1976, *33*, 48–54.

26. A. Beitel and R. D. Parke, "Maternal Attitudes as a Determinant of Father Involvement" (University of Illinois, 1993).

27. G. Russell, *The Changing Role of Fathers* (St. Lucia, Australia: Queensland University Press, 1983).

28. R. D. Parke and S. O'Leary, "Father-Mother-Infant Interaction in the Newborn Period"; Parke and Sawin, "The Father's Role in Infancy: A Reevaluation"; Parke and Sawin, "The Family in Early Infancy."

29. J. Dickie and S. Carnahan, "Training in Social Competence: The Effect on Mothers, Fathers and Infants," *Child Development*, 1980, *51*, 1248–1251; R. D. Parke, S. Hymel, T. G. Power, and B. R. Tinsley, "Fathers and Risk: A Hospital-Based Model Intervention," in D. B. Sawin, R. C.

Hawkins, L. O. Walker, and J. H. Penticuff, eds., *Psychosocial Risks in Infant-Environment Transactions* (New York: Bruner/Mazel, 1980); P. R. Zelazo, M. Kotelchuck, L. Barber, and J. David, "Fathers and Sons: An Experimental Facilitation of Attachment Behaviors" (paper presented at the biennial meeting of the Society for Research in Child Development, New Orleans, March 1977); R. D. Parke and A. Beitel, "Hospital-Based Interventions for Fathers," in M. E. Lamb, ed., *Fatherhood: Applied Perspectives* (New York: Wiley, 1986).

30. "Facts at a Glance," Child Trends Inc., Washington, D.C., February 1995.

31. A. J. Cherlin, *Marriage, Divorce, and Remarriage* (Cambridge, Mass.: Harvard University Press, 1992).

32. R. Collins and S. Coltrane, *Sociology of Marriage and the Family*, 4th ed. (Chicago: Nelson-Hall, 1994).

33. Cherlin, *Marriage, Divorce, and Remarriage.*

34. Ibid.

35. K. A. McCluskey, J. Killarney, and D. R. Papini, "Adolescent Pregnancy and Parenthood: Implications for Development," in E. C. Callahan and K. A. McCluskey, eds., *Life-Span Developmental Psychology: Non-Normative Life Events* (New York: Academic Press, 1983).

36. F. F. Furstenberg, Jr., J. Brooks-Gunn, and L. Chase-Lansdale, "Teenaged Pregnancy and Childbearing," *American Psychologist*, 1989, *44*, 313–320.

37. R. I. Lerman, "A National Profile of Young Unwed Fathers," in R. I. Lerman and T. J. Ooms, eds., *Young Unwed Fathers* (Philadelphia: Temple University Press, 1993), pp. 27–51.

38. Furstenberg, Brooks-Gunn, and Chase-Lansdale, "Teenaged Pregnancy and Childbearing."

39. Lerman and Ooms, *Young Unwed Fathers.*

40. F. Mott, "Absent Fathers and Child Development: Emotional and Cognitive Effects at Ages Five to Nine" (Ohio State University, 1993).

41. B. E. Robinson and R. L. Barret, *The Developing Father* (New York: Guilford Press, 1986).

42. M. L. Sullivan, "Young Fathers and Parenting in Two

Inner-City Neighborhoods," in Lerman and Ooms, *Young Unwed Fathers*, pp. 52–73.

43. Ibid.

44. Ibid., p. 62.

45. Lerman and Ooms, *Young Unwed Fathers*; M. E. Lorenzi, L. V. Klerman, and J. F. Jekel, "School-Age Parents: How Permanent a Relationship," *Adolescent*, 1977, *45*, 13–22.

46. Lerman and Ooms, *Young Unwed Fathers*.

47. F. F. Furstenberg and K. M. Harris, "When and Why Fathers Matter: Impacts of Father Involvement on Children of Adolescent Mothers," in Lerman and Ooms, *Young Unwed Fathers*, pp. 117–138.

48. Ibid.

49. Lerman and Ooms, *Young Unwed Fathers*.

50. R. D. Parke and B. Neville, "The Male Adolescent's Role in Adolescent Pregnancy and Childrearing," in S. Hoffreth and C. D. Hayes, eds., *Adolescent Pregnancy and Childbearing*, vol. 2 (Washington, D.C.: National Academy Press, 1987), pp. 145–173.

51. J. Brooks-Gunn and F. F. Furstenberg, "The Children of Adolescent Mothers: Physical, Academic, and Psychological Outcomes," *Developmental Review*, 1986, *6*, 224–251.

52. Furstenberg, Brooks-Gunn, and Chase-Lansdale, "Teenaged Pregnancy and Childbearing."

53. S. Hoffreth, "The Children of Teen Childbearers," in Hoffreth and Hayes, *Adolescent Pregnancy and Childbearing*, vol. 2.

54. Brooks-Gunn and Furstenberg, "The Children of Adolescent Mothers."

55. R. D. Parke and B. Neville, "Late-Timed Fatherhood: Determinants and Consequences for Children and Families," in J. Shapiro, M. Diamond, and M. Greenberg, eds., *Becoming a Father: Social, Emotional, and Psychological Perspectives* (New York: Springer, 1995), pp. 104–116.

56. B. J. Tinsley and R. D. Parke, "The Contemporary Impact of the Extended Family on the Nuclear Family: Grandparents as Support and Socialization Agents," in M. Le-

wis, ed., *Beyond the Dyad* (New York: Plenum, 1984); B. J. Tinsley and R. D. Parke, "The Role of Grandfathers in the Context of the Family," in Bronstein and Cowan, *Fatherhood Today*, pp. 236–250.

57. A. L. Yarrow, *Latecomers: Children of Parents over 35* (New York: Free Press, 1991).

58. C. N. Nydegger, "Timing of Fatherhood: Role Perception and Socialization" (Ph.D. diss., Pennsylvania State University, 1973).

59. J. Bloom-Feshbach, "The Beginnings of Fatherhood" (Ph.D. diss., Yale University, 1979).

60. Daniels and Weingarten, *Sooner or Later*.

61. T. M. Cooney, F. A. Pedersen, S. Indelicato and R. Paklowitz, "Timing of Fatherhood: Is 'On-Time' Optimal?" *Journal of Marriage and the Family*, 1993, *55*, 205–215.

62. S. Coltrane and M. Ishii-Kuntz, "Men's Housework: A Life Course Perspective," *Journal of Marriage and the Family*, 1992, *54*, 43–57.

63. K. MacDonald and R. D. Parke, "Parent-Child Physical Play: The Effects of Sex and Age of Children and Parents," *Sex Roles*, 1986, *7–8*, 367–379.

64. B. Neville and R. D. Parke, "Waiting for Paternity: Interpersonal and Contextual Implications of the Timing of Fatherhood" (University of Washington, 1995); Parke and Neville, "Late-Timed Fatherhood."

65. Volling and Belsky, "Multiple Determinants of Father Involvement."

66. Neville and Parke, "Waiting for Paternity."

67. B. J. Tinsley and R. D. Parke, "Grandparents as Interactive and Social Support Agents for Families with Young Infants," *International Journal of Aging and Human Development*, 1988, *25*, 261–279.

68. L. W. Hoffman, "Changes in Family Roles, Socialization, and Sex Differences," *American Psychologist*, 1977, *32*, 644–658.

69. Parke and O'Leary, "Father-Mother-Infant Interaction in the Newborn Period"; Parke and Sawin, "Infant Characteristics and Behavior as Elicitors of Maternal and Pater-

nal Responsivity"; E. B. Thoman, P. H. Leiderman, and
J. P. Olson, "Neonate-Mother Interaction during Breast
Feeding," *Developmental Psychology,* 1972, *6,* 110–118; E. B.
Thoman, C. Barnett, and P. H. Leiderman, "Feeding Behaviors of Newborn Infants as a Function of Parity of
the Mother," *Child Development,* 1971, *42,* 1471–1483;
M. Siegal, "Are Sons and Daughters Treated More Differently by Fathers than by Mothers?" *Developmental Review,*
1987, *7,* 183–209.

70. Parke and Sawin, "The Family in Early Infancy."

71. Kotelchuck, "The Infant's Relationship to the Father";
Power and Parke, "Play as a Context for Early Learning."

72. J. Rubin, F. J. Provenzano, and Z. Luria, "The Eye of the
Beholder: Parents' Views on Sex of Newborns," *American
Journal of Orthopsychiatry,* 1974, *43,* 720–731.

73. M. Stern and K. H. Karraker, "Sex Stereotyping of Infants:
A Review of Gender Labeling Studies," *Sex Roles,* 1989,
20, 501–522.

74. Cowan and Cowan, *When Partners Become Parents.*

75. A. C. Crouter and M. S. Crowly, "School-Age Children's
Time Alone with Fathers in Single- and Dual-Earner
Families: Implications for the Father-Child Relationship,"
Journal of Early Adolescence, 1990, *10,* 296–312.

76. Ibid., p. 309.

77. K. M. Harris and S. P. Morgan, "Fathers, Sons, and
Daughters: Differential Paternal Involvement in Parenting," *Journal of Marriage and the Family,* 1991, *53,* 531–544
at 540.

78. H. B. Gewirtz and J. G. Gewirtz, "Visiting and Caretaking
Patterns for Kibbutz Infants: Age and Sex Trends," *Ameri-
can Journal of Orthopsychiatry,* 1968, *38,* 427–443; M. M.
West and M. J. Konner, "The Role of the Father: An
Anthropological Perspective," in Lamb, *The Role of the
Father in Child Development,* pp. 345–385.

79. W. K. Redican, "Adult Male–Infant Interactions in Nonhuman Primates," in Lamb, *The Role of the Father in Child
Development,* p. 217.

80. M. A. Straus, *Beating the Devil out of Them: Corporal Pun-*

ishment in American Families (Lexington, Mass.: Lexington Books, 1994).

81. E. M. Hetherington, M. S. Hagan, and E. R. Anderson, "Marital Transitions: A Child's Perspective," *American Psychologist*, 1989, *44*, 303–312.

82. Z. Hossain and J. L. Roopnarine, "Division of Household Labor and Child Care in Dual-Earner African-American Families with Infants," *Sex Roles*, 1993, *29*, 571–583.

83. J. L. Roopnarine, J. Brown, P. Snell-White, N. B. Riegraf, D. Crossley, Z. Hossain, and W. Webb, "Father Involvement in Child Care and Household Work in Common-Law Dual-Earner and Single-Earner Jamaican Families," *Journal of Applied Developmental Psychology*, 1995, *16*, 35–52.

84. Ishii-Kuntz, "Paternal Involvement and Perception toward Family Roles," p. 43.

85. H. Lytton and D. M. Romney, "Parents' Differential Socialization of Boys and Girls: A Meta-Analysis," *Psychological Bulletin*, 1991, *109*, 267–296; some recent reviewers have questioned the differential treatment of boys and girls by fathers.

86. J. H. Pleck, *Husbands and Wives: Paid Work, Family Work ,and Adjustment* (Wellesley, Mass.: Wellesley College Center for Research on Women, 1982); R. P. Quinn and G. L. Staines, *The 1977 Quality of Employment Survey* (Ann Arbor: Survey Research Center, 1979).

87. M. E. Lamb, "The Changing Roles of Fathers," in Lamb, *The Father's Role: Applied Perspectives*, pp. 3–27.

88. J. Dickie and S. C. Gerber, "Training in Social Competence: The Effect of Mothers, Fathers, and Infants," *Child Development*, 1980, *51*, 1248–1251.

89. Beitel and Parke, "Maternal Attitudes as a Determinant of Father Involvement."

90. R. D. Parke, quoted in V. Secunda, *Women and Their Fathers* (New York: Delacorte Press, 1992), p. 58.

91. S. S. Feldman, S. C. Nash, and B. G. Aschenbrenner, "Antecedents of Fathering," *Child Development*, 1983, *54*, 1628–1636.

92. J. Belsky, B. Gilstrap, and M. Rovine, "The Pennsylvania Infant and Family Development Project, I: Stability and Change in Mother-Infant and Father-Infant Interaction in a Family Setting at One, Three, and Nine Months," *Child Development*, 1984, *55*, 692–705.

93. J. R. Dickie and P. Matheson, "Mother-Father-Infant: Who Needs Support?" (paper presented at the meeting of the American Psychological Association, Toronto, August 1984).

94. M. E. Lamb and A. B. Elster, "Adolescent Mother-Infant-Father Relationships," *Developmental Psychology*, 1985, *21*, 768–773.

95. J. Belsky, L. Youngblade, M. Rovine, and B. Volling, "Patterns of Marital Change and Parent-Child Interaction," *Journal of Marriage and the Family*, 1991, *53*, 487–498.

96. S. S. Feldman, S. C. Nash, and B. G. Aschenbrenner, "Antecedents of Fathering," *Child Development*, 1983, *54*, 1628–1636, at 1634.

97. M. Ahmeduzzaman and J. L. Roopnarine, "Sociodemographic Factors, Functioning Style, Social Support, and Father's Involvement with Preschoolers in African-American Families," *Journal of Marriage and the Family*, 1992, *54*, 699–707.

98. A. E. Gottfried and A. W. Gottfried, *Maternal Employment and Children's Development: Longitudinal Research* (New York: Plenum Press, 1988); L. A. Gilbert, "Current Perspectives on Dual-Career Families," *Current Perspectives in Psychological Science*, 1994, 101–105.

99. D. J. Hernandez, *America's Children* (New York: Russell Sage, 1993).

100. Coltrane, *Family Man*.

101. M. M. Ferree, "The Gender Division of Labor in Two-Earner Marriages: Dimensions of Variability and Change," *Journal of Family Issues*, 1991, *12*, 158–180; J. Robinson, "Who's Doing the Housework?" *American Demographics*, 1988, *10*, 24–28; B. A. Shelton, *Women, Men, and Time: Gender Differences in Paid Work, Housework, and Leisure* (New York: Greenwood, 1992); L. Thompson and A. J. Walker, "Gender in Families," *Journal of Marriage and*

Family, 1989, *51*, 845–871; M. Biernat and C. Wortman, "Sharing of Home Responsibilities between Professionally Employed Women and Their Husbands," *Journal of Personality and Social Psychology*, 1991, *60*, 844–860.

102. Coltrane, *Family Man*; L. W. Hoffman, "Effects of Maternal Employment in the Two-Parent Family," *American Psychologist*, 1989, *44*, 283–292; Ferree, "The Gender Division of Labor in Two-Earner Marriages."

103. Robinson, *How Americans Use Time*; G. Russell, "Fathers as Caregivers: Possible Antecedents and Consequences" (paper presented to a study group on The Role of the Father in Child Development, Social Policy, and the Law, University of Haifa, Israel, July 1980).

104. K. Walker and M. Woods, *Time Use: A Measure of Household Production fo Family Goods and Services* (Washington, D.C.: American Home Economics Association, 1976).

105. G. Russell, "Shared-Caregiving Families: An Australian Study," in Lamb, *Nontraditional Families*.

106. A. C. Crouter, M. Perry-Jenkins, T. L. Huston, and S. M. McHale, "Processes Underlying Father Involvement in Dual-Career and Single-Earner Families," *Developmental Psychology*, 1987, *23*, 431–440.

107. A. E. Gottfried and A. W. Gottfried, eds., *Redefining Families: Implications for Children's Development* (New York: Plenum Press, 1993), p. 93.

108. M. O'Connell, *Where's Papa? Father's Role in Child Care: Population Trends and Public Policy* (Washington, D.C.: Population Reference Bureau, 1993).

109. Bloom-Feshbach, "The Beginnings of Fatherhood."

110. F. A. Pedersen, B. J. Anderson, and R. L. Cain, Jr., "Parent-Infant and Husband-Wife Interactions Observed at Age Five Months," in Pedersen, *The Father-Infant Relationship*.

111. P. L. Chase-Lansdale and M. T. Owen, "Maternal Employment in a Family Context: Effects on Infant-Mother and Infant-Father Attachments," *Child Development*, 1987, *58*, 1505–1512.

112. Field, "Interaction Behaviors of Primary versus Secondary Caretaker Fathers."

113. S. M. McHale, A. C. Crouter, and W. T. Bartko, "Traditional and Egalitarian Patterns of Parental Involvement: Antecedents, Consequences, and Temporal Rhythms," in R. Lerner and D. Featherman, eds., *Advances in Life-Span Development* (Hillsdale, N.J.: Erlbaum, 1991), vol. 9.

114. M. E. Lamb and S. K. Bronson, "The Role of the Father in Child Development: Past Presumptions, Present Realities, and the Future Potential" (paper presented at a conference on Fatherhood and the Male Single Parent, Omaha, November 1978).

115. W. R. Gove and C. Zeiss, "Multiple Roles and Happiness," in F. Crosby, ed., *Spouse, Parent, Worker* (New Haven, Conn.: Yale University Press, 1987), pp. 125–137.

116. E. Hock and D. DeMeis, "Depression in Mothers of Infants: The Role of Maternal Employment," *Developmental Psychology*, 1990, *26*, 285–291.

117. G. K. Baruch and R. C. Barnett, "Role Quality and Psychological Well-Being," in Crosby, *Spouse, Parent, Worker*, pp. 63–84; W. A. Goldberg and M. A. Easterbrooks, "Maternal Employment When Children Are Toddlers and Kindergartners," in Gottfried and Gottfried, *Maternal Employment and Children's Development*, pp. 121–154.

118. C. Ross, "The Division of Labor at Home," *Social Forces*, 1987, *65*, 816–833.

119. Ishii-Kuntz, "Paternal Involvement and Perception toward Family Roles."

120. R. C. Barnett, N. L. Marshall, and J. H. Pleck, "Men's Multiple Roles and Their Relationship to Men's Psychological Distress," *Journal of Marriage and the Family*, 1992, *54*, 358–367.

121. A. C. Crouter, "Processes Linking Families and Work: Implications for Behavior and Development in Both Settings," in R. D. Parke and S. Kellam, eds., *Exploring Family Relationships with Other Social Contexts* (Hillsdale, N.J.: Erlbaum, 1994).

122. R. L. Repetti, "Short-Term and Long-Term Processes Linking Perceived Job Stressors to Father-Child Interaction," *Social Development*, 1994, *3*, 1–15.

123. F. K. Grossman, W. S. Pollack, and E. Golding, "Fathers and Children: Predicting the Quality and Quantity of Fathering," *Developmental Psychology*, 1988, *24*, 82–91.

124. M. L. Kohn and C. Schooler, *Work and Personality: An Inquiry into the Impact of Social Stratification* (Norwood, N.J.: Ablex, 1983); D. R. Miller and G. E. Swanson, *The Changing American Parent* (New York: Wiley, 1954).

125. E. Greenberger and R. O'Neil, "Characteristics of Fathers' and Mothers' Jobs: Implications for Parenting and Children's Social Development" (paper presented at the biennial meeting of the Society for Research in Child Development, Seattle, April 1991).

126. Ibid., p. 13.

127. N. Bolger, A. DeLongis, R. C. Kessler, and E. Wethington, "The Contagion of Stress across Multiple Roles," *Journal of Marriage and the Family*, 1989, *51*, 175–183.

128. Barnett, Marshall, and Pleck, "Men's Multiple Roles."

129. Ibid., p. 366.

130. E. E. Maccoby and C. N. Jacklin, "Gender Segregation in Childhood," in H. Reese, ed., *Advances in Child Behavior and Development*, vol. 20 (New York: Academic Press, 1987), pp. 239–287.

131. E. E. Maccoby, "Gender and Relationships: A Developmental Account," *American Psychologist*, 1990, *45*, 513–520.

132. P. W. Berman and V. Goodman, "Age and Sex Differences in Children's Responses to Babies: Effects of Adults' Caregiving Requests and Instructions," *Child Development*, 1984, *55*, 1071–1077.

133. J. J. Goodnow, "Children's Household Work: Its Nature and Functions," *Psychological Bulletin*, 1988, *103*, 5–26.

134. E. A. Rotundo, "American Fatherhood: A Historical Perspective," *American Behavioral Scientist*, 1985, *29*, 7–25, at 17; Rotundo, *American Manhood*.

135. Furstenberg, "Good Dads, Bad Dads," p. 193.

136. Parke and Stearns, "Fathers and Child-Rearing."

137. S. Coltrane and K. Allan, "New Fathers and Old Stereotypes: Representations of Masculinity in 1980's Television Advertising," *Masculinities*, 1994, *2*, 43–66.

138. Ibid.
139. Coltrane, *Family Man.*
140. R. La Rossa, "Fatherhood and Social Change," *Family Relations*, 1988, *37*, 451–457.

5 / SOCIALIZATION AND SOCIABILITY

1. Schaffer, *Mothering*, p. 98.
2. A. Macfarlane, "Olfaction in the Development of Social Preferences in the Human Neonate," in *Parent-Infant Interaction*, CIBA Foundation Symposium 33, new series (Amsterdam: Associated Scientific Publishers, 1975); D. Mauer and C. Mauer, *The World of the Newborn* (New York: Basic Books, 1988).
3. T. M. Field, "Gaze Behavior of Normal and High Risk Infants during Early Interactions," *Journal of the American Academy of Child Psychology*, 1981, *20*, 308–317.
4. See R. Karen, *Becoming Attached* (New York: Warner Books, 1994), for a review of the history of attachment research.
5. H. R. Schaffer and P. E. Emerson, "The Development of Social Attachments in Infancy," *Monographs of the Society for Research in Child Development*, 1964 *29*, no. 3 (serial no. 94).
6. F. A. Pedersen and K. S. Robson, "Father Participation in Infancy," *American Journal of Orthopsychiatry*, 1969, *39*, 466–472.
7. M. Kotelchuck, "The Infant's Relationship to the Father: Experimental Evidence," in Lamb, *The Role of the Father in Child Development.*
8. Lamb, "Father-Infant and Mother-Infant Interaction in the First Year of Life."
9. Kotelchuck, "The Infant's Relationship to the Father: Experimental Evidence."
10. Pedersen and Robson, "Father Participation in Infancy."
11. M. J. Cox, M. T. Owen, V. K. Henderson, and N. A. Margand, "Prediction of Infant-Father and Infant-Mother Attachment," *Developmental Psychology*, 1992, *28*, 474–483.

12. R. D. Parke, "Parent-Infant Interaction: Progress Paradigms and Problems," in G. Sackett, ed., *Observing Behavior*, vol. 1, *Theory of Applications in Mental Retardation* (Baltimore: University Park Press, 1978), pp. 69–94; J. Goodnow and A. Collins, *Ideas According to Parents* (Hillsdale, N.J.: Erlbaum, 1990).

13. See Parke, "Parent-Infant Interaction."

14. E. Rendina and J. D. Dickerscheid, "Father Involvement with First-Born Infants," *Family Coordinator*, 1976, 25, 373–379; A. M. Frodi, M. E. Lamb, M. Frodi, C. P. Hwang, B. Forstrom, and T. Corry, "Stability and Change in Parental Attitudes Following an Infant's Birth into Traditional and Nontraditional Swedish Families" (University of Michigan, 1980); P. Hwang, "The Changing Role of Swedish Fathers," in Lamb, *The Father's Role: Cross-Cultural Perspectives*.

15. M. J. Cox, M. T. Owen, J. T. Lewis, and V. K. Henderson, "Marriage, Adult Adjustment, and Early Parenting," *Child Development*, 1989, 60, 1015–1024.

16. Lamb and Elster, "Adolescent Mother-Infant-Father Relationships"; M. E. Durrett, M. Otaki, and P. Richards, "Attachment and the Mother's Perception of Support from the Father," *International Journal of Behavioral Development*, 1984, 7, 167–176; Dickie and Matheson, "Mother-Father-Infant: Who Needs Support?"; W. A. Goldberg and M. A. Easterbrook, "The Role of Marital Quality in Toddler Development," *Developmental Psychology*, 1984, 20, 504–514.

17. Cox, Owen, Lewis, and Henderson, "Marriage, Adult Adjustment, and Early Parenting."

18. M. Rutter and M. Rutter, *Developing Minds* (New York: Basic Books, 1993), p. 272.

19. F. A. Pedersen, J. Rubinstein, and L. J. Yarrow, "Infant Development in Father-Absent Families," *Journal of Genetic Psychology*, 1979, 135, 51–61.

20. Kotelchuck, "The Infant's Relationship to the Father: Experimental Evidence."

21. Ibid.

22. Clarke-Stewart, "The Father's Contribution to Children's Cognitive and Social Development."

23. B. M. M. Kotelchuk, E. Spelke, M. J. Sellers, and R. E. Klein, "Separation Protest in Guatemalan Infants: Cross-Cultural and Cognitive Findings," *Developmental Psychology*, 1974, *10*, 79–85.

24. M. D. Ainsworth, *Infancy in Uganda: Infant Care and the Growth of Love* (Baltimore: Johns Hopkins University Press, 1967).

25. R. L. Harwood, J. G. Miller, and N. L. Irizarry, *Culture and Attachment* (New York: Guilford Press, 1995); M. H. van Jzendoorn and P. M. Kroonenberg, "Cross-Cultural Patterns of Attachment: A Meta-Analysis of the Strange Situation," *Child Development*, 1988, *59*, 147–156.

26. M. Main and D. R. Weston, "The Quality of the Toddler's Relationship to Mother and Father: Related to Conflict Behavior and Readiness to Establish New Relationships," *Child Development*, 1981, *52*, 932–940.

27. For a general discussion of this issue, see M. D. Ainsworth, "The Development of Infant-Mother Attachment," in B. M. Caldwell and H. N. Ricciuti, eds., *Review of Child Development Research*, vol. 3 (Chicago: University of Chicago Press, 1973); M. D. S. Ainsworth, M. C. Blehar, E. Waters, and S. Wall, *Patterns of Attachment: A Psychological Study of the Strange Situation* (Hillsdale, N.J.: Erlbaum, 1978); Karen, *Becoming Attached*.

28. Main and Weston, "The Quality of the Toddler's Relationship to Mother and Father."

29. Z. Hossain, T. Field, J. Gonzalez, J. Malphurs, C. Del Valle, and J. Pickens, "Infants of 'Depressed' Mothers Interact Better with Their Non-Depressed Fathers," *Infant Mental Health Journal*, 1994, *15*, 348–357.

30. L. Tannenbaum and R. Forehand, "Maternal Depressive Mood: The Role of the Father in Preventing Adolescent Problem Behaviors," *Behavior Research and Therapy*, 1994, *32*, 321–326.

31. L. Hirshberg and M. Svejda, "When Infants Look to Their Parents: Infant Social Referencing of Mothers Compared to Fathers," *Child Development*, 1990, *61*, 1175–1186.

32. S. Dickstein and R. D. Parke, "Social Referencing in Infancy: A Glance at Fathers and Marriage," *Child Development*, 1988, *59*, 506–511.

33. L. M. Stolz, *Father Relations of War-Born Children: The Effect of Postwar Adjustment of Fathers on the Behavior and Personality of First Children Born While the Fathers Were at War* (Stanford: Stanford University Press, 1954); D. B. Lynn and W. L. Sawrey, "The Effects of Father Absence on Norwegian Boys and Girls," *Journal of Abnormal and Social Psychology*, 1959, *59*, 258–262.

34. F. L. Mott, "Absent Fathers and Child Development."

35. Ibid., p. 207.

36. Ibid.

37. J. Elicker, B. Egeland, and L. A. Sroufe, "Predicting Peer Competence and Peer Relationships from Early Parent-Child Relationships," in R. D. Parke and G. W. Ladd, *Family-Peer Relationships: Modes of Linkage* (Hillsdale, N.J.: Erlbaum, 1992).

38. G. J. Suess, K. E. Grossman, L. A. Sroufe, "Effects of Infant Attachment to Mother and Father on Quality of Adaptation to Preschool: from Dyadic to Individual Organization of Self," *International Journal of Behavioral Development*, 1992, *15*, 43–65.

39. MacDonald and Parke, "Bridging the Gap."

40. R. D. Parke, K. MacDonald, V. Burks, J. Carson, N. Bhavnagri, J. Barth, and A. Beitel, "Family-Peer Systems: In Search of the Linkages," in K. Kreppner and R. M. Lerner, eds., *Family Systems and Life Span Development* (Hillsdale, N.J.: Erlbaum, 1989), pp. 65–92.

41. J. Barth and R. D. Parke, "Parent-Child Relationship Influences on Children's Transition to School," *Merrill Palmer Quarterly*, 1993, *39*, 173–195.

42. E. W. Lindsey, D. Moffett, M. Clawson, and J. Mize, "Father-Child Play and Children's Competence" (paper presented at the biennial meeting of the Southwestern Society for Research in Human Development, Austin, April 1994).

43. L. M. Youngblade and J. Belsky, "Parent-Child Antecedents of 5-Year-Olds' Close Friendships: A Longitudi-

nal Analysis," *Developmental Psychology*, 1992, *28*, 700–713.

44. R. D. Parke, J. Cassidy, V. M. Burks, J. L. Carson, and L. Boyum, "Familial Contribution to Peer Competence among Young Children: The Role of Interactive and Affective Processes," in Parke and Ladd, *Family-Peer Relationships*, pp. 107–134.

45. J. Carson and R. D. Parke, "The Exchange of Affect in Parent-Child Interactions: Predicting Peer Outcomes" (University of California, Berkeley, 1995).

46. L. Boyum and R. D. Parke, "Family Emotional Expressiveness and Children's Social Competence," *Journal of Marriage and the Family*, 1995, *57*, 593–608.

47. S. Isley, R. O'Neil, and R. D. Parke, "Parent-Child Affect and Children's Social Competence," *Early Education and Development*, 1996, *7*, 7–23.

48. W. Roberts, "The Socialization of Emotional Expression: Relations with Competence in Preschool" (paper presented at the meetings of the Canadian Psychological Association, Penticton, B.C., June 1994).

49. C. Hooven, J. M. Gottman, and L. F. Katz, "Parental Meta-Emotion Structure Predicts Family and Child Outcomes," *Cognition and Emotion*, in press.

50. J. M. Gottman and L. F. Katz, "Effects of Marital Discord on Young Children's Peer Interaction and Health," *Developmental Psychology*, 1989, *25*, 373–381.

51. L. F. Katz and J. M. Gottman, "Patterns of Marital Conflict Predict Children's Internalizing and Externalizing Behavior," *Developmental Psychology*, 1993, *29*, 940–950.

52. J. Bowlby, *Separation and Loss* (New York: Basic Books, 1973).

53. M. Main, N. Kaplan, and J. Cassidy, "Security in Infancy, Childhood, and Adulthood: A Move to the Level of Representation," in I. Bretherton and E. Waters, eds., "Growing Points in Attachment Theory and Research," *Monographs of the Society for Research in Child Development*, 1985, *50*, 1–2 (series no. 209).

54. K. Grossmann and E. Fremmer-Bombik, "Fathers' Attachment Representations and the Quality of Their Interac-

tions with Their Children in Infancy and Childhood" (poster presentation at the meeting of the International Society for the Study of Behavioral Development, Amsterdam, June 1994).

55. P. A. Cowan, D. A. Cohn, C. P. Cowan, and J. L. Pearson, "Parents' Attachment Histories and Children's Internalizing and Externalizing Behavior: Exploring Family Systems Models of Linkage," *Journal of Consulting and Clinical Psychology*, 1996, *64*, 1–11.

56. Ibid.

57. Ibid.

58. C. Gilligan, *In a Different Voice* (Cambridge, Mass.: Harvard University Press, 1982).

59. S. Shulman and M. M. Klein, "Distinctive Role of the Father in Adolescent Separation-Individuation," in Shulman and Collins, *Father-Adolescent Relationships*, pp. 41–57.

60. Ibid., p. 53.

61. S. T. Hauser, B. K. Book, J. Houlinahn, S. Powers, B. Weiss-Perry, D. Follansbee, A. M. Jacobson and G. Noam, "Sex Differences within the Family: Studies of Adolescent and Parent Family Interaction," *Journal of Youth and Adolescence*, 1987, *16*, 199–213.

62. W. Madsen, *The Mexican-American of South Texas* (New York: Holt, Rinehart and Winston, 1973).

63. R. Koestner, C. E. Franz, J. Weinberger, "The Family Origins of Empathic Concern: A 26-Year Longitudinal Study," *Journal of Personality and Social Psychology*, 1990, *58*, 709–717.

64. C. E. Franz, D. McClelland, J. Weinberger, "Childhood Antecedents of Conventional Social Accomplishment in Midlife Adults: A 26-Year Prospective Study," *Journal of Personality and Social Psychology*, 1991, *60*, 586–595.

65. S. McLanahan and G. Sandefur, *Growing Up with a Single Parent* (Cambridge, Mass.: Harvard University Press, 1994); M. R. Stevenson and K. N. Black, "Paternal Absence and Sex Role Development: A Meta Analysis," *Child Development*, 1988, *52*, 1246–1254.

66. E. M. Hetherington, "Effects of Paternal Absence on Sex-

Typed Behaviors in Negro and White Preadolescent Males," *Journal of Personality and Social Psychology*, 1966, 4, 87–91.

67. B. Biller, *Paternal Deprivation* (Lexington, Mass.: D. C. Heath, 1974); E. M. Hetherington and J. Deur, "The Effects of Father Absence on Child Development," in W. W. Hartup, ed., *The Young Child*, vol. 2 (Washington, D.C.: National Association for the Education of Young Children, 1972); C. Leaper, L. Smith, R. Sprague, and R. Schwartz, "Single Parent Mothers, Married Mothers, Married Fathers, and the Socialization of Gender in Preschool Children" (paper presented at the biennial meeting of the Society for Research in Child Development, Seattle, April 1991).

68. E. M. Hetherington, M. Stanley-Hagen, and E. R. Anderson, "Marital Transitions: A Child's Perspective," *American Psychologist*, 1989, 44, 303–312.

69. C. R. Beal, *Boys and Girls: The Development of Gender Roles* (New York: McGraw Hill, 1994), p. 82.

70. W. Mischel, Y. Shoda, and P. K. Peake, "The Nature of Adolescent Competencies Predicted by Preschool Delay of Gratification," *Journal of Personality and Social Psychology*, 1988, 54, 687–696.

71. J. W. Santrock, "Relation of Type and Onset of Father-Absence on Cognitive Development," *Child Development*, 1972, 43, 455–469.

72. M. E. Brenes, N. Eisenberg, and G. C. Holmstadter, "Sex Role Development of Preschoolers from Two-Parent and One-Parent Families," *Merrill Palmer Quarterly*, 1985, 31, 33–46.

73. Beal, *Boys and Girls*, p. 83.

74. M. M. Johnson, "Sex Role Learning in the Nuclear Family," *Child Development*, 1963, 34, 315–333; M. M. Johnson, *Strong Mothers, Weak Wives* (Berkeley: University of California Press, 1988).

75. E. M. Hetherington, "Effects of Father Absence on Personality Development in Adolescent Daughters," *Developmental Psychology*, 1972, 7, 313–326.

76. E. E. Maccoby, "Different Reproductive Strategies in Males and Females," *Child Development,* 1991, *62,* 676–681.
77. F. A. Pedersen, "Does Research on Children Reared in Father-Absent Families Yield Information on Father Influence?" *The Family Coordinator,* 1976, *25,* 459–464.
78. E. M. Hetherington, "A Developmental Study of the Effects of Sex of the Dominant Parent on Sex Role Preference, Identification, and Imitation in Children," *Journal of Personality and Social Psychology,* 1965 2, 188–194.
79. S. F. Fisher, *The Female Orgasm: Psychology, Physiology, Fantasy* (New York: Basic Books, 1973).
80. J. H. Langlois and A. C. Downs, "Mothers, Fathers, and Peers as Socialization Agents of Sex-Typed Play Behaviors in Young Children," *Child Development,* 1980, *51,* 1217–1247.
81. R. D. Parke and D. B. Sawin, "Children's Privacy in the Home: Developmental, Ecological and Child-Rearing Determinants," *Environment and Behavior,* 1979, *11,* 87–104.

6 / INTELLECTUAL DEVELOPMENT

1. T. D. Wachs, *The Nature of Nurture* (Newbury Park, Calif.: Sage, 1992).
2. L. J. Yarrow, J. L. Rubinstein, and F. A. Pedersen, *Infant and Environment: Early Cognitive and Motivational Development* (New York: Halsted Press, 1975), p. 86.
3. C. S. Dweck, "Achievement," in P. H. Mussen, ed., *Handbook of Child Psychology,* vol. 4 (New York: Wiley, 1983); C. S. Dweck and E. L. Leggett, "A Social Cognitive Approach to Motivation and Personality," *Psychological Review,* 1988, 256–273.
4. F. A. Pedersen, J. L. Rubinstein, and L. J. Yarrow, "Infant Development in Father-Absent Families," *Journal of Genetic Psychology,* 1979, *135,* 51–61.
5. Ibid., p. 60.
6. J. K. Nugent, "Cultural and Psychological Influences on the Father's Role in Infant Development," *Journal of Marriage and the Family,* 1991, *53,* 475–485.

7. Clarke-Stewart, "And Daddy Makes Three"; K. A. Clarke-Stewart, "The Father's Contribution to Children's Cognitive and Social Development in Early Childhood," in Pedersen, *The Father-Infant Relationship*.
8. Wachs, *The Nature of Nurture*.
9. B. L. White, B. Kaban, B. Shapiro, and J. Attonucci, "Competency and Experience," in I. C. Uzgiris and F. Weizmann, eds., *The Structuring of Experience* (New York: Plenum Press, 1976), pp. 150–151.
10. J. Newson and E. Newson, "Family and Sex Roles in Middle Childhood," in D. J. Hargreaves and A. M. Colley, eds., *The Psychology of Sex Roles* (London: Harper and Row, 1986), pp. 142–158; A. C. Huston, "Sex Typing," in Mussen, *Handbook of Child Psychology*, vol. 4, p. 387–467.
11. L. W. Hoffman, "Changes in Family Roles, Socialization, and Sex Differences," *American Psychologist*, 1977, *32*, 649.
12. R. W. Blanchard and H. B. Biller, "Father Availability and Academic Performance among Third Grade Boys," *Developmental Psychology*, 1971, *4*, 301–305.
13. H. B. Biller, *Father, Child, and Sex Role* (Lexington, Mass.: D. C. Heath, 1971), p. 59.
14. M. Shinn, "Father Absence and Children's Cognitive Development," *Psychological Bulletin*, 1978, *85*, 295–324.
15. F. Mott, "Absent Fathers and Child Development."
16. L. J. Crockett, D. J. Eggebeen, and A. J. Hawkins, "Fathers' Presence and Young Children's Behavioral and Cognitive Adjustment," *Journal of Family Issues*, 1993, *14*, 355–377.
17. McLanahan and Sandefur, *Growing Up with a Single Parent*.
18. F. F. Furstenberg and K. M. Harris, "When and Why Fathers Matter: Impacts of Father Involvement on Children of Adolescent Mothers," in Lerman and Ooms, *Young Unwed Fathers*, pp. 117–138.
19. E. Thomson, S. S. McLanahan, and R. B. Curtin, "Family Structure, Gender, and Parental Socialization," *Journal of Marriage and the Family*, 1992, *54*, 368–378.
20. McLanahan and Sandefur, *Growing Up with a Single Parent*.
21. P. H. Leiderman and G. F. Leiderman, "Familial Infant

Development in an East African Agricultural Community," in E. J. Anthony and C. Koupernik, eds., *The Child in His Family: Children at Psychiatric Risk,* vol. 3 (New York: John Wiley and Sons, 1974).

22. R. B. Zajonc, "Family Configuration and Intelligence," *Science,* 1976, *192,* 227–236; R. B. Zajonc, "Validating the Confluence Model," *Psychological Bulletin,* 1983, *93,* 457–480.

23. N. Radin, "The Influence of Fathers upon Sons and Daughters and Implications for School Social Work," *Social Work in Education,* 1986, *8,* 77–91; N. Radin, "Primary Caregiving Fathers in Intact Families," in Gottfried and Gottfried, *Redefining Families.*

24. H. S. Goldstein, "Father's Absence and Cognitive Development of 12- to 17-Year-Olds," *Psychological Reports,* 1982, *51,* 843–848.

25. N. Radin, Testimony before the Select Committee on Children, Youth and Families of the U.S. House of Representatives, June 1991, p. 6.

26. N. Radin, E. Williams, and K. Coggins, "Paternal Involvement in Childrearing and the School Performance of Native American Children: An Exploratory Study," *Family Perspectives,* 1993, *27,* 375–391.

27. Ibid., p. 386.

28. T. E. Smith, "Mother-Father Differences in Parental Influence on School Grades and Educational Goals," *Sociological Inquiry,* 1989, *59,* 88–98.

29. S. S. Feldman and K. R. Wentzel, "Relations among Family Interaction Patterns, Classroom Self-Restraint and Academic Achievement in Preadolescent Boys," *Journal of Educational Psychology,* 1990, *82,* 813–819; K. R. Wentzel and S. S. Feldman, "Parental Predictors of Boys' Self-Restraint and Motivation to Achieve at School: A Longitudinal Study," *Journal of Early Adolescence,* 1993, *13,* 183–203.

30. K. R. Wentzel, "Family Functioning and Academic Achievement in Middle School: A Social-Emotional Perspective," *Journal of Early Adolescence,* 1994, *14,* 268–291.

31. D. A. Cohn and P. A. Cowan, "Links between Parents' Attachment Histories, Marital and Parenting Quality, and Their Children's School Difficulties" (paper presented at the biennial meeting of the Society for Research in Child Development, New Orleans, March 1993), p. 10.

32. Ibid., p. 10.

33. M. P. Honzik, "Environmental Correlates of Mental Growth: Prediction from the Family Setting at Twelve Months," *Child Development,* 1967, *38,* 337–364; N. Radin, "The Role of the Father in Cognitive, Academic, and Intellectual Development," in Lamb, *The Role of the Father in Child Development,* p. 259.

34. J. H. Block, "Another Look at Sex Differentiation in the Socialization Behaviors of Mothers and Fathers," in *Psychology of Women: Future Directions of Research* (New York: Psychological Dimensions, 1979), p. 25.

35. Hoffman, "Changes in Family Roles."

36. K. W. Bartz and E. S. Levine, "Childbearing by Black Parents: A Description and Comparison to Anglo and Chicano Parents," *Journal of Marriage and the Family,* 1978, *40,* 709–719; J. L. McAdoo, "Changing Perspectives on the Role of the Black Father," in Bronstein and Cowan, *Fatherhood Today,* pp. 79–92.

37. D. B. Downey and B. Powell, "Do Children in Single-Parent Households Fare Better Living with Same-Sex Parents," *Journal of Marriage and the Family,* 1993, *55,* 55–71.

38. McLanahan and Sandefur, *Growing Up with a Single Parent.*

39. Snarey, *How Fathers Care for the Next Generation.*

40. Ibid., p. 185.

41. Radin, "The Role of the Father," p. 253.

42. M. Hennig and N. Jardim, *The Managerial Woman* (Garden City, N.Y.: Anchor Press, 1977).

43. P. B. Coats and S. J. Overman, "Childhood Play Experiences of Women in Traditional and Nontraditional Professions," *Sex Roles,* 1992, *26,* 261–271.

44. M. C. Rau, *Indira Priyadarshini* (New Delhi: Popular Book Services, 1966), cited in M. L. Hamilton, *The Father's Influence on Children* (Chicago: Nelson-Hall, 1977), p. 33.

45. M. Mead, *Blackberry Winter* (New York: Morrow, 1972), pp. 40, 41, 44.

7 / DIVORCE, CUSTODY, AND REMARRIAGE

1. C. Sorrentino, "The Changing Family in International Perspective," *Monthly Labor Review,* 1990, *113,* 41–46; E. E. Maccoby and R. H. Mnookin, *Dividing the Child: Social and Legal Dilemmas of Custody* (Cambridge, Mass.: Harvard University Press, 1992); A. J. Cherlin, *Marriage, Divorce, and Remarriage* (Cambridge, Mass.: Harvard University Press, 1992).
2. J. A. Sweet and L. L. Bumpass, *American Families and Households* (New York: Russell Sage Foundation, 1987).
3. E. E. Maccoby, C. E. Depner, and R. H. Mnookin, "Custody of Children Following Divorce," in E. M. Hetherington and J. D. Arasteh, eds., *Impact of Divorce, Single Parenting, and Stepparenting on Children* (Hillsdale, N.J.: Erlbaum, 1988); R. H. Mnookin, E. E. Maccoby, C. F. Depner, and C. R. Albiston, "Private Ordering Revisited: What Custodial Arrangements Are Parents Negotiating?" in S. Sugarman and H. Kay, eds., *Divorce Reform at the Crossroads* (New Haven, Conn.: Yale University Press, 1990); Maccoby and Mnookin, *Dividing the Child.*
4. E. M. Hetherington, "Divorce: A Child's Perspective," *American Psychologist,* 1979, *34,* 851.
5. E. M. Cummings and P. Davies, *Children and Marital Conflict* (New York: Guilford, 1994).
6. E. M. Hetherington, M. Cox, and R. Cox, "Effects of Divorce on Parents and Children," in Lamb, *Nontraditional Families,* pp. 233–288.
7. P. S. Morgan, D. N. Lye, and G. A. Condron, "Sons, Daughters, and the Risk of Marital Disruption," *American Journal of Sociology,* 1988, *94,* 110–129.
8. E. M. Hetherington, M. Cox, and R. Cox, "The Aftermath of Divorce," in Stevens and Mathews, *Mother-Child, Father-Child Relations.*
9. L. J. Weitzman, *The Divorce Revolution: The Unexpected*

Social and Economic Consequences for Women and Children in America (New York: Free Press, 1985).

10. G. J. Duncan and S. D. Hoffman, "Economic Consequences of Marital Instability," in M. David and J. Smeeding, eds., *Horizontal Equity, Uncertainty, and Economic Well-Being,* (Chicago: University of Chicago Press, 1985), pp. 427–470.

11. U.S. Bureau of the Census, Current Populations Reports, 1992, p. 23, N181.

12. F. F. Furstenberg and A. J. Cherlin, *Divided Families* (Cambridge, Mass.: Harvard University Press, 1991).

13. Duncan and Hoffman, "Economic Consequences of Marital Instability."

14. D. J. Hernandez, "Demographic Trends and the Living Arrangement of Children," in Hetherington and Arasteh, *Impact of Divorce, Single Parenting, and Stepparenting on Children,* pp. 3–22; D. J. Hernandez, *America's Children* (New York: Russell Sage Foundation, 1993).

15. Hetherington, Cox and Cox, "Effects of Divorce."

16. E. M. Hetherington, M. Cox, and R. Cox, "Aftermath of Divorce," in Stevens and Mathews, *Mother-Child, Father-Child Relations,* p. 163.

17. Ibid., p. 170.

18. Morgan, Lye, and Condron, "Sons, Daughters, and the Risk of Marital Disruption."

19. E. M. Hetherington, M. Cox, and R. Cox, "Play and Social Interaction in Children Following Divorce," *Journal of Social Issues,* 1979, *35,* 26–49.

20. Ibid., p. 38.

21. J. L. Singer, "Television, Imaginative Play, and Cognitive Development: Some Problems and Possibilities" (paper presented at the meeting of the American Psychological Association, San Francisco, September 1977), p. 10.

22. E. M. Hetherington, M. Stanley-Hagan, and E. R. Anderson, "Marital Transitions: A Child's Perspective," *American Psychologist,* 1989, *44,* 303–312.

23. E. M. Hetherington, "Coping with Family Transitions: Winners, Losers, and Survivors," *Child Development,* 1989, *60,* 1–14.

24. S. Newcomber and J. R. Udry, "Parental Marital Status Effects on Adolescent Sexual Behavior," *Journal of Marriage and the Family*, 1987, *49*, 235–240; P. L. Chase-Lansdale and E. M. Hetherington, "The Impact of Divorce on Life-Span Development: Short- and Long-Term Effects," in D. Featherman and R. M. Lerner, eds., *Life-Span Development and Behavior*, vol. 10 (Orlando, Fla.: Academic Press, 1990), pp. 105–150; M. T. Zazlow, "Sex Differences in Children's Response to Parental Divorce: Research Methodology and Post-Divorce Forms," *American Journal of Orthopsychiatry*, 1988, *58*, 355–378.

25. E. M. Hetherington, "Long-Term Impact of Divorce on Children's Marital Stability" (University of Virginia, 1987).

26. S. McLanahan and L. Bumpass, "Intergenerational Consequences of Marital Disruption," *American Journal of Sociology*, 1988, *94*, 130–152.

27. McLanahan and Sandefur, *Growing Up with a Single Parent*.

28. H. S. Freidman, J. S. Tucker, J. E. Schwartz, C. Tomlinson-Keasey, L. R. Martin, D. L. Wingard, and M. H. Criqui, "Psychosocial and Behavioral Predictors of Longevity," *American Psychologist*, 1995, *50*, 69–78.

29. Hetherington, Stanley-Hagan, and Anderson, "Marital Transitions."

30. Ibid.

31. J. S. Wallerstein and J. B. Kelly, *Surviving the Break-up: How Children Actually Cope with Divorce* (New York: Basic Books, 1980).

32. F. F. Furstenberg and P. D. Allison, "How Marital Dissolution Affects Children: Variations by Age and Sex" (University of Pennsylvania, 1985).

33. Wallerstein and Kelly, *Surviving the Break-up*.

34. Hetherington, "Divorce: A Child's Perspective," p. 853.

35. Chase-Lansdale and Hetherington, "The Impact of Divorce on Life-Span Development."

36. J. H. Block, J. Block, and P. F. Gjerde, "The Personality of Children prior to Divorce: A Prospective Study," *Child Development*, 1986, *57*, 827–840.

37. A. J. Cherlin, F. F. Furstenberg, P. L. Chase-Lansdale, K. E. Kienan, P. K. Robbins, D. R. Morrison, and J. O. Teitler, "Longitudinal Studies of Effects of Divorce on Children in Great Britain and the United States," *Science,* 1991, *252,* 1386–1389.

38. R. E. Emery and R. Forehand, "Parental Divorce and Children's Well-Being: A Focus on Resilience," in R. J. Haggerty, L. R. Sherrod, N. Garmezy, and M. Rutter, eds., *Stress, Risk, and Resilience in Children and Adolescents* (New York: Cambridge University Press, 1994).

39. Hetherington, "Coping with Family Transitions."

40. Cummings and Davies, *Children and Marital Conflict.*

41. Hetherington, Cox, and Cox, "Effects of Divorce."

42. J. A. Fulton, "Parental Reports of Children's Post-Divorce Adjustment," *Journal of Social Issues,* 1979, *35,* 126–139.

43. G. Spanier and L. Thompson, *Parting: The Aftermath of Separation and Divorce* (Beverly Hills, Calif.: Sage, 1984).

44. F. F. Furstenberg, C. W. Nord, J. L. Peterson, and N. Zill, "The Life Course of Children and Divorce: Marital Disruption and Parental Conflict," *American Sociological Review,* 1983, *48,* 656–668.

45. J. A. Seltzer and S. M. Bianchi, "Children's Contact with Absent Parents," *Journal of Marriage and the Family,* 1988, *50,* 663–678.

46. Maccoby and Mnookin, *Dividing the Child.*

47. R. A. Thompson, "Fatherhood and Divorce," in L. S. Quinn, ed., *The Future of Children: Children and Divorce* (1994), p. 4.

48. Seltzer and Bianchi, "Children's Contact with Absent Parents."

49. Furstenberg and Cherlin, *Divided Families,* p. 34.

50. Ibid.

51. Hetherington, Stanley-Hagan, and Anderson, "Marital Transitions."

52. Fulton, "Parental Reports of Children's Post-Divorce Adjustment," p. 134.

53. McLanahan and Sandefur, *Growing Up with a Single Parent.*

54. U.S. Bureau of the Census, Current Population Reports, Series P-60, No. 173, Child Support and Alimony, 1989, U.S. Government Printing Office, Washington, D.C., 1991.
55. J. D. Treachman, "Contributions to Children by Divorced Fathers," Social Problems, 1991, 38, 358–371.
56. J. A. Seltzer, "Relationships between Fathers and Children Who Live Apart: The Father's Role after Separation," Journal of Marriage and the Family, 1991, 52, 79–101.
57. Ibid., p. 97.
58. I. Garfinkel, Assuring Child Support (New York: Russell Sage, 1992).
59. McLanahan and Sandefur, Growing Up with a Single Parent, p. 25.
60. E. M. Hetherington, M. Cox, and R. Cox, "Family Interaction and the Social, Emotional, and Cognitive Development of Children Following Divorce," in V. Vaughn and T. B. Brazelton, eds., The Family: Setting Priorities (New York: Science and Medicine, 1979), p. 20.
61. R. D. Hess and K. A. Camara, "Post-Divorce Relationships as Mediating Factors in the Consequences of Divorce for Children," Journal of Social Issues, 1979, 35, 79–96.
62. Morgan, Lye, and Condron, "Sons, Daughters, and the Risk of Marital Disruption."
63. Hess and Camara, "Post-Divorce Relationships as Mediating Factors," pp. 93–94.
64. Hetherington, Stanley-Hagan, and Anderson, "Marital Transitions."
65. Ibid.
66. J. S. Wallerstein and J. B. Kelly, "California's Children of Divorce," Psychology Today, 1980, 13, 71–72.
67. Ibid., p. 71.
68. Hetherington, Stanley-Hagan, and Anderson, "Marital Transitions."
69. Wallerstein and Kelly, "California's Children of Divorce," p. 71.
70. Hess and Camara, "Post-Divorce Relationships as Mediating Factors," p. 94.
71. J. W. Santrock and R. Warshak, "Father Custody and

Social Development in Boys and Girls," *Journal of Social Issues*, 1979, 35, 113.

72. Cited in Levine, *Who Will Raise the Children*, p. 45.

73. Maccoby and Mnookin, *Dividing the Child*.

74. Weitzman, *The Divorce Revolution*.

75. McLanahan and Sandefur, *Growing Up with a Single Parent*, p. 72.

76. K. E. Gersick, "Fathers by Choice: Divorced Men Who Receive Custody of Their Children," in G. Levinger and O. C. Moles, eds., *Divorce and Separation* (New York: Basic Books, 1979), p. 320.

77. Levine, *Who Will Raise the Children*, p. 48.

78. H. A. Mendes, "Single Fathers," *The Family Coordinator*, 1976, 25, 439–444.

79. Maccoby and Mnookin, *Dividing the Child*.

80. Santrock and Warshak, "Father Custody and Social Development."

81. A. Clarke-Stewart and C. Hayward, "Advantages of Father Custody and Contact for the Psychological Well-Being of School-Age Children" (University of California, Irvine, 1994).

82. P. R. Amato and B. Keith, "Parental Divorce and the Well-being of Children: A Meta-Analysis," *Psychological Bulletin*, 1991, 110, 26–46.

83. J. L. Peterson and N. Zill, "Marital Disruption, Parent-Child Relationships, and Behavior Problems in Children," *Journal of Marriage and the Family*, 1986, 48, 295–307.

84. H. Zimiles and V. E. Lee, "Adolescent Family Structure and Educational Progress," *Developmental Psychology*, 1991, 27, 314–320.

85. Santrock and Warshak, "Father Custody and Social Development," pp. 116–117.

86. D. B. Downey and B. Powell, "Do Children in Single-Parent Households Fare Better with Same-Sex Parents?"

87. A. De Maris and G. L. Grief, "The Relationships between Family Structure and Parent-Child Relationship Problems in Single Father Households," *Journal of Divorce and Re-*

marriage, 1992, *18,* 55–78; B. J. Risman, "Can Men 'Mother'? Life as a Single Father," *Family Relations,* 1986, *35,* 95–102.

88. N. F. Marks and S. S. McLanahan, "Brave New Families and Their Kin: Who Gives and Who Gets?" (paper presented at the annual meeting of the American Sociological Association, Pittsburgh, 1992).

89. Clarke-Stewart and Hayward, "Advantages of Father Custody."

90. Peterson and Zill, "Marital Disruption, Parent-Child Relationships."

91. Hetherington, Stanley-Hagan, and Anderson, "Marital Transitions."

92. K. M. Rosenthal and H. F. Keshet, *Fathers without Partners: A Study of Fathers and the Family after Marital Separation* (Totowa, N.J.: Rowman and Littlefield, 1980), p. 71.

93. Ibid., p. 69.

94. Thompson, *Fatherhood and Divorce,* p. 17.

95. Maccoby and Mnookin, *Dividing the Child.*

96. Ibid.

97. Ibid., p. 114.

98. Ibid., pp. 246–247.

99. Ibid., p. 248.

100. C. M. Buchanan, E. E. Maccoby, and S. M. Dornbusch, "Caught between Parents: Adolescents' Experience in Divorced Families," *Child Development,* 1991, *62,* 1008–1029.

101. Ibid., p. 1024.

102. D. A. Luepnitz, *Child Custody: A Study of Families after Divorce* (Lexington, Mass.: Lexington Books, 1982).

103. S. A. Wolchik, S. L. Braver, and I. W. Sandler, "Maternal versus Joint Custody: Children's Postseparation Experiences and Adjustment," *Journal of Clinical Child Psychology,* 1985, *14,* 118–141.

104. R. E. Emery, *Marriage, Divorce, and Children's Adjustment* (Newbury Park, Calif.: Sage, 1988), p. 93.

105. P. C. Glick, "The Family Life Cycle and Social Change," *Family Relations,* 1989a, *38,* 123–129.

106. P. C. Glick, "Remarried Families, Stepfamilies and Step-children: A Brief Demographic Profile," *Family Relations,* 1989b, *38*, 24–47.
107. T. Arendell, *Mothers and Divorce: Legal, Economic, and Social Dilemmas* (Berkeley: University of California Press, 1986), pp. 116–117.
108. Furstenberg and Cherlin, "Divided Families."
109. E. M. Hetherington and G. Clingempeel, eds., "Coping with Marital Transitions," *Monographs of the Society for Research in Child Development,* 1992, *57*, Serial no. 227.
110. Furstenberg, Nord, Peterson, and Zill, "The Life Course of Children and Divorce"; F. F. Furstenberg, "Child Care after Divorce and Remarriage," in Hetherington and Arasteh, *Impact of Divorce, Single Parenting, and Stepparenting on Children,* pp. 245–261.
111. Cherlin, *Marriage, Divorce, and Remarriage.*
112. Furstenberg and Cherlin, *Divided Families,* pp. 83–84.
113. Hetherington, "Coping with Family Transitions," p. 8.
114. J. Bernard, *Remarriage: A Study of Marriage* (New York: Dryden Press, 1956).
115. Hetherington and Clingempeel, "Coping with Marital Transitions."
116. H. B. Biller and D. L. Meredith, *Father Power* (New York: David McKay, 1974), pp. 292, 293.
117. Furstenberg and Cherlin, *Divided Families;* P. D. Allison and F. F. Furstenberg, "How Marital Dissolution Affects Children: Variations by Age and Sex," *Developmental Psychology,* 1989, *25*, 540–549; N. Zill, "Behavior, Achievement, and Health Problems among Children in Stepfamilies: Findings from a National Survey of Child Health," in Hetherington and Arasteh, *Impact of Divorce, Single Parenting, and Stepparenting on Children.*
118. Hetherington and Clingempeel, "Coping with Marital Transitions."
119. Wallerstein and Kelly, "California's Children of Divorce," p. 74.
120. Ibid., p. 76.

121. C. Longfellow, "Divorce in Context: Its Impact on Children," in Levinger and Moles, *Divorce and Separation,* p. 289.

122. N. Zill, "Divorce, Marital Happiness, and the Mental Health of Children: Findings from the Foundation for Child Development National Survey of Children" (paper prepared for National Institute of Mental Health Workshop on Divorce and Children, Bethesda, Md., 1978).

8 / INNOVATIONS IN FATHERING

1. L. Haas, "Nurturing Fathers and Working Mothers: Changing Gender Roles in Sweden," in J. C. Hood, ed., *Men, Work and Family* (Newbury Park, Calif.: Sage, 1993).

2. J. H. Pleck, "Fathers and Infant Care Leave," in E. Zigler and M. Franks, eds., *The Parental Leave Crisis: Toward a National Policy* (New Haven, Conn.: Yale University Press, 1988), pp. 177–191.

3. S. L. Hyland, "Helping Employees with Family Care," *Monthly Labor Review,* 1990, *113,* 22–26; K. Christensen, "Flexible Staffing and Scheduling in U.S. Corporations," Conference Board, New York, 1989, cited in J. H. Pleck, "Are Family-Supportive Employer Policies Relevant to Men?" in Hood, *Men, Work and Families.*

4. "Report on a National Study of Parental Leaves," Catalyst, New York, 1986.

5. D. Vrazo, "Paternity Leaves Offered More Often," *Providence Journal,* 1990, p. 17, cited in Pleck, "Are Family-Supportive Employer Policies Relevant to Men?"

6. Pleck, "Are Family-Supportive Employer Policies Relevant to Men?"

7. J. T. Bond, E. Galinsky, M. Lord, G. L. Staines, and K. R. Brown, *Beyond the Parental Leave Debate: The Impact of Laws in Four States* (New York: Families and Work Institute, 1991).

8. Pleck, "Are Family-Supportive Employer Policies Relevant to Men?"

9. Ibid., p. 229.
10. Haas, "Nurturing Fathers and Working Mothers"; J. S. Hyde, M. J. Essex, and F. Horton, "Fathers and Parental Leave," *Journal of Family Issues*, 1993, *14*, 616–641.
11. Green, *Fathering*, p. 216.
12. R. A. Lee, "Flextime and Conjugal Roles," *Journal of Occupational Behavior*, 1983, *4*, 297–315.
13. R. A. Winett and M. S. Neale, "Results of Experimental Study on Flextime and Family Life," *Monthly Labor Review*, 1980, *113*, 29–32.
14. H. Bohen and A. Viveros-Long, *Balancing Jobs and Family Life: Do Flexible Work Schedules Help?* (Philadelphia: Temple University Press, 1981).
15. Levine, *Who Will Raise the Children*, p. 91.
16. Hewitt Associates, 1995, cited in *Los Angeles Times*, November 6, 1995.
17. E. Gronseth, "Work-Sharing: Adaptations of Pioneering Families with Husband and Wife in Part-Time Employment," *Acta Sociologia*, 1975, *18*, 218.
18. Ibid., p. 219.
19. D. Maklan, "The Four-Day Workweek: Blue-Collar Adjustment to a Nonconventional Arrangement of Work and Leisure Time" (Ph.D. diss., University of Michigan, 1976), cited in Robinson, *How Americans Use Time*.
20. Russell, "Fathers as Caregivers" (all quotes from pp. 126–131).
21. Ibid.
22. A. Hochschild, *The Second Shift* (New York: Viking, 1989).
23. Russell, "Fathers as Caregivers."
24. Ibid.
25. K. D. Pruett, *The Nurturing Father* (New York: Warner Books, 1987).
26. A. Sagi, "Antecedents and Consequences of Various Degrees of Paternal Involvement in Childrearing"; Sagi, Koren, and Weinberg, "Fathers in Israel"; Sagi, Lamb, Shoham, Dvir, and Lewkowicz, "Parent-Infant Interaction in Families on Israeli Kibbutzim."

27. N. Radin, "Primary Caregiver and Role-Sharing Fathers," in Lamb, *Nontraditional Families*, pp. 173–204.

28. N. Radin, "Primary Caregiving Fathers of Long Duration," in Bronstein and Cowan, *Fatherhood today*, pp. 127–143.

29. Ibid.

30. E. Williams, N. Radin, and T. Allegro, "Sex-Role Attitudes of Adolescents Raised Primarily by Their Fathers," *Merrill-Palmer Quarterly*, 1992, *38*, 457–476 at 475.

31. E. Williams and N. Radin, "Paternal Involvement, Maternal Employment, and Adolescent Academic Achievement," *American Journal of Orthopsychiatry*, 1993 *63*, 306–312.

32. Radin, "Primary Caregiving Fathers in Intact Families," p. 475.

33. Russell, "Fathers as Caregivers."

34. J. S. Chafetz, *Masculine, Feminine, or Human* (Itasca, Ill.: F. E. Peacock, 1978), p. 197.

35. A. J. Hawkins, S. L. Christiansen, K. P. Sargent, and E. J. Hill, "Rethinking Fathers' Involvement in Child Care: A Developmental Perspective," *Journal of Family Issues*, 1993, *14*, 531–549.

36. P. W. Berman, L. C. Monda, and R. P. Myerscough, "Sex Differences in Young Children's Responses to an Infant: An Observation within a Day-Care Setting," *Child Development*, 1977, *48*, 711–715; C. R. Beal, *Boys and Girls: The Development of Gender Roles* (New York: McGraw Hill, 1994).

37. D. G. Kilinman and R. Kohl, *Fatherhood USA* (New York: Garland, 1984); J. A. Levine, D. T. Murphy, and S. Wilson, *Getting Men Involved* (New York: Scholastic, 1993); R. F. Levant, "Education for Fatherhood," in Bronstein and Cowan, *Fatherhood Today*, pp. 253–275; R. F. Levant, "Toward the Reconstruction of Masculinity," *Journal of Family Psychology*, 1992, *5*, 370–402; F. R. Levant and J. Kelly, *Between Father and Child* (New York: Penguin, 1989).

38. A. S. Wente and S. Crockenberg, "Transition to Father-

hood: Lamaze Preparation, Adjustment Difficulty, and the Husband-Wife Relationship," *The Family Coordinator,* 1976, *25*, 356.

39. Lind, "Observations after Delivery of Communication between Mother-Infant-Father."
40. Parke, Hymel, Power, and Tinsley, "Fathers and Risk."
41. B. A. McBride, "Parent Education and Support Programs for Fathers: Outcomes on Paternal Involvement," *Early Child Development and Care,* 1991, *67*, 73–85.
42. J. Dickie and S. Carnahan Gerber, "Training in Social Competence: The Effect on Mothers, Fathers, and Infants," *Child Development,* 1980, *51*, 1248–1251.
43. Zelazo, Kotelchuck, Barber, and David, "Fathers and Sons."
44. A. J. Hawkins, T. Roberts, S. L. Christiansen, and C. M. Marshall, "An Evaluation of a Program to Help Dual-Earner Couples Share the Second Shift," *Family Relations,* 1994, *43*, 213–220.
45. R. F. Levant, "Education for Fatherhood," in Bronstein and Cowan, *Fatherhood Today,* pp. 253–275.
46. Cowan and Cowan, *When Partners Become Parents.*
47. Ibid., pp. 179–180.
48. Levine, Murphy, and Wilson, *Getting Men Involved.*
49. Ibid., pp. 9–10.
50. Ibid.
51. D. R. Powell, "Including Latin Fathers in Parent Education and Support Programs," in R. E. Zambrana, ed., *Understanding Latino Families* (Thousand Oaks, Calif.: Sage, 1995), pp. 85–106.
52. J. Sander, "Service Programs to Help Unwed Fathers," in Lerman and Ooms, *Young Unwed Fathers,* pp. 297–315.
53. Ibid., p. 300.
54. Ibid., p. 309.
55. F. F. Furstenberg, "Fathering in the Inner City: Paternal Participation and Public Policy," in W. Marsiglio, ed., *Fatherhood: Contemporary Theory, Research, and Social Policy* (Thousand Oaks, Calif.: Sage, 1995), pp. 119–147.
56. Snarey, *How Fathers Care for the Next Generation.*

57. Ibid., p. 111.
58. Shapiro, *The Measure of a Man.*
59. Snarey, *How Fathers Care for the Next Generation,* pp. 18–19.
60. Ibid.
61. D. H. Heath and H. E. Heath, *Fulfilling Lives: Paths to Maturity and Success* (San Francisco: Jossey-Bass, 1991).
62. G. Valliant, *Adaptation to Life* (Boston: Little, Brown, 1977).
63. Snarey, *How Fathers Care for the Next Generation,* p. 98.
64. Ibid., p. 117–118.
65. Ibid., p. 119.

Suggested Reading

Henry Biller and Robert J. Trotter, *The Father Factor* (New York: Pocket Books, 1994). A volume directed mainly to parents that offers practical advice based on recent research in the area.

Frederick W. Bozett and Shirley M. H. Hanson, eds., *Fatherhood and Families in Cultural Context* (New York: Springer, 1991). This scholarly volume describes historical, ethnic, and cross-cultural variations in fathering.

Phyllis Bronstein and Carolyn Pape Cowan, eds., *Fatherhood Today: Men's Changing Role in the Family* (New York: Wiley, 1988). This edited collection offers fresh perspectives on the father's role in the family, ethnic variations, intergenerational analyses and prevention and intervention programs for fathers.

Scott Coltrane, *Family Man* (New York: Oxford University Press, 1996). An in-depth look at how contemporary parents are attempting to share family work and paid work.

Robert L. Griswold, *Fatherhood in America* (New York: Basic Books, 1993). A volume that traces the history of fatherhood in the United States.

Jane C. Hood, ed., *Men, Work and Family* (Newbury Park, Calif.: Sage, 1993). A series of scholarly essays that explore men's changing roles in the family and the world of work.

Michael E. Lamb, ed., *The Father's Role: Applied Perspectives* (New York: Wiley, 1986). This scholarly collection offers comprehensive essays concerning the legal, clinical, and social policy issues that pertain to fathering.

Michael E. Lamb, ed., *The Father's Role: Cross-Cultural Perspectives* (Hillsdale, N.J.: Erlbaum, 1987). This volume offers a rich source of information on father's roles in other cultures.

William Marsiglio, ed., *Fatherhood: Contemporary Theory, Research, and Social Policy* (Thousand Oaks, Calif.: Sage, 1995). A set of essays by leading scholars in the field that address cross-cultural, socioeconomic, and policy issues concerning contemporary fatherhood.

Index